BRIEF HISTORY OF THE INDIAN PEOPLES

BRIEF HISTORY OF THE INDIAN PEOPLES

W. W. HUNTER

GYAN

Published by

GYAN

Gyan Publishing House
5, Ansari Road
Daryaganj, New Delhi-110002
Phone: 011-47034999, 9811692060
E-mail: books@gyanbooks.com

Distribution Network
gyanbooks.com
India, USA, Canada, UK, Australia, France

ISBN : 978-81-212-3155-8 (PB)

2nd Impression 2020

Printed at: Gyan Press, Delhi.

Brief History of the Indian Peoples
Author: W. W. Hunter

A BRIEF HISTORY OF THE INDIAN PEOPLES

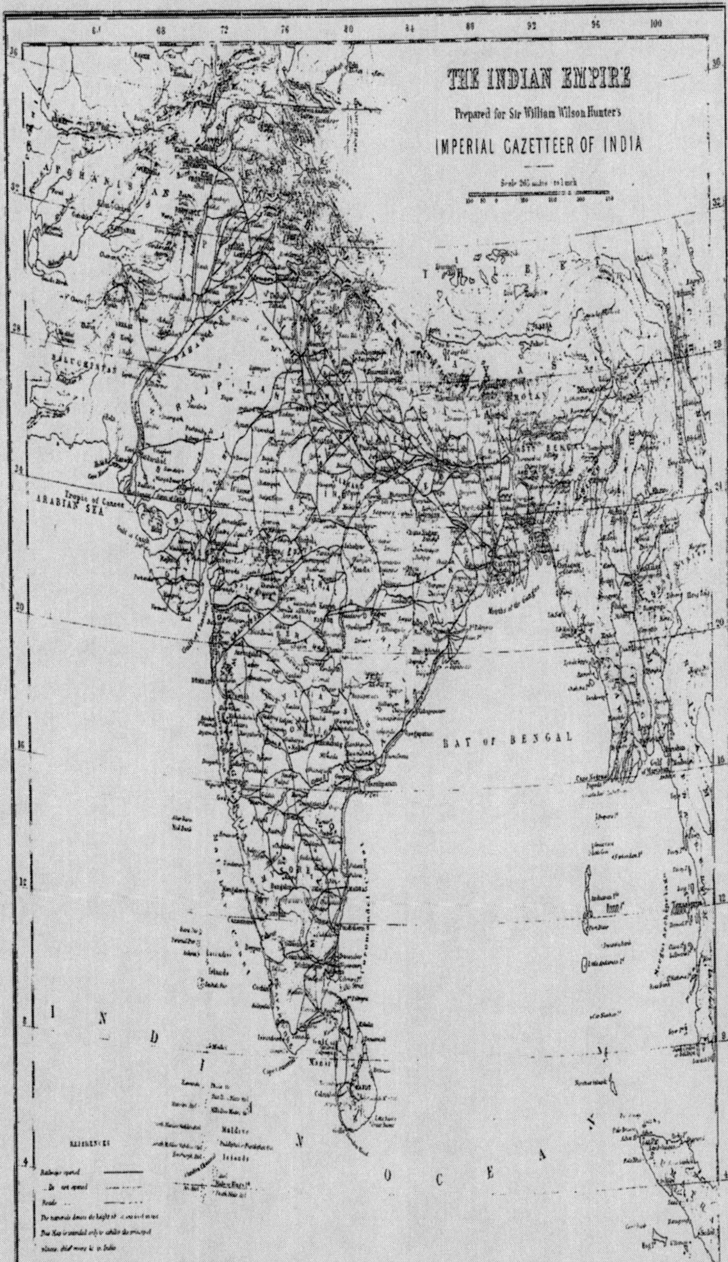
THE INDIAN EMPIRE
Prepared for Sir William Wilson Hunter's
IMPERIAL GAZETTEER OF INDIA
ARABIAN SEA
BAY OF BENGAL
I N D I A N O C E A N

A BRIEF HISTORY OF THE INDIAN PEOPLES

BY SIR WILLIAM WILSON HUNTER, K.C.S.I., C.I.E.

M.A. OXON., LL.D. CAMBRIDGE

A VICE-PRESIDENT OF THE ROYAL ASIATIC SOCIETY

TWENTY-FOURTH EDITION. NINETY-SECOND THOUSAND

OXFORD: AT THE CLARENDON PRESS: 1907

PREFACE

IN this book I try to exhibit the growth of the Indian peoples, to show what part they have played in the world's progress, and what sufferings they have endured from other nations. Short Indian histories, as written by Englishmen, usually dismiss the first two thousand years of their narrative in a few pages, and start by disclosing India as a conquered country. This plan is not good, either for Europeans in India or for the Indians themselves; nor does it accord with the facts. As long as Indian history is presented to the Indian youth as nothing but a dreary record of disunion and subjection, our Anglo-Indian Schools can scarcely become the nurseries of a self-respecting nation. I have therefore tried to put together, from original sources, a brief narrative of what I believe to be the true history of the peoples of India. These sources have been carefully examined in my larger works. This little book merely states, without discussing, the results arrived at by the labour of thirty years.

I have tried to show how an early gifted race, ethnically akin to our own, welded the primitive forest tribes into settled communities. How the nobler stock, set free from the severer struggle for life by the bounty of the Indian soil, created a language, a literature and a religion, of rare stateliness and beauty. How the very absence of that strenuous striving with nature, which is so necessary a discipline for nations, unfitted them for the great conflicts which await all races. How, among the most intellectual class, the spiritual and contemplative aspects of life overpowered the practical and the political. How Hinduism, while sufficing to organize the Indian communities into social and religious confederacies, failed to knit them together into a coherent nation.

India was destined, by her position, to receive the human overflow from the ancient breeding-grounds of Central Asia. Waves of conquest from the north were as inevitable in early times as are the tidal waves from the ocean at the present day. But such conquests, although rapid, were seldom enduring; and although widespread, were never complete. The religious and social organization of Hinduism never succumbed. The greatest of India's conquerors, the Mughals, were being hemmed in by Hindu confederacies before their supremacy had lasted $1\frac{3}{4}$ centuries. So far as can now be estimated, the advance of the British alone saved the Delhi Empire from dismemberment by three Hindu military powers, the Maráthás, Rájputs, and Sikhs. The British Rule has endured, because it is wielded in the joint interest of the Indian races.

But while these thoughts have long been present in my mind, I have not obtruded them on my pages. For I hope that this little book will reach the hands of many who look on history as a record of events, rather than as a compendium of philosophy. The greatest service which an Indian historian can at present render to India, is to state the facts accurately and in such a way that they will be read. If my story is found to combine truth with simplicity, it will have attained all that I aimed at. If it teaches young Englishmen and young Natives of India to think more kindly of each other, I shall esteem myself richly rewarded.

PREFACE TO THE TWENTY-FIRST EDITION

I AM grateful to my critics in many countries for the reception which they have given to this book. It has been translated into five languages, including a literal rendering in Burmese, and a poetical version in Urdu. The English issue alone has reached its eighty-second thousandth copy, and from 1886 onwards for many years the Calcutta University prescribed the work as a text-book for its Entrance Examination. The present edition incorporates suggestions kindly forwarded to me by Directors of Public Instruction, and other educational authorities in India. To Mr. Griffith, formerly Director of Public Instruction in the North-Western Provinces, and to Professor A. A. Macdonell, Deputy Professor of Sanskrit at Oxford, I am specially indebted for a revision of the earlier chapters. The whole proof-sheets have been kindly revised for me by Mr. Morse Stephens, B.A., Lecturer on Indian History to the University of Cambridge.

On my own part, no pains have been spared to render this edition an improvement on its predecessors. Although compressed into a small size, it essays to embody the latest results of Indian historical research, and of that more critical examination of the Indian Records which forms so important a feature of recent Indian work. My endeavour has been to present the history of India in an attractive and accurate narrative, yet within a compass which will place it within reach of the ordinary English and American reader, and render it available as a text-book for English and Indian colleges or schools. The Twenty-first Edition includes the population returns of the latest Indian Census in 1891, and brings down the chronicle of events to the Chitral Expedition of 1895.

W. W. HUNTER.

OAKEN HOLT, CUMNOR, near OXFORD,
1895.

NOTE TO THE TWENTY-THIRD EDITION

IN preparing the revised edition which has become necessary, I have altered nothing in Sir William Hunter's work but what time has rendered incorrect. The figures of the Census of 1901 have been inserted, and the last chapter has been revised where this was necessary, and brought up to the Coronation Darbár of 1903. Where it was possible, I have adopted the words of distinguished public servants in describing the events of the last few years. What it has been my privilege to do is only what the accomplished and deeply regretted author would himself have done. I trust that, touching it with reverence, I have not damaged his work.

W. H. HUTTON.

ST. JOHN'S COLLEGE, OXFORD,
May, 1903.

TABLE OF CONTENTS

CHAPTER I.

CHAPTER II.

CHAPTER III.

CHAPTER IV.

CHAPTER V.

CHAPTER VI.

CHAPTER VII.

CHAPTER VIII.

CHAPTER IX.

CHAPTER X.

CHAPTER XI.

CHAPTER XII.

CHAPTER XIII.

CHAPTER XIV.

CHAPTER XV.

CHAPTER XVI.

NOTE.

The orthography of proper names follows my system adopted by the Indian Government for the *Imperial Gazetteer of India.* That system, while adhering to the popular spelling of very well-known places, such as Punjab, Lucknow, &c., employs in all other cases the vowels with the following uniform sounds :—

a, as in wom*a*n : *á*, as in f*a*ther : *i*, as in p*i*n : *í*, as in intr*i*gue : *o*, as in c*o*ld : *u*, as in b*u*ll : *ú*, as in r*u*ral : *e*, as in gr*e*y.

A BRIEF HISTORY OF THE INDIAN PEOPLES.

CHAPTER I.

The Country.

Situation and Size.—India is a great three-cornered country, stretching southward from mid-Asia into the ocean. Its northern base rests upon the Himálaya ranges; the chief part of its western side is washed by the Arabian Sea, and the chief part of its eastern side by the Bay of Bengal. But while thus guarded along the whole length of its boundaries by nature's defences, the mountains and the ocean, it has on its north-eastern and on its north-western frontiers two opposite sets of gateways which connect it with the rest of Asia. On the north-east it is bounded by the wild hill-regions between Burma and the Chinese Empire or Tibet; on the north-west by the Muhammadan States of Afghánistán and Balúchistán; and two streams of population of widely diverse types have poured into India by the passes at these north-eastern and north-western corners.

India extends from the eighth to the thirty-sixth degree of north latitude,—that is, from the hot regions near the equator to far within the temperate zone. The capital, Calcutta, lies in 88 degrees of E. longitude; so that, when the sun sets at six o'clock there, it is just past mid-day in England. The length of India from north to south, and its greatest breadth from east to west, are both about 1900 miles; but it tapers with a pear-shaped curve to a point at Cape Comorin, its southern extremity. To this compact dominion the English have added Burma, or the country on the eastern shores of the Bay of Bengal. The whole territory thus described contains over 1½ millions of square miles, and 288 millions of inhabitants. India, therefore, has an area almost equal to, and a population in excess of, the area and population of all Europe, less Russia.

The Four Regions.—This noble empire is rich in varieties of scenery and climate, from the highest mountains in the world to vast river-deltas, raised only a few inches above the level of the sea. It teems with the products of nature, from the fierce beasts and tangled jungles of the tropics, to the stunted barley crop which the hillman rears, and the small furred animal which he traps, within sight of the eternal snow. But if we could look down on the whole from a balloon, we should find that India is made up of four well-defined tracts. The first includes the Himálayan mountains, which shut India out from the rest of Asia on the north; the second stretches southwards from their foot, and comprises the plains of the great rivers which issue from the Himálayas; the third tract slopes upwards again from the southern edge of the river-plains, and consists of a high, three-sided tableland, dotted with peaks, and covering the southern half of India; the fourth is Burma on the east of the Bay of Bengal.

First Region: The Himálayas.—The first of these four regions is composed of the Himálayas and their offshoots to the southward. The Himálayas (meaning, in Sanskrit, the Abode of Snow) form two irregular mountain walls, running nearly parallel to each other east and west, with a hollow trough or valley beyond. The southernmost of these walls rises steeply from the plains of India to over 20,000 feet, or four miles in height. It culminates in Mount Everest, 29,002 feet, the highest peak in the world. The crests then subside on the northward into a series of dips, lying about 13,000 feet above the sea. Behind these dips rises the inner range of the Himálayas, a second wall of mountains and snow. Beyond the double wall thus formed, is the great trough or line of valleys in which the Indus, the Sutlej, and the Brahmaputra gather their waters. From the northern side of these valleys rises the tableland of Tibet, 16,000 feet above the sea. The Himálayas shut out India from the rest of Asia. Their heights between Tibet and India are crowned with eternal snow; while vast glaciers, one of which is known to be sixty miles in length, slowly move their masses of ice downwards to the valleys. This wild region is in many parts impenetrable to man, and nowhere yields a route for an army. But bold parties of traders, wrapped in sheepskins, force their way across its passes, 18,000 feet high. The bones of worn-out mules and ponies mark their path. The little yak cow, whose bushy tail is manufactured in Europe into lace, is employed in the Himálayas as a beast of burden, and patiently toils up the steepest gorges with a heavy load on her back. The sheep are also used to carry bags of borax to markets near the plains. They are then shorn of their fleeces and eaten as mutton. A few return into the inner mountains laden with sugar and cloth.

Offshoots of the Himálayas.—The Himálayas not only form a double wall along the north of India, but at both ends send out hilly offshoots southwards, which protect its north-eastern and north-western boundaries. On the north-east, these offshoots, under the name of the Nága and Patkoi mountains, form a barrier between the civilized British Districts and the wild tribes of Upper Burma. But the barrier is pierced, just at the corner where it strikes southwards from the Himálayas, by a passage through which the Brahmaputra river rushes into the Assam valley. On the opposite or north-western frontier of India, the hilly offshoots run down the entire length of the British boundary from the Himálayas to the sea. As they proceed southwards, they are in turn known as the Safed Koh, the Suláimán range, and the Hála mountains. This western barrier has peaks over 11,000 feet in height; but it is pierced at the corner where it strikes southwards from the Himálayas by an opening, the Kháibar pass, near which the Kábul river flows into India. The Kháibar pass, with the Kuram pass to the south of it, the Gwalarí pass near Dera Ismáil Khán, and the famous Bolán pass, still further south, form the gateways from India to Afghánistán and Balúchistán.

Himálayan Water-Supply.—The rugged Himálayas, while thus keeping out enemies, are a source of food and wealth to the Indian people. They collect and store up water for the hot plains below. Throughout the summer, vast quantities of moisture are exhaled from the distant tropical seas. This moisture gathers into vapour, and is carried northward by the monsoon, or regular wind, which sets in from the south in the month of June. The monsoon drives the masses of vapour northwards before it across the length and breadth of India,—sometimes in the form of long processions of clouds, which a native poet has likened to flights of great white birds; sometimes in the shape of rain-storms, which crash through the forests, and leave a line of unroofed villages and flooded fields on their track. The moisture which does not fall as rain on its aerial voyage over India, is at length dashed against the Himálayas. These stop its further progress northwards, and the moisture descends as rain on their outer slopes, or is frozen into snow in its attempts to cross their inner heights. Very little moisture passes beyond them, so that while their southern sides receive the heaviest rainfall in the world, and pour it down in torrents to the Indian rivers, the great plain of Tibet on the north gets scarcely any rain. At Cherra Púnjí, where the monsoon first strikes the hills in Assam, 523 inches of rain fall annually; while in one year (1861) as many as 805 inches are reported to have poured down, of which 366 inches fell in the single month of June. While, therefore, the yearly rainfall in London is about two feet, and that of the plains of India from one to seven, the usual rainfall at Cherra Púnjí is thirty feet, or enough to float the largest man-of-war; while in one year sixty-seven feet of water fell from the sky, or sufficient to drown a high three-storeyed house.

Himálayan Products and Scenery.—This heavy rainfall renders the southern slopes of the Himálayas very fertile. Their upper ranges form bare grey masses, but wherever there is any depth of soil a forest springs up; and the damp belt of lowland at their foot, called the Tarái, is covered with dense fever-breeding jungle, habitable only by a few rude tribes and wild beasts. Thickets of tree-ferns and bamboos adorn their eastern ranges; tracts of rhododendron, which here grows into a forest tree, blaze red and pink in the spring; the deodar, or Himálayan cedar, rises in dark stately masses. The branches of the trees are themselves clothed with mosses, ferns, and flowering creepers or orchids. In the autumn, crops of red and yellow millet run in ribands of brilliant colour down the hill-sides. The chief saleable products of the Himálayas are timber and charcoal; barley, small grains or millets, grown in the hot valleys and upon terraces formed with much labour on the slopes; potatoes, other vegetables, and honey. Strings of ponies and mules straggle with their burdens along the narrow paths, at places cut out of the sheer precipice. The muleteers and their hard-working wives load themselves also with pine stems and conical baskets of grain.

The Destruction of the Forests.—The high price of wood on the plains has caused many of the hills to be stripped of their forests, so that the rainfall now rushes quickly down their bare slopes, and no new woods can spring up. The potato crop, introduced from England, leads to a further destruction of timber. The hillman clears his potato ground by burning a ring round the stems of the great trees, and laying out the side of the mountain into terraces. In a few years the bark drops off the trees, and the forest stands bleached and ruined. Some of the trees rot on the ground, like giants fallen in a confused fight; others still remain upright, with white trunks and skeleton arms. In the end, the rank green potato crop marks the spot where a forest has been slain and buried. Several of the ruder hill tribes follow an even more wasteful mode of tillage. Destitute of either ploughs or cattle, they burn down the jungle, and exhaust the soil by a quick succession of crops, raised by the hoe. In a year or two the whole settlement moves off to a fresh patch of jungle, which they clear and exhaust, and then desert in like manner.

The Himálayan River System.—The special feature of the Himálayas, however, is that they send down the rainfall from their northern as well as from their southern slopes upon the Indian plains. For, as we have seen, they form a double mountain-wall, with a deep trough or valley beyond. Even the rainfall which passes beyond their outer or southern heights is stopped by their inner or northern ridges, and drains into the trough behind. Of the three great rivers of India,—the two longest—namely, the Indus and the Brahmaputra—take their rise in this trough lying on the north of the double wall of the Himálayas; while the third, the Ganges, receives its waters from their southern slopes.

Indus and Sutlej.—The Indus, with its mighty feeder the Sutlej, and the Brahmaputra rise not very far from each other, in lonely valleys, which are separated from India by mountain barriers 15,000 feet high. The Indus and the Sutlej first flow westwards. Then, turning south, through openings in the Himálayas, they join with shorter rivers in the Punjab, and their united stream falls into the Indian Ocean after a course of 1800 miles.

Brahmaputra.—The Brahmaputra, on the other hand, strikes to the east, flowing behind the Himálayas until it searches out a passage for itself through their clefts at the north-eastern corner of Assam. It then turns sharply round to the west, and afterwards to the south, and so finally reaches the Bay of Bengal. Like the Indus, it has a course of about 1800 miles. Thus, while the Indus and the Brahmaputra rise close to each other behind the Himálayas, and run an almost equal course, their mouths lie 1500 miles apart, on the opposite sides of India. Both of them have a long secret existence in the trough between the double mountain wall before they pierce through the hills; and they bring to the Indian plains the drainage from the northern slopes of the Himálayas. Indeed, the first part of the course of the Brahmaputra is still unexplored. It bears the name of the Sampu for nearly a thousand miles of its passage behind the Himálayan wall, and it is not till it bursts through the mountains into India that the noble stream receives its Sanskrit name of Brahmaputra, the son of Brahmá or God.

The Ganges and its great tributary the Jumna collect the drainage from the southern slopes of the Himálayas; they join their waters to those of the Brahmaputra as they approach the sea, and, after a course of 1500 miles, enter the Bay of Bengal by a vast network of channels.

Second Region: The River Plains.—The wide plains watered by the Himálayan rivers form the second of the four regions into which I have divided India. They extend from the Bay of Bengal on the east to the Indian Ocean on the west, and contain the richest and most densely-crowded provinces of the Indian Empire. One set of invaders after another have, from very ancient times, entered by the passes at their north-eastern and north-western corners, and, following the courses of the rivers, pushed the earlier comers south towards the sea. About 150 millions of people now live on and around these river plains, in the provinces known as the Lieutenant-Governorship of Bengal, Assam, Oudh, the North-Western Provinces, the Punjab, Sind, Rájputána, and other Native States. The Indus brings water from the Himálayas to the western side of the river plains of Northern India, the Brahmaputra to their eastern, while the Ganges and its feeders fertilize their central region.

The Indus, after it unites the five rivers of the Punjab, ceases to obtain further tributaries, and the great desert of Rájputána stretches from its left bank. The Brahmaputra, on the extreme east of the plains, passes down the still thinly-inhabited valley of Assam; and it is only in the lower part of its course, as it approaches the Ganges, that a dense population is found on its margin. But the Ganges and its great tributary the Jumna flow for nearly a thousand miles almost parallel to the Himálayas, and receive many streams from them. They do the work of water-carrier for most of Northern India, and the people reverence the bountiful rivers which fertilize their fields. The sources of the Ganges and Jumna in the mountains are held sacred; their point of junction at Allahábád is yearly visited by thousands of pilgrims; and a great religious gathering takes place each January on Ságar island, where the united stream formerly poured into the sea. To bathe in Mother Ganges, as she is lovingly called, purified from sin during life; and the devout Hindu died in the hope that his ashes would be borne by her waters to the ocean. The Ganges is also a river of great cities. Calcutta, Patná, and Benares are built on her banks; Agra and Delhi on those of her tributary the Jumna; and Allahábád on the tongue of land where the two sister streams unite.

The Work done by the Rivers.—In order to understand

the Indian plains, we must have a clear idea of the part played by these great rivers; for the rivers first create the land, then fertilize it, and finally distribute its produce. The plains were in many parts upheaved by volcanic forces, or deposited in an aqueous era, long before man appeared on the earth. But in other parts the plains of Northern India have been formed out of the silt which the rivers bring down from the mountains, and at this day we may stand by and watch the ancient, silent process of land-making go on. A great Bengal river like the Ganges has two distinct stages in its career from the Himálayas to the sea. In the first stage of its course, it runs along the bottom of valleys, receives the drainage and mud of the country on both sides, absorbs tributaries, and rushes forward with an ever-increasing volume of water and silt. But by the time that the Ganges reaches the middle of Lower Bengal, it enters on the second stage of its life. Finding its speed checked by the equal level of the plains, it splits out into several channels, like a jet of water suddenly obstructed by the finger, or a jar of liquid dashed on the floor. Each of the new streams thus created throws off its own set of channels to left and right.

The Bengal Delta.—The country which these numerous channels or offshoots enclose and intersect, forms the Delta of Bengal. The network of streams struggles slowly across this vast flat; and the currents are no longer able, owing to their diminished speed, to carry along the silt or sand which the more rapid parent river had brought down from Northern India. The sluggish split-up rivers of the delta accordingly drop their burden of silt in their channels or on their margins, producing almond-shaped islands, and by degrees raising their beds above the surrounding plains. In this way the rivers of a delta build themselves up, as it were, into high-level canals, which in the rainy season overflow their banks, and leave their silt upon the low country on either side. Thousands of square miles in Lower Bengal thus receive each autumn a top-dressing of new soil, brought free of cost by the river-currents from the distant Himálayas,—a system of natural manuring which yields a constant succession of rich crops.

The Rivers as Land-makers.—As the rivers creep further

down the delta, they become more and more sluggish, and raise their beds still higher above the adjacent plains. Each set of channels has a depressed tract or swamp on both sides, so that the lowest levels in a delta lie often about half-way between the rivers. The stream overflows into these depressed tracts, and gradually fills them up with its silt. The water which rushes from the rivers into the swamps is sometimes yellow from the quantity of silt or sand which it carries. When it has stood a few days in the swamps, and the river-flood subsides, the water flows back from the swamps into the river-channels; but it has dropped all its silt, and is of a clear dark-brown hue. The silt remains in the swamp, and by degrees fills it up, thus slowly creating new land.

River Estuaries.—The last scene in the life of an Indian river is a wilderness of forest and swamp at the end of its delta, amid whose malarious solitudes the network of channels merges into the sea. Here all the secrets of land-making stand disclosed. The streams, finally checked by the dead weight of the sea, deposit their remaining silt, which rises above the surface of the water in the shape of banks or curved headlands. The ocean-currents also find themselves impeded by the down-flow from the rivers, and drop the burden of sand which the tides sweep along the coast. In this way, while the shore gradually grows out into the sea, owing to the deposit of river silt, islands or bars are formed around the river mouths from the sand dropped by the ocean-currents, and a double process of land-making goes on.

The Rivers as Irrigators and Highways.—The great Indian rivers, therefore, not only supply new ground by depositing islands in their beds, and by filling up the low-lying tracts or swamps beyond their margins, but also by forming banks and capes and masses of land at their mouths. They slowly construct their deltas by driving back the sea. The land which they thus create, they also fertilize. In the lower parts of their course, their overflow affords a natural system of irrigation and manuring; in the higher parts, man has to step in, and to bring their water by canals to the fields. They form, moreover, cheap highways for carrying the produce of the country to the towns and seaports; and what the arteries are to the human body, the rivers are to the plains of Bengal.

The Rivers as Destroyers.—But the very vastness of their energy causes terrible calamities. Scarcely a year passes without floods, which sweep off cattle and grain stores, and the thatched cottages, with anxious families perched on their roofs. In the upper part of their courses, where their water is carried by canals to the fields, the rich irrigated lands sometimes breed fever, and are in places destroyed and rendered sterile by a saline crust called *reh.* Further down, the uncontrollable rivers wriggle across the face of the country, deserting their old beds, and searching out new channels for themselves, it may be at a distance of many miles. During these restless changes, they drown the lands and villages that lie in their path; and a Bengal proprietor has sometimes to look on helplessly while his estate is being converted into the new bed of a broad, deep stream. Even in their quiet moods the rivers steadily steal land from the old owners, and give it capriciously to a fresh set. Each autumn the mighty currents undermine, and then rend away, the fields and hamlets on their margins. Their activity in land-making stops up their channels with newly formed islands, and has thus left high and dry in ruin many a once important city along their banks. The ancient harbours at their mouths have in like manner been land-locked and shut off from the sea, by islands and bars formed from the silt or sand jointly deposited by the rivers and the ocean-currents.

Crops and Scenery of the Northern River Plains.—Throughout the river plains of Bengal, two harvests, and in some provinces three, are reaped each year. In many districts, indeed, the same fields have to yield two crops within the twelve months. Wheat and various grains, pease, pulses, oil-seeds, and green crops of many sorts are reaped in spring; the early rice crops in September; the great rice harvest of the year and other grains in November or December. Before these last have been gathered in, it is time to prepare the ground again for the spring crops; and the husbandman knows no rest except during the hot weeks of May, when he is anxiously waiting for the rains. The northern and drier regions, along the higher courses of the rivers, roll upwards from their banks into fertile plains, dotted with mud-built villages, and adorned with noble trees. Mango groves scent the air with their blossom in spring, and yield their abundant fruit in summer. The spreading banian with its colonnades of hanging roots, the stately *pípal* with its masses of foliage, the leafless wild cotton-tree laden with its heavy red flowers, the tall feathery tamarind, and the quick-growing *babúl*, rear their heads above the crop fields. As the rivers approach the coast, the palms begin to take possession of the scene.

Crops of the Delta.—The ordinary landscape in the Bengal Delta is a flat stretch of rice fields, fringed round with evergreen masses of bamboos, cocoa-nuts, *areca*, and other coroneted palms. . This densely-peopled tract seems at first sight bare of villages, for each hamlet is hidden amid its own grove of plantains and wealth-giving trees. The crops also change as we sail down the rivers. In the north, the principal grains are wheat, barley, and millets, such as *joár* and *bájra*. The two last form the food of the masses, rice, in Northern Bengal, being only grown on irrigated lands, and consumed by the rich. In the delta, on the other hand, rice is the staple crop and the universal diet. More than a hundred varieties of it are known to the Bengal peasant. Sugar-cane, oil-seeds, cotton, tobacco, indigo, and many precious spices and dyes grow both in the north and the south. The tea-plant is reared on several hilly ranges which skirt the plains, but chiefly around Dárjíling or in the Dwárs and Assam; the opium poppy, about half-way down the Ganges, near Benares and Patná; the silkworm mulberry, still further down in Lower Bengal; while the jute fibre is essentially a crop of the delta, and would exhaust any soil not fertilized by river floods. Even the jungles yield the costly lac dye and *tasar* silk cocoons. To name all the crops of the river plains would weary the reader. Nearly every vegetable product which feeds and clothes a people, or enables it to trade with foreign nations, abounds.

Third Region: The Southern Tableland.—Having thus glanced at the leading features of the Himálayas on the north, and of the great river plains at their base, I come now to the third division of India, namely, the three-sided tableland which covers the southern half of the peninsula. This tract, known in ancient times as The Deccan, or 'The South' (*dakshin*), comprises the Central Provinces, Berar, Madras, and Bombay, and the native territories of the Nizám, Mysore, Sindhia, Holkar, and other feudatory princes. It slopes upwards from the southern edge of the Gangetic plains. Two sacred mountains stand as outposts on the extreme east and west, with confused ranges stretching eight hundred miles between. At the western extremity, Mount Abu, famous for its exquisite Jain temples, rises 5650 feet from the Rájputána plains, like an island out of the sea. The Arávalli chain, the Vindhya mountains, the Sátpura and Káimur ranges, with other highland tracts, run across the country eastwards until they abut on the Ganges valley, under the name of the Rájmahál hills. On the eastern edge of the central mountainous region, Mount Párasnáth, also sacred to Jain rites, towers 4400 feet above the level of the Gangetic plains.

Scenery of the Southern Tableland.—These various ranges form, as it were, the northern wall and buttresses on which rests the central tableland of India. Now pierced by road and rail, they stood in former times as a barrier of mountain and jungle between Northern and Southern India, and greatly increased the difficulty of welding the whole into one empire. The three-cornered tableland forms a vast mass of forests, ridges, and peaks, broken by cultivated valleys and high-lying plains. Its eastern and western sides are known as the Gháts, a word applied to a flight of steps up a river bank or to a mountain pass. The Eastern Gháts run in fragmentary spurs and ranges down the Madras side of India, sometimes receding inland, and leaving broad plains between them and the coast. The Western Gháts form a great sea-wall for the Bombay Presidency, with only a narrow strip between them and the shore. At places they rise in magnificent precipices and headlands almost out of the ocean, and truly look like colossal 'landing-stairs' from the sea. The Eastern and Western Gháts meet at an angle near Cape Comorin at the southern extremity of India, and so complete the three sides of the tableland. The inner plateau itself lies far below the snow line, and its ordinary elevation seldom exceeds 2000 to 3000 feet. Its best-known hills are the Nílgiris (Blue Mountains), which contain the summer capital of Madras, Utakamand, 7000 feet above the sea. The highest point is Dodábetta peak, 8760 feet, at the southern extremity of Mysore.

Rivers of the Southern Tableland.—This inner region of highlands sends its waters chiefly to the eastern coast. The drainage from the northern or Vindhyan edge of the three-sided tableland falls into the Ganges. The Narbadá runs along the southern base of the Vindhyas, and carries their southern drainage due west into the Gulf of Cambay. The Tápti flows almost parallel to the Narbadá, a little to the southward, and bears to the Gulf of Cambay the waters from the Sátpura hills. But from this point, as we proceed southwards, the Western Gháts rise into a high unbroken barrier between the Bombay coast and the waters of the inner tableland. The drainage has therefore to make its way right across India to the eastwards, now twisting round hill ranges, now rushing down the valleys between them, until the rain, which the Bombay sea-breeze dropped upon the Western Gháts, finally falls into the Bay of Bengal. In this way the three great rivers of the Madras Presidency—namely, the Godávari, the Krishna (Kistna), and the Káveri—rise in the mountains overhanging the Bombay coast, and traverse the whole breadth of the central tableland before they reach the ocean on the eastern shores of India.

Forests of the Southern Tableland.—The ancient Sanskrit poets speak of the southern tableland as buried under forests; and *sál*, ebony, *sissu*, teak, and other great trees still abound. The Gháts, in particular, are covered with magnificent vegetation wherever a sapling can take root. But tillage has now driven back the jungle to the hilly recesses; and fields of wheat, and many kinds of smaller grain or millets, tobacco, cotton, sugar-cane, and pulses, spread over the open country. The black soil of Southern India is proverbial for its fertility; and the lowlands between the Gháts and the sea rival even Lower Bengal in their fruit-bearing palms, rice harvests, and rich succession of crops. The inner tableland is, however, very liable to droughts; and the people have devised a varied system of irrigation, in some districts from wells, in others from tanks, or from artificial lakes formed by damming up the mouths of river valleys. They thus store the rain brought during a few months by the northern and southern monsoons, and husband it for use throughout the whole year. The food of the common people consists chiefly of small grains or millets, such as *joár*, *bájra*, and *rágí*. The principal exports are cotton and wheat.

Minerals of the Tableland.—It is, moreover, on the three-sided tableland, and among the hilly spurs which project from it, that the mineral wealth of India lies hid. Coal-mining now forms a great industry, both on the north-eastern edge of the tableland in Bengal, and in the valleys of the Central Provinces. Beds of iron ore and limestone hold out a prospect of metal-smelting on a large scale in the future; copper and other metals exist in small quantities. The diamonds of Golconda were long famous. Gold-dust has from very ancient times been washed out of many of the river beds; and gold-mining is now being attempted on scientific principles in Madras and Mysore.

Burma.—Burma, which the English have incorporated into the Indian Empire, consists mainly of the valley of the Irawadi, and a strip of coast along the east side of the Bay of Bengal. It stretches north and south, with the sea on the west, a backbone of lofty ranges running down the middle, and the mountainous frontier of the Chinese Empire and Siam on the east. The central backbone of ranges in Burma is formed by the Yoma mountains. They are covered with dense forests, and separate the Irawadi valley from the strip of coast. The river floats down an abundant supply of teak from the north. A thousand creeks indent the seaboard; and the whole of the level country, both on the coast and in the Irawadi valley, forms a vast rice-field. Tobacco of an excellent quality supplies the cigars which all Burmese men and women smoke; and large quantities of tobacco leaf are also brought over from the Madras Presidency. Until 1886 British Burma was divided into three Provinces—Arakan, or the northern coast strip; Pegu, or the Irawadi valley in the middle; and Tenasserim, or the narrow maritime tract and islands running down from the south of the Irawadi Delta. In 1886 Upper Burma, or the old kingdom of Ava, was added to the British Empire. Arakan and Pegu contain mineral oil springs. Tenasserim is rich in tin mines, and in iron ores equal to the finest Swedish, besides gold and copper in smaller quantities, and a very pure limestone. Rice and timber form the staple exports of Burma, and rice is also the universal food of the people.

MATERIALS FOR REFERENCE.

The materials for a complete study of the physical aspects of India will be found in (1) *The Imperial Gazetteer of India*, 14 vols. 2nd ed. This again is condensed from the Statistical Survey of India in about 120 volumes. (2) The printed Records of the Geological Survey of India. (3) Blanford's *Meteorological Memoirs* and *Meteorology of India.*

CHAPTER II.

The People.

General Survey of the People.—India is divided into two classes of territories; first, Provinces under British rule; second, States under Native Chiefs. The population of the whole amounted in 1901 to over 294 millions, or more than double the number estimated for the Roman Empire in the height of its power. But the English, even more than the Romans, have respected the rights of Native Chiefs who are willing to govern well. Such Chiefs still rule on their own account nearly one-third of the area of India, with over 62 millions of subjects, or more than a quarter of the whole Indian people. The British territories, therefore, comprise about two-thirds of the area of India, and over three-quarters, or more than 231 millions, of its inhabitants.

The Native States.—The Native princes govern their States with the help and under the advice of a British Resident, whom the Viceroy stations at their courts. Some of them reign almost as independent sovereigns; others have less power. They form a great body of feudatory rulers, possessed of revenues and armies of their own. The more important exercise the power of life and death over their subjects; but the authority of all is limited by treaties, by which they acknowledge their 'subordinate dependence' to the British Government. The British Government, as Suzerain in India, does not allow its feudatories to make war upon each other, or to form alliances with foreign States. It interferes when any Chief misgoverns his people; rebukes, and if needful dethrones, the oppressor; protects the weak, and imposes peace upon all.

The British Provinces.—The British possessions are distributed into fourteen Provinces. Each has its own Governor or head; but all are controlled by the supreme Government of India, consisting of a Governor-General in Council. The Governor-General also bears the title of Viceroy. He holds his court and government at Calcutta in the cold weather; and during summer at Simla, in the Himálayas, 7,000 feet above the level of the sea. The Viceroy of India is appointed by the King of England; so also are the Governors of Madras and Bombay. The heads of the other Provinces are chosen for their merit from the Anglo-Indian services, almost always from the Civil Service, and are nominated by the Viceroy, subject in the case of the Lieutenant-Governorships to the approval of the Secretary of State. The King of England is Emperor of India, and is spoken of both officially and commonly in India as 'the King-Emperor.'

Area and Population.—The two tables following show the area and population, first, of the fourteen Provinces of British India, including Aden and the Andaman Islands; and, second, the area and population of the Feudatory States arranged in thirteen groups.

The first table gives the population counted by the Census Officers in British India, inclusive of Aden and the Andaman Islands, in 1901. But, as shown in the footnotes to the table, certain additions have to be made for districts in which the population could only be roughly enumerated or estimated. But, remembering this, we find that the actual total population of British India, inclusive of Aden and the Andaman Islands, amounted to nearly 232 millions in 1901.

In the second table it must be observed that certain areas can only be roughly counted. Making, then, some additions, the actual population of Feudatory or Native India in 1901 was nearly 62½ millions. Adding this number to the actual population of nearly 232 millions in British India, we find that the total population of British and Feudatory India in 1901 (inclusive of Aden and the Andaman Islands) was in round figures 294⅓ millions.

PROVINCE, STATE, OR AGENCY.	Area in square miles.	Total population, 1901.	Number of Persons per square mile.
1. Ajmere	2,711	476,912	176
2. Andaman and Nicobars .	3,188	24,649	7
3. Assam *	56,243	6,126,343	108
4. Balúchistán † (district and administered territory)	45,804	308,246	6
5. Bengal . . .	151,185	74,744,866	494
6. Berar . . .	17,710	2,754,016	154
7. Bombay (Presidency)	123,064	18,559,561	158
Bombay	75,918	15,301,677	201
Sind . . .	47,066	3,210,910	68
Aden .	80	43,974	549
8. Burma ‡ . . .	236,738	10,489,924	44
9. Central Provinces . .	86,614	9,876,646	114
10. Coorg .	1,582	180,607	114
11. Madras	141,726	38,209,436	269
12. North-West Frontier Province § . . .	16,466	2,125,480	129
13. Punjab . . .	97,209	20,330,339	209
14. United Provinces of Agra and Oudh . . .	107,164	47,691,782	445
Agra . . .	83,198	34,858,705	418
Oudh	23,966	12,833,077	538
Total for British India .	1,087,404	231,898,807	213

* Includes South Luchai and Manipur.

† Certain areas were imperfectly enumerated owing to tribal disputes.

‡ Includes Shan States, Chin Hills, and Karrenni.

§ This province was formed in 1901 out of certain Punjab districts and areas not previonsly included in India.

Feudatory India.

States and Agencies.	Area in square miles.	Total population, 1901.	Number of Persons per square mile.
1. Balúchistán (agency tracts)*	86,511	502,500	5
2. Baroda State	8,099	1,952,692	241
3. Bengal Native States	38,652	3,748,544	97
4. Bombay Native States	65,761	6,908,648	105
5. Central India Agency	78,772	8,628,781	109
6. Central Provinces States	29,435	1,996,383	67
7. Haidarábád (Nizám's Dominions)	82,698	11,141,142	134
8. Kashmír State	80,900	2,905,578	35
9. Madras Native States	9,969	4,188,086	420
10. Mysore States	29,444	5,539,399	188
11. Punjab Native States	36,532	4,424,398	121
12. Rájputána Agency	127,541	9,723,301	76
13. United Provinces Native States	5,079	802,097	157
Total for Feudatory India	679,393	62,461,549	91

* Certain areas imperfectly enumerated owing to tribal disputes.

If to the figures in the foregoing tables of the population actually counted by the Census Officers for British and Feudatory India we add the French and Portuguese possessions, we obtain the total for all India. Thus—

All India, including Burma.

	Area in square miles.	Population.	Number of Persons per square mile.
British India (1901)	1,087,404	231,898,807	213
Feudatory India (1901)	679,393	62,461,549	91
French Possessions (March 1, 1901)	178	273,185	Chiefly in towns or suburbs.
Portuguese Possessions (Dec. 1, 1900)	1,086	329,223	
Total for all India, including Burma	1,768,061	294,962,764	166

Density of the Population.—British India is very thickly peopled; and some parts are so overcrowded that the inhabitants can with difficulty obtain land to cultivate. Each square mile of the British Provinces has to feed, on an average, 229 persons. Each square mile of the Native States has to feed, on an average, only 110 persons, or less than one-half. If we exclude the outlying Provinces of Burma and Assam, the people in British India average 279 to the square mile; so that British India is two and a half times more thickly inhabited than the Native States. How thick this population is, may be realized from the fact that, in 1886, France only had 187 people to the square mile; while even in crowded England, wherever the density approaches 200 to the square mile the population ceases to be rural, and has to live by manufactures, by mining, or by city industries.

Few Large Towns in India.—Unlike England, India has few large towns. Thus, in England and Wales, more than one-half of the population, in 1901, lived in towns with upwards of 20,000 inhabitants, while in British India less than one-fifteenth of the people lived in such towns. India, therefore, is almost entirely a rural country; and many of the so-called towns are mere groups of villages, in the midst of which the cattle are driven a-field, and ploughing and reaping go on.

Overcrowded Districts.—We see, therefore, in India a dense population of husbandmen. Wherever their numbers exceed 1 to the acre, or 640 to the square mile—excepting near towns or in irrigated tracts—they find it difficult to raise sufficient crops from the land to supply them with food. Yet many millions of peasants in India are struggling to live off half an acre apiece. In such districts, if the rain falls short by a few inches, the people suffer great distress; if the rain fails to a large extent, thousands die of famine.

Under-peopled Districts.—In some parts of India, therefore, there are more husbandmen than the land can feed. In other parts, vast tracts of fertile soil still await the cultivator. In England, people move freely from over-populated to the thinly-inhabited districts. In India, though emigration is beginning, the peasant generally does not move: he parcels his fields among his children, even when his family has grown too numerous to live upon the crops. If the Indian husbandmen will learn to migrate to tracts where spare land abounds, they will do more than the utmost efforts of Government can accomplish to better themselves and to prevent famines.

Distribution of the People.—It is not stupidity that makes the Indian peasant cling to his hereditary fields. In old days he could move to other districts or provinces only with great difficulty and danger. Roads for carts or wheeled traffic were few and far between; and in many parts of India only existed along the chief military routes. During the century of confusion and Native misrule which preceded the establishment of the British Power, travelling even by such roads as did exist was perilous owing to robbers and armed bands. Railways and steamboats, which are the great modern distributors of population, were altogether unknown in India under Native rule, and have only been introduced into India in our own generation. By the help of roads, railways and river-steamers, it is now possible for the first time for the Indian peasants in overcrowded districts to move to districts where there is still spare land. The Indian cultivators are slowly but surely learning this, and they are moving in large numbers to thinly peopled districts in Eastern and Northern Bengal, Assam, and the Central Provinces.

The Nomadic System of Husbandry.—Throughout many of the hill and frontier tracts land is so plentiful that it yields no rent. The hillmen settle for a few years in some fertile spot, which they clear of jungle. They then exhaust the soil by a rapid succession of crops, and leave it to relapse into forest. In such tracts no rent is charged; but each family of wandering husbandmen pays a poll-tax to the Chief, under whose protection it dwells. As the inhabitants increase, this nomadic system of cultivation gives place to regular tillage. Throughout Burma we see both methods at work side by side; while on the thickly-peopled plains of India the 'wandering husbandmen' have disappeared, and each peasant family remains rooted to the same plot of ground during many generations.

Rise in Rents.—Yet only a hundred years ago there was more land even in Bengal than there were cultivators to till it.

The landlords had to tempt husbandmen to settle on their estates, by giving them land at low rents. Now the cultivators have grown so numerous, that in some districts they will offer any rent for a piece of ground. The Government has, therefore, had to pass laws to prevent too great a rise in rents. These laws recognize the rights of the cultivators in the fields which they have long tilled; and the rents of such hereditary husbandmen cannot be raised above fair rates, fixed by the Courts.

Serfdom abolished.—In the old times the scarcity of people made each family of cultivators of great value to their landlord. In many parts of India, when once a peasant had settled in a village, he was not allowed to go away. In hill districts where the nomadic or wandering system of husbandry still survives, no family is allowed by the Native Chief to quit his territory; for each household pays a poll-tax to the Chief, and the Chief cannot afford to lose this money. In some Provinces the English found the lower classes of husbandmen attached like serfs to the soil. Our officers in South-Eastern Bengal almost raised a rebellion by their efforts to liberate the rural slaves. The descendants of the old serfs still survive; but they are now freemen.

Fourfold Division of the People.—European writers formerly divided the Indian population into two races,—the Hindus and the Muhammadans. But when we look more closely at the people, we find that they consist of four elements. These are—First, the Non-Aryan Tribes, called the Aborigines, who numbered in 1872 (when the first Census of India was taken) about 18 millions in the British Provinces.* Second, the descendants of the Aryan or Sanskrit-speaking Race, now called Bráhmans and Rájputs, who numbered in 1872 about 16 millions. Third, the great Mixed Population, generally known as the Hindus, which has grown out of the Aryan and non-Aryan elements (chiefly from the latter), and numbered in 1872 about 121 millions. Fourth, the Muhammadans, who began to come to India about 1000 A.D., and who numbered in 1872 over

* For the new system of classification adopted by the Census of 1881 and 1891 see *post*, p. 50.

45 millions. These made up the 200 millions of the people under British rule in 1872. Since then the population of British India has grown to over 231 millions in 1901. All the four sections of the population above mentioned have contributed to this increase. But many of the non-Aryan or Aboriginal tribes have during the past twenty years been converted to the Hindu religion, and are now reckoned in the Census as Hindus. The same fourfold division applies to the population of the 62 millions in Feudatory India, but we do not know the numbers of the different classes.

The Two Chief Races of Prehistoric India.—The great sources of the Indian population were, therefore, the non-Aryans and the Aryans; and we must first try to get a clear view of these ancient peoples. Our earliest glimpses of India disclose two races struggling for the soil. The one was a fair-skinned people, which had lately entered by the north-western passes,—a people who called themselves ARYAN, literally of 'noble' lineage, speaking a stately language, worshipping friendly and powerful gods. These Aryans became the Bráhmans and Rájputs of India. The other race was of a lower type, who had long dwelt in the land, and whom the lordly new-comers drove back into the mountains, or reduced to servitude on the plains. The comparatively pure descendants of these two races are now nearly equal in numbers; the intermediate castes, sprung chiefly from the ruder stock, make up the great mass of the Indian population. We shall afterwards see that a third race, the Scythians, also played an important part in India, about the beginning of the Christian era. The Muhammadans belong to a period a thousand years later.

MATERIALS FOR REFERENCE.

Full particulars as to the population of India, according to their birthplace, sex, race, age, religion, their distribution into town and country, and their ability to read and write, are given in the Appendices to my *Indian Empire* (Third edition, 1893). [See also the full tables given in *Statistical Abstracts relating to British India from* 1891–2 *to* 1900–1, 1902.]

CHAPTER III.

The non-Aryans.

The non-Aryans or Aborigines.—The oldest dwellers in India consisted of many tribes, who, in the absence of a race-name of their own, are called the non-Aryans or Aborigines. They have left no written records; indeed, the use of letters, or of any simplest hieroglyphics, was to them unknown. The sole works of their hands which have come down to us are rude stone circles, and the upright slabs and mounds beneath which, like the primitive peoples of Europe, they buried their dead. From the remains found in these tombs, we only discover that, at some far distant but unfixed period, they knew how to make round pots of hard thin earthenware, not inelegant in shape; that they fought with iron weapons and wore ornaments of copper and gold. Earlier remains prove, indeed, that these ancient tomb-builders formed only one link in a chain of primeval races. Before them, India was peopled by tribes unacquainted with the metals, who hunted and warred with polished flint axes and other deftly wrought implements of stone, similar to those found in Northern Europe. And even these were the successors of yet ruder beings, who have left their agate knives and rough flint weapons in the Narbadá valley. In front of this far-stretching background of the Early-Metal and Stone Ages, we see the so-called Aborigines being beaten down by the newly-arrived Aryan race.

The non-Aryans as described by the Aryans.—The victorious Aryans from Western or West-Central Asia called the earlier tribes whom they found in India *Dasyus*, or 'enemies,' and *Dásas*, or 'slaves.' The Aryans entered India from the colder north, and prided themselves on their fair complexion. Their Sanskrit word for 'colour' (*varna*) came to mean 'race' or 'caste.' The old Aryan poets, who composed the Veda at least 3000 and perhaps 4000 years ago, praised their bright gods, who, 'slaying the Dasyus, protected the *Aryan colour*';

who 'subjected the black-skin to the Aryan man.' They tell us of their own 'stormy deities, who rush on like furious bulls and scatter the black-skin.' Moreover, the Aryan, with his finely-formed features, loathed the squat Mongolian faces of the Aborigines. One Vedic poet speaks of the Dasyus or non-Aryans as 'noseless' or flat-nosed, while another praises his own 'beautiful-nosed' gods. The same unsightly feature was noticed with regard to a non-Aryan Asiatic tribe, by the companions of Alexander the Great on his Indian expedition, more than a thousand years later. But indeed the Vedic hymns abound in scornful epithets for the primitive races of India, as 'disturbers of sacrifices,' 'gross feeders on flesh,' 'raw-eaters,' 'lawless,' 'not-sacrificing,' 'without gods,' and 'without rites.' As time went on, and these rude tribes were driven back into the forest, they were painted in still more hideous shapes, till they became the 'monsters' and 'demons' of the Aryan poet and priest. Their ancient race-name, Dasyu, or 'enemy,' thus grew to signify goblin or devil, as the old Teutonic word for enemy or 'the hater' (modern German *feind*) has become the English 'fiend.'

More Civilized non-Aryan Tribes.—Nevertheless all the non-Aryan tribes of ancient India could not have been savages. We hear of wealthy Dasyus or non-Aryans; and the Vedic hymns speak of their 'seven castles' and 'ninety forts.' The Aryans afterwards made alliance with non-Aryan tribes; and some of the most powerful kingdoms of India were ruled by non-Aryan kings. Nor were the non-Aryans devoid of religious rites, or of cravings after a future life. 'They adorn,' says an ancient Sanskrit book, 'the bodies of their dead with gifts, with raiment, with ornaments; imagining that thereby they shall attain the world to come.' These ornaments are the bits of bronze, copper, and gold which we now dig up from beneath their rude stone monuments. In the Rámáyana, the Sanskrit epic which narrates the advance of the Aryans into Southern India, a non-Aryan chief describes his race as of fearful swiftness, unyielding in battle, in colour like a dark-blue cloud.'

The non-Aryans as they are.—Let us now examine these primitive peoples as they exist at the present day. Thrust back by the Aryan invaders from the plains, they have lain hidden away in the mountains, like the remains of extinct animals found in hill-caves. India thus forms a great museum of races, in which we can study man from his lowest to his highest stages of culture. The specimens are not fossils or dry bones, but living tribes, each with its own set of curious customs and religious rites.

The Andaman Islanders.—Among the rudest fragments of mankind are the isolated Andaman islanders, or non-Aryans of the Bay of Bengal. The Arab and early European voyagers described them as dog-faced man-eaters. The English officers sent to the islands in 1855 to establish a settlement, found themselves in the midst of naked cannibals; who daubed their bodies at festivals with red earth, and mourned for their dead friends by plastering themselves with dark mud. They used a noise like *crying* to express friendship or joy; bore only names of common gender, which they received before birth, and which therefore had to be applicable to either sex; and their sole conception of a god was an evil spirit, who spread disease. For five years they repulsed every effort at intercourse with showers of arrows; but our officers slowly brought them to a better frame of mind, by building sheds near the settlement, where some of these poor beings might find shelter and receive medicines and food.

The Hillmen of Madras.—The Anamalai hills, in Southern Madras, form the refuge of many non-Aryan tribes. The long-haired, wild-looking Puliyárs live on jungle products, mice, or any small animals they can catch; and worship demons. Another clan, the Mundavers, have no fixed dwellings, but wander over the innermost hills with their cattle. They shelter themselves in caves or under little leaf sheds, and seldom remain in one spot more than a year. The thick-lipped, small-bodied Kaders, 'Lords of the Hills,' are a remnant of a higher race. They live by the chase, and wield some influence over the ruder forest-folk. These hills abound in the great stone monuments (kistvaens and dolmens) which the ancient non-Aryans erected over their dead. The Nairs, the old military non-Aryan ruling race of South-Western India, still keep up the ancient system of polyandry, according to which one woman is the wife of several husbands, and a man's property descends not to his own sons, but to his sister's children. This system also appears among the non-Aryan tribes of the Himálayas at the opposite extremity of India.

Non-Aryans of the Vindhya Ranges.—Many wild tribes inhabit the mountain ranges which separate Northern from Southern India. The best-known of these rude races are perhaps the Bhíls, who dwell in the Vindhya hills, from Udaipur State far north of the Narbadá river, southwards to the Khándesh Agency in the Bombay Presidency. They move about with their herds of sheep and goats through the jungly highlands, and eke out a spare livelihood by the chase and the natural products of the forest. In Udaipur State, they are settled in little hamlets, each homestead being built on a separate hillock, so as to render it impossible for their enemies to surprise a whole village at once. A single family may be seized, but the shouts which it raises give the alarm to all the rest, and in a few minutes the war-cry spreads from hill to hill, and swarms of half-naked savages rush together in arms to beat off the intruder. Before the British rule the Bhíls were the terror of the neighbouring country, plundering and burning villages far and wide; while the Native Governments revenged themselves from time to time by fearful Bhíl massacres. In 1818 the East India Company obtained the neighbouring Bombay District of Khándesh, but its first expedition against the Bhíls failed miserably; one-half of our men having perished of fever in the jungles. Soon afterwards Sir James Outram took these wild tribes in hand. He made friends with them by means of feasts and tiger-hunts. Nine Bhíl warriors, who were his constant companions in tracking the beasts of chase, formed the beginning of a regular Bhíl corps which numbered 600 men in 1827, and fought boldly for the British Government. These loyal Bhíls put a stop to plundering among their wilder fellow-countrymen, and they have proved themselves so trustworthy that they are now employed as policemen and treasury-guards throughout a large tract in the Khándesh Political Agency.

Non-Aryans of the Central Provinces.—In the Central Provinces, the non-Aryan races form a large part of the population. In certain localities they amount to one-half of the inhabitants. Their most important race, the Gonds, have made advances in civilization; but the wilder tribes still cling to the forest, and live by the chase. Some of them used, within the present generation, flint points for their arrows. They wield bows of great strength, which they hold with their feet, while they draw the string with both hands. They can send an arrow right through the body of a deer. The Márís fly from their grass-built huts on the approach of a stranger. Once a year a messenger comes to them from the local Rájá to take their tribute, which consists chiefly of jungle products. He does not, however, enter their hamlets, but beats a drum outside, and then hides himself. The shy Márís creep forth from their huts, place what they have to give in an appointed spot, and run back again into their retreats.

The 'Leaf-wearers' of Orissa.—Farther to the north-east, in the Tributary States of Orissa, there is a poor tribe, about 10,000 in number, of Juángs or Patuas, literally the 'leaf-wearers.' Until twenty years ago, their women wore no clothes, but only a few strings of beads around the waist, with a bunch of leaves before and behind. In 1871, the English officer called together the clan, and, after a speech, handed out strips of cotton for the women to put on. They then passed in single file before him in their new clothes, and made obeisance. Finally, they gathered the bunches of leaves, which had formed their sole clothing, into a great heap, and solemnly set fire to it.

Himálayan Tribes.—Proceeding to the northern boundary of India, we find the slopes and spurs of the Himálayas peopled by a great variety of rude non-Àryan tribes. Some of the Assam hillmen have no word for expressing distance by miles or by any land-measure, but reckon the length of a journey by the number of plugs of tobacco or betel-leaf which they chew upon the way. They hate work; and, as a rule, they are fierce, black, undersized, and ill-fed. In old times they earned a scanty livelihood by plundering the hamlets of the Assam valley. We now use them as a sort of police, to keep the peace of the border, in return for a yearly gift of cloth, hoes, and grain. Their very names bear witness to their former wild life. One tribe, the Akas of Assam, is divided into two clans, whose names literally mean 'The eaters of a thousand hearths,' and 'The thieves who lurk in the cotton-field.'

More advanced non-Aryan Tribes.—Many of the aboriginal tribes, therefore, remain in the same early stage of human progress as that ascribed to them by the Vedic poets more than 3000 years ago. But others have made great advances, and form communities of a well-developed type. These higher races, like the ruder ones, are scattered over the length and breadth of India, and I must confine myself to a very brief account of two of them,—the Santáls and the Kandhs.

The Santáls.—The Santáls have their home among the hills which abut on the valley of the Ganges in Lower Bengal. They dwell in villages of their own, apart from the people of the plains, and, when first counted by British officers, numbered about a million. Although still clinging to many customs of a hunting forest tribe, they have learned the use of the plough, and have settled down into skilful husbandmen. Each hamlet is governed by its own headman, who is supposed to be a descendant of the original founder of the village, and who is assisted by a deputy headman and a watchman. The boys of the hamlet had their separate officers, and were strictly controlled by their own headman and his deputy till they entered the married state. The Santáls know not the cruel distinctions of Hindu caste, but trace their tribes, usually fixed at seven, to the seven sons of the first parents. The whole village feasts, hunts, and worships together. So strong is the bond of race, that expulsion from the tribe used to be the only Santál punishment. A heinous criminal was cut off from 'fire and water' in the village, and sent forth alone into the jungle. Smaller offences were forgiven upon a public reconciliation with the tribe; to effect which the guilty one had to provide a feast, with much rice-beer, for his clansmen.

Santál Ceremonies.—The Santáls do not allow of child-weddings. They marry about the age of 15 to 17, when the young people are old enough to choose for themselves. At the end of the ceremony the girl's relatives pound burning charcoal with the household pestle, and extinguish it with water, in token of the breaking up of her former family ties. The Santáls respect their women, and do not take a second wife during the life of the first, except when the first is childless. They solemnly burn their dead, and whenever possible they used to float three fragments of the skull down the Dámodar river, the sacred stream of the race.

Santál Religion.—The Santál has no knowledge of bright and friendly gods, such as the Vedic singers of the Aryan Indians worshipped. Still less can he imagine one omnipotent and beneficent Deity, who watches over mankind. Hunted and driven back before the Hindus and Muhammadans, the Santál does not understand how a Being can be more powerful than himself without wishing to harm him. 'What,' said a Santál to an eloquent missionary who had been discoursing on the omnipotence of the Christian God,—'what if that strong One should eat me?' He thinks that the earth swarms with demons, whose ill-will he tries to avert by the sacrifice of goats, cocks, and chickens. There are the ghosts of his forefathers, river-spirits, forest-spirits, well-demons, mountain-demons, and a mighty host of unseen beings, whom he must keep in good humour. These dwell chiefly in the ancient *sál* trees which shade his village. In some hamlets the people dance round every tree, so that they may not by evil chance miss the one in which the village-spirits happen to be dwelling.

Santál History.—Until near the end of the last century, the Santáls lived by plundering the adjacent plains. But under British rule they settled down into peaceful cultivators. To prevent disputes between them and the Hindu villagers of the lowlands, our officers set up in 1832 a boundary of stone pillars. But the Hindu money-lender soon came among them; and the simple hillmen plunged into debt. Their strong love of kindred prevented them from running away, and they sank into serfs to the Hindu usurers. The poor Santál gave over his whole crop each year to the money-lender, and was allowed just enough food to keep his family at work. When he died, the life-long burden descended to his children; for the high sense of honour among the Santáls compels a son to take upon himself his father's debts. In 1848 three entire villages threw up their clearings, and fled in despair to the jungle. In 1855 the Santáls started in a body of 30,000 men, with their bows and arrows, to walk to Calcutta and lay their condition before the Governor-General. At first they were orderly; but the way was long; they had to live, and the hungry ones began to plunder. Quarrels broke out between them and the British police; and within a week they were in armed rebellion. The rising was put down, not without mournful bloodshed. Their complaints were carefully inquired into, and a simple system of government, directly under the eye of a British officer, was granted to them. They are now a prosperous people. But their shyness and superstition make them dread any new thing. A few of them took up arms to resist the Census of 1881.

The Kandhs or Kondhs.—The Kandhs, literally 'The Mountaineers,' a tribe about 100,000 strong, inhabit the steep and forest-covered ranges which rise from the Orissa coast. Their system of government is purely patriarchal. The family is strictly ruled by the father. The grown-up sons have no property during his life, but live in his house with their wives and children, and all share the common meal prepared by the grandmother. The head of the tribe is usually the eldest son of the patriarchal family; but if he be not fit for the post he is set aside, and an uncle or a younger brother is appointed. He enters on no undertaking without calling together the elders of the tribe.

Kandh Wars and Punishments.—Up to 1835, when the English introduced milder laws, the Kandhs punished murder by blood-revenge. The kinsmen of the dead man were bound to kill the slayer, unless appeased by a payment of grain or cattle. Any one who wounded another had to maintain the sufferer until he recovered from his hurt. A stolen article must be returned, or its value paid; but the Kandh twice convicted of theft was driven forth from his tribe—the greatest punishment known to the race. Disputes were settled by duels, or by deadly combats between armed bands, or by the ordeal of boiling oil or heated iron, or by taking a solemn oath on an ant-hill, or on a tiger's claw, or on a lizard's skin. If a housefather died leaving no sons, his land was parcelled out among the other male heads of the village; for no woman was allowed to hold land, nor indeed any Kandh who could not with his own arms defend it.

Kandh Agriculture.—The Kandh system of tillage represents a stage half way between the migratory cultivation of the ruder non-Aryan tribes and the settled agriculture of the Hindus. The Kandhs do not, like the ruder non-Aryans, merely burn down a patch in the jungle, take a few crops off it, and then move on to fresh clearings. Nor, on the other hand, do they go on cultivating the same fields, like the Hindus, from father to son. When their lands show signs of exhaustion, they desert them; and it was a rule in some of the Kandh settlements to change their village sites once in fourteen years.

Kandh Marriages by 'Capture.'—A Kandh wedding consists of forcibly carrying off the bride in the middle of a feast. The boy's father pays a price for the girl, and usually chooses a strong one, several years older than his son. In this way Kandh maidens are married about fourteen, Kandh boys about ten. The bride remains as a servant in her new father-in-law's house till her boy-husband grows old enough to live with her. She generally acquires a great influence over him; and a Kandh may not marry a second wife during the life of his first one, except with her consent.

Serfs of the Kandh Village.—The Kandh engages only in husbandry and war, and despises all other work. But attached to each village is a row of hovels inhabited by a lower race, who are not allowed to hold land, to go forth to battle, or to join in the village worship. These poor people do the dirty work of the hamlet, and supply families of hereditary weavers, blacksmiths, potters, herdsmen, and distillers. They are kindly treated, and a portion of each feast is left for them. But they can never rise in the social scale. No Kandh could engage in their work without degradation, nor eat food prepared by their hands. They are supposed to be the remnants of a ruder race, whom the Kandhs found in possession of the hills, when they themselves were pushed backwards by the Aryans from the plains.

Kandh Human Sacrifices.—The Kandhs, like the Santáls, have many deities, race-gods, tribe-gods, family-gods, and a multitude of malignant spirits and demons. But their great divinity is the earth-god, who represents the productive energy of nature. Twice each year, at sowing-time and at harvest, and in all seasons of special calamity, the earth-god required a human sacrifice. The duty of kidnapping victims from the plains rested with the lower race attached to the Kandh village. Bráhmans and Kandhs were the only classes exempted from sacrifice, and an ancient rule ordained that the offering *must be bought with a price.* The victim, on being brought to the hamlet, was welcomed at every threshold, daintily fed, and kindly treated till the fatal day arrived. He was then solemnly sacrificed to the earth-god, the Kandhs shouting in his dying ear, 'We bought you with a price; no sin rests with us!' His flesh and blood were portioned out among the village lands.

The Kandhs under British Rule.—In 1835 the Kandhs passed under our rule, and human sacrifices were put down. Roads have been made through their hills, and fairs established. The English officers interfere as little as possible with their customs; and the Kandhs are now a peaceable and well-to-do race.

The Three non-Aryan Stocks.—Whence came these primitive peoples, whom the Aryan invaders found in the land more than 3000 years ago, and who are still scattered over India, the fragments of a prehistoric world? Written annals they do not possess. Their traditions tell us little. But from their languages we find that they belong to three stocks. First, the Tibeto-Burman tribes, who entered India from the north-east, and still cling to the skirts of the Himálayas. Second, the Kolarians, who also seem to have entered Bengal by the north-eastern passes. They dwell chiefly along the north-eastern ranges of the central tableland which covers the southern half of India. Third, the Dravidians, who appear, on the other hand, to have found their way into the Punjab by the north-western passes. They now inhabit the southern part of the three-sided tableland as far down as Cape Comorin, the southernmost point of India.

Character of the non-Aryans.—As a rule, the non-Aryan races, when fairly treated, are truthful, loyal, and kind. Those in the hills make good soldiers; while even the thieving tribes of the plains can be turned into clever police. The non-Aryan low-castes of Madras supplied the troops which conquered Southern India for the British; and some of them fought at the battle of Plassey, which won for us Bengal. The gallant Gúrkhas, a non-Aryan tribe of the Himálayas, now rank among the bravest regiments in our Indian army, and have covered themselves with honour in every recent war, from Afghánistán to Burma.

The Future of the Non-Aryans.—In many countries of the world, the ruder tribes have been crushed, or killed off by superior races. This has been the case, to a large extent, with the primitive peoples of Mexico and Peru, with the Red Indians of North America, and with the Aborigines of Australia and, to some extent, in New Zealand. But the non-Aryan tribes of India are prospering instead of decreasing under British rule. Hill-fairs and roads through their mountains and jungles have opened up to them new means of livelihood; and the Census, both in 1872 and 1881, showed that they have a larger proportion of children than the other Indian races. As they grow rich, they adopt Hindu customs, and numbers of them every year pass within the pale of Hinduism. Others become converts to Christianity, and it seems likely that in the course of two or three generations there will be but a small remnant of the non-Aryan races which still cling to their aboriginal customs and rites. The Census in 1881 and 1891 included many of them among the low caste Hindus, and returned a much smaller number of pure Aborigines than the figures which I have given at page 38 for the aboriginal population, from the Census of 1872. This arises partly from the fact that the aboriginal races are merging into the Hindu community: partly because the system of classification adopted in 1872 exhibited the Aborigines more fully according to their race than the later Census enumerations in 1881 and 1891. The returns of 1901 do not give details, but there is no reason to doubt that they continue as time goes on to abandon their ancient customs and to become merged, socially and religiously, in the general population.

Materials for Reference.

Particulars will be found regarding the various aboriginal races in the *Imperial Gazetteer of India*, 2nd ed., under the heading of their respective localities. Dalton's *Ethnology of Bengal*, Hislop's *Aboriginal Tribes of the Central Provinces*, Sir Henry Elliot's *Races of the North Western Provinces of India* (Beames' edition), Sir William Hunter's *Annals of Rural Bengal*, Ibbetson's *Census Report for the Punjab*, 1881, Bishop Caldwell's *Comparative Grammar of the Dravidian or South Indian Languages*, and Risley's *Tribes and Castes of Bengal* are the standard authorities.

CHAPTER IV.

The Aryans in India

The Aryan Stock.—At a very early period we catch sight of a nobler race from the north-west, forcing its way in among the primitive peoples of India. This race belonged to the splendid Aryan or Indo-Germanic stock, from which the Bráhman, the Rájput, and the Englishman alike descend. Its earliest home seems to have been in Western Asia. From that common camping-ground certain branches of the race started for the east, others for the further west. One of the western offshoots built Athens and Sparta, and became the Greek nation; another went on to Italy, and reared the city on the Seven Hills, which grew into Imperial Rome. A distant colony of the same race excavated the silver ores of prehistoric Spain; and when we first catch a sight of ancient England, we see an Aryan settlement fishing in wattle canoes, and working the tin mines of Cornwall. Meanwhile other branches of the Aryan stock had gone forth from the primitive Asiatic home to the east. Powerful bands found their way through the passes of the Himálayas into the Punjab, and spread themselves, chiefly as Bráhmans and Rájputs, over India.

The Aryans conquer the Early Races in Europe and Asia.—The Aryan offshoots, alike to the east and to the west, asserted their superiority over the earlier peoples whom they found in possession of the soil. The history of ancient Europe is the story of the Aryan settlements around the shores of the Mediterranean; and that wide term, modern civilization, merely means the civilization of the western branches of the same race. The history of India consists in like manner of the history of the eastern offshoots of the Aryan stock who settled in that land.

The Aryans in their Primitive Home.—We know little regarding these noble Aryan tribes in their early camping-ground in Western Asia. From words preserved in the languages of their long-separated descendants in Europe and India, scholars infer that they roamed over the grassy steppes with their cattle, making long halts to raise crops of grain. They had tamed most of the domestic animals; were acquainted with iron; understood the arts of weaving and sewing; wore clothes; and ate cooked food. They lived the hardy life of the comparatively temperate zone; and the feeling of cold seems to be one of the earliest common remembrances of the eastern and the western branches of the race.

European and Indian Languages merely Varieties of Aryan Speech.—The forefathers of the Greek and the Roman, of the English and the Hindu, dwelt together in Western Asia, spoke the same tongue, worshipped the same gods. The languages of Europe and India, although at first sight they seem wide apart, are merely different growths from the original Aryan speech. This is especially true of the common words of family life. The names for *father*, *mother*, *brother*, *sister*, and *widow* are the same in most of the Aryan languages, whether spoken on the banks of the Ganges, of the Tiber, or of the Thames. Thus the word *daughter*, which occurs in nearly all of them, has been derived from the Aryan root *dugh*, which in Sanskrit has the form of *duh*, to milk; and perhaps preserves the memory of the time when the daughter was the little milkmaid in the primitive Aryan household.

Common Origin of European and Indian Religions.—The ancient religions of Europe and India had a common origin. They were to some extent made up of the sacred stories or myths, which our joint-ancestors had learned while dwelling together in Asia. Several of the Vedic gods were also the gods of Greece and Rome; and to this day the Divinity is adored by names derived from the same old Aryan word (*deva*, the Shining One), by Bráhmans in Calcutta, by the Protestant clergy of England, and by Roman Catholic priests in Peru.

The Indo-Aryans on the March.—The Vedic hymns exhibit the Indian branch of the Aryans on their march to the south-east, and in their new homes. The earliest songs disclose the race still to the north of the Kháibar pass, in Kábul; the later ones bring them as far as the Ganges. Their victorious advance eastwards through the intermediate tract can be traced in the Vedic writings almost step by step. The steady supply of water among the five rivers of the Punjab, led the Aryans to settle down from their old state of wandering half-pastoral tribes into regular communities of husbandmen. The Vedic poets praised the rivers which enabled them to make this great change—perhaps the most important step in the progress of a race. 'May the Indus,' they sang, 'the far-famed giver of wealth, hear us; (fertilizing our) broad fields with water.' The Himálayas, through whose south-western passes they had reached India, and at whose southern base they long dwelt, made a lasting impression on their memory. The Vedic singer praised 'Him whose greatness the snowy ranges, and the sea, and the aerial river declare.' The Aryan race in India never forgot its northern home. There dwelt its gods and holy singers; and there eloquence descended from heaven among men; while high amid the Himálayan mountains lay the paradise of deities and heroes, where the kind and the brave for ever repose.

The Rig-Veda.—The Rig-Veda forms the great literary memorial of the early Aryan settlements in the Punjab. The age of this venerable hymnal is unknown. Orthodox Hindus believe, without evidence, that it existed 'from before all time,' or at least from 3001 years B.C. European scholars have inferred from astronomical data that its composition was going on about 1400 B.C. But the evidence might have been calculated backwards, and inserted later in the Veda. We only know that the Vedic religion had been at work long before the rise of Buddhism in the sixth century B.C. The Rig-Veda is a very old collection of 1017 short poems, chiefly addressed to the gods, and containing 10,580 verses. Its hymns show us the Aryans on the banks of the Indus, divided into various tribes, sometimes at war with each other, sometimes united against the 'black-skinned' Aborigines. Caste, in its later sense, is unknown. Each father of a family is the priest of his own household. The chieftain acts as father and priest to the tribe; but at the greater festivals he chooses some one specially learned in holy offerings to conduct the sacrifice in the name of the people. The king himself seems to have been elected; and his title of Vis-pati, literally 'Lord of the Settlers,' survives in the old Persian Vis-paiti, and as the Lithuanian Wiéz-patis in east-central Europe at this day. Women enjoyed a high position; and some of the most beautiful hymns were composed by ladies and queens. Marriage was held sacred. Husband and wife were both 'rulers of the house' (*dampati*); and drew near to the gods together in prayer. The burning of widows on their husbands' funeral pile was unknown; and the verses in the Veda which the Bráhmans afterwards distorted into a sanction for the practice, have the very opposite meaning. 'Rise, woman,' says the Vedic text to the mourner; 'come to the world of life. Come to us. Thou hast fulfilled thy duties as a wife to thy husband.'

Aryan Civilization in the Veda.—The Aryan tribes in the Veda have blacksmiths, coppersmiths, and goldsmiths among them, besides carpenters, barbers, and other artisans. They fight from chariots, and freely use the horse, although not yet the elephant, in war. They have settled down as husbandmen, till their fields with the plough, and live in villages or towns. But they also cling to their old wandering life, with their herds and 'cattle-pens.' Cattle, indeed, still form their chief wealth—the coin in which payment of fines is made—reminding us of the Latin word for money, *pecunia*, from *pecus*, a herd. One of the Vedic words for war literally means 'a desire for cows.' Unlike the modern Hindus, the Aryans of the Veda ate beef; used a fermented liquor or beer, made from the *soma* plant; and offered the same strong meat and drink to their gods. Thus the stout Aryans spread eastwards through Northern India, pushed on from behind by later arrivals of their own stock, and driving before them, or reducing to bondage, the earlier 'black-skinned' races. They marched in whole communities from one river valley to another; each house-father a warrior, husband-man, and priest; with his wife, and his little ones, and his cattle.

The Gods of the Veda.—These free-hearted tribes had a great trust in themselves and their gods. Like other conquering races, they believed that both themselves and their deities were altogether superior to the people of the land, and to their poor, rude objects of worship. Indeed, this noble self-confidence is a great aid to the success of a nation. Their divinities—*devas*, literally 'the shining ones,' from the Sanskrit root *div*, 'to shine'—were the great powers of nature. They adored the Father-heaven,—*Dyaush-pitar* in Sanskrit, the *Dies-piter* or *Jupiter* of Rome, the *Zeus* of Greece; and the Encompassing Sky—*Varuna* in Sanskrit, *Uranus* in Latin, *Ouranos* in Greek. Indra, or the Aqueous Vapour that brings the precious rain on which plenty or famine still depends each autumn, received the largest number of hymns. By degrees, as the settlers realized more and more keenly the importance of the periodical rains to their new life as husbandmen, he became the chief of the Vedic gods. 'The gods do not reach unto thee, O Indra, nor men; thou overcomest all creatures in strength.' Agni, the God of Fire (Latin *ignis*), ranks perhaps next to Indra in the number of hymns addressed to him. He is 'the Youngest of the Gods,' 'the Lord and Giver of Wealth.' The Maruts are the Storm Gods, 'who make the rock to tremble, who tear in pieces the forest.' Ushas, 'the High-born Dawn' (Greek *Eos*), 'shines upon us like a young wife, rousing every living being to go forth to his work.' The Asvins, the 'Horsemen' or fleet outriders of the dawn, are the first rays of sunrise, 'Lords of Lustre.' The Solar Orb himself (Súrya), the Wind (Váyu), the Sunshine or Friendly Day (Mitra), the intoxicating fermented juice of the Sacrificial Plant (Soma), and many other deities are invoked in the Veda—in all, about thirty-three gods, 'who are eleven in heaven, eleven on earth, and eleven dwelling in glory in mid-air.'

The Vedio Idea of God.—The Aryan settler lived on excellent terms with his bright gods. He asked for protection, with an assured conviction that it would be granted. At the same time, he was deeply stirred by the glory and mystery of the earth and the heavens. Indeed, the majesty of nature so filled his mind, that when he praises any one of his Shining Gods, he can think of none other for the time being, and adores him as the supreme ruler. Verses may be quoted declaring each of the greater deities to be the One Supreme: 'Neither gods nor men reach unto thee, O Indra.' Another hymn speaks of Soma as 'king of heaven and earth, the conqueror of all.' To Varuna also it is said, 'Thou art lord of all, of heaven and earth; thou art king of all those who are gods, and of all those who are men.' The more spiritual of the Vedic singers, therefore, may be said to have worshipped One God, though not One alone.

A Vedic Hymn.—'In the beginning there arose the Golden Child. He was the one born lord of all that is. He established the earth and this sky. Who is the God to whom we shall offer our sacrifice?

'He who gives life, he who gives strength; whose command all the Bright Gods revere; whose shadow is immortality, whose shadow is death. Who is the God to whom we shall offer our sacrifice?

'He who, through his power, is the one king of the breathing and awakening world. He who governs all, man and beast. Who is the God to whom we shall offer our sacrifice?

'He through whom the sky is bright and the earth firm; he through whom the heaven was established, nay, the highest heaven; he who measured out the light and the air. Who is the God to whom we shall offer our sacrifice?

'He who by his might looked even over the water-clouds; he who alone is God above all gods. Who is the God to whom we shall offer our sacrifice?'

Burning of the Dead.—While the aboriginal races buried their dead in the earth or under rude stone monuments, the Aryan—alike in India, in Greece, and in Italy—made use of the funeral-pile. Several exquisite Sanskrit hymns bid farewell to the dead:—'Depart thou, depart thou by the ancient paths to the place whither our fathers have departed. Meet with the Ancient Ones; meet with the Lord of Death. Throwing off thine imperfections, go to thy home. Become united with a body; clothe thyself in a shining form.' 'Let him depart to those for whom flow the rivers of nectar. Let him depart to those who, through meditation, have obtained the victory; who, by fixing their thoughts on the unseen, have gone to heaven. Let him depart to the mighty in battle, to the heroes who have laid down their lives for others, to those who have bestowed their goods on the poor.' The doctrine of transmigration was at first unknown. The circle round the funeral-pile sang with a firm assurance that their friend went direct to a state of blessedness and reunion with the loved ones who had gone before. 'Do thou conduct us to heaven,' says a hymn of the later Atharva-Veda; 'let us be with our wives and children.' 'In heaven, where our friends dwell in bliss—having left behind the infirmities of the body, free from lameness, free from crookedness of limb —there let us behold our parents and our children.' 'May the water-shedding Spirits bear thee upwards, cooling thee with their swift motion through the air, and sprinkling thee with dew.' 'Bear him, carry him; let him, with all his faculties complete, go to the world of the righteous. Crossing the dark valley which spreadeth boundless around him, let the unborn soul ascend to heaven. Wash the feet of him who is stained with sin; let him go upwards with cleansed feet. Crossing the gloom, gazing with wonder in many directions, let the unborn soul go up to heaven.'

Later Vedic Literature.—By degrees the old collection of hymns, or the Rig-Veda, no longer sufficed. Three other collections or service-books were therefore added, making the Four Vedas. The word Veda is from the same root as the Latin *vid-ere*, to see: the early Greek *feid-enai*, infinitive of *oida*, I know: and the English *wisdom*, or I *wit*. The Bráhmans taught that the Veda was divinely inspired, and that it was literally 'the *wisdom* of God.' There was, first, the Rig-Veda, or the hymns in their simplest form. Second, the Sáma-Veda, made up of hymns of the Rig-Veda to be used at the Soma sacrifice. Third, the Yajur-Veda, consisting not only of Rig-Vedic hymns, but also of prose sentences, to be used at the great sacrifices; and divided into two editions, the Black and White Yajur. The fourth, or Atharva-Veda, was compiled from the least ancient hymns at the end of the Rig-Veda, very old religious spells, and later sources. Some of its spells have a similarity to the ancient German and Lithuanian charms, and appear to have come down from the most primitive times, before the Indian and European branches of the Aryan race struck out from their common home.

The Bráhmanas.—To each of the four Vedas were attached

prose works, called Bráhmanas, in order to explain the sacrifices and the duties of the priests. Like the four Vedas, the Bráhmanas were held to be the very word of God. The Vedas and the Bráhmanas form the revealed Scriptures of the Hindus—the *sruti*, literally 'Things *heard* from God.' The Vedas supplied their divinely-inspired psalms, and the Bráhmanas their divinely-inspired theology or body of doctrine. To them were afterwards added the Sútras, literally '*Strings* of pithy sentences' regarding laws and ceremonies. Still later the Upanishads were composed, treating of God and the soul; the Aranyakas, or 'Tracts for the forest recluse'; and, after a very long interval, the Purános, or 'Traditions from of old.' All these ranked, however, not as divinely-inspired knowledge, or things 'heard from God' (*sruti*), like the Vedas and Bráhmanas, but only as sacred traditions—*smriti*, literally 'The things *remembered*.'

The Four Castes formed.—Meanwhile the Four Castes had been formed. In the old Aryan colonies among the Five Rivers of the Punjab, each house-father was a husbandman, warrior, and priest. But by degrees certain gifted families, who composed the Vedic hymns or learned them off by heart, were always chosen by the king to perform the great sacrifices. In this way probably the priestly caste sprang up. As the Aryans conquered more territory, fortunate soldiers received a larger share of the lands than others, and cultivated it not with their own hands, but by means of the vanquished non-Aryan tribes. In this way the Four Castes arose. First, the Priests or Bráhmans. Second, the warriors or fighting companions of the king, called Rájputs or Kshattriyas, literally 'of the *royal* stock.' Third, the Aryan agricultural settlers, who kept the old name of Vaisyas, from the root *vis*, which in the primitive Vedic period had included the whole Aryan people. Fourth, the Súdras, or conquered non-Aryan tribes, who became serfs. The three first castes were of Aryan descent, and were honoured by the name of the Twice-born Castes. They could all be present at the sacrifices, and they worshipped the same Bright Gods. The Súdras were 'the slave-bands of black descent' of the Veda. They were distinguished from their 'Twice-born' Aryan conquerors as being only 'Once-born,' and by many contemptuous epithets. They were not allowed to be present at the great national sacrifices, or at the feasts which followed them. They could never rise out of their servile condition; and to them was assigned the severest toil in the fields, and all the hard and dirty work of the village community.

The Bráhman Supremacy established.—The Bráhmans or priests claimed the highest rank. But they seem to have had a long struggle with the Kshattriya or warrior caste, before they won their proud position at the head of the Indian people. They afterwards secured themselves in that position, by teaching that it had been given to them by God. At the beginning of the world, they said, the Bráhman proceeded from the mouth of the Creator, the Kshattriya or Rájput from his arms, the Vaisya from his thighs or belly, and the Súdra from his feet. This legend is true so far, that the Bráhmans were really the brain-power of the Indian people, the Kshattriyas its armed hands, the Vaisyas the food-growers, and the Súdras the down-trodden serfs. When the Bráhmans had established their power, they made a wise use of it. From the ancient Vedic times they recognized that if they were to exercise spiritual supremacy, they must renounce earthly pomp. In arrogating the priestly function, they gave up all claim to the royal office. They were divinely appointed to be the guides of nations and the counsellors of kings, but they could not be kings themselves. As the duty of the Súdra was to serve, of the Vaisya to till the ground and follow middle-class trades or crafts; so the business of the Kshattriya was to fight the public enemy, and of the Bráhman to propitiate the national gods.

Stages of a Bráhman's Life.—Each day brought to the Bráhmans its routine of ceremonies, studies, and duties. Their whole life was mapped out into four clearly-defined stages of discipline. For their existence, in its full religious significance, commenced not at birth, but on being invested at the close of childhood with the sacred thread of the Twice-born. Their youth and early manhood were to be entirely spent in learning the Veda by heart from an older Bráhman, tending the sacred fire, and serving their preceptor. Having completed his long studies, the young Bráhman entered on the second stage of his life, as a householder. He married, and commenced a course of family duties. When he had reared a family, and gained a practical knowledge of the world, he retired into the forest as a recluse, for the third period of his life; feeding on roots or fruits, practising his religious duties with increased devotion. The fourth stage was that of the ascetic or religious mendicant, wholly withdrawn from earthly affairs, and striving to attain a condition of mind which, heedless of the joys, or pains, or wants of the body, is intent only on its final absorption into the deity. The Bráhman, in this fourth stage of his life, ate nothing but what was given to him unasked, and abode not more than one day in any village, lest the vanities of the world should find entrance into his heart. This was the ideal life prescribed for a Bráhman, and ancient Indian literature shows that it was to a large extent practically carried out. Throughout his whole existence the true Bráhman practised a strict temperance; drinking no wine, using a simple diet, curbing the desires; shut off from the tumults of war, as his business was to pray, not to fight, and having his thoughts ever fixed on study and contemplation. 'What is this world?' says a Bráhman sage. 'It is even as the bough of a tree, on which a bird rests for a night, and in the morning flies away.'

The Modern Bráhmans.—The Bráhmans, therefore, were a body of men who, in an early stage of this world's history, bound themselves by a rule of life the essential precepts of which were self-culture and self-restraint. The Bráhmans of the present India are the result of 3000 years of hereditary education and temperance; and they have evolved a type of mankind quite distinct from the surrounding population. Even the passing traveller in India marks them out, alike from the bronze-cheeked, large-limbed, leisure-loving Rájput or Kshattriya, the warrior caste of Aryan descent; and from the dark-skinned, flat-nosed, thick-lipped low castes of non-Aryan origin, with their short bodies and bullet heads. The Bráhman stands apart from both, tall and slim, with finely-modelled lips and nose, fair complexion, high forehead, and slightly cocoa-nut shaped skull—the man of self-centred refinement. He is an example of a class becoming the ruling power in a country, not by force of arms, but by the vigour of hereditary culture and temperance. One race has swept across India after another, dynasties have risen and fallen, religions have spread themselves over the land and disappeared. But since the dawn of history the Bráhman has calmly ruled; swaying the minds and receiving the homage of the people, and accepted by foreign nations as the highest type of Indian mankind. The position which the Bráhmans won resulted in no small measure from the benefits which they bestowed. For their own Aryan countrymen they developed a noble language and literature. The Bráhmans were not only the priests and philosophers, but also the lawgivers, the men of science, and the poets of their race. Their influence on the aboriginal peoples, the hill and forest races of India, was even more important. To these rude remnants of the flint and stone ages they brought, in ancient times, a knowledge of the metals and the gods.

Bráhman Theology.—The Bráhmans, among themselves, soon began to see that the old gods of the Vedic hymns were in reality not supreme beings, but poetic fictions. For when they came to think the matter out, they found that the Sun, the Aqueous Vapour, the Encompassing Sky, the Wind, and the Dawn could not each be separate and supreme creators, but must have all proceeded from one First Cause. They did not shock the more ignorant castes by any public rejection of the Vedic deities. They accepted the old 'Shining Ones' of the Veda as beautiful manifestations of the divine power, and continued to decorously conduct the sacrifices in their honour. But among their own caste the Bráhmans taught the unity of God. The mass of the people were left to believe in four castes, four Vedas, and many deities. But the higher thinkers among the Bráhmans recognized that in the beginning there was but one caste, one Veda, and one God.

The Hindu Trinity.—The confused old groups of deities or Shining Ones in the Veda thus gave place to the grand conception of one God, in his three solemn manifestations as Brahmá the Creator, Vishnu the Preserver, and Siva the Destroyer and Reproducer. Each of these had his prototype among the Vedic deities; and they remain to this day the three persons of the

Hindu trinity. Brahmá, the Creator, or first person of the trinity, was too abstract an idea to be a popular god. Vishnu, the second person of the trinity, was a more useful and friendly deity. He is said to have ten times come down from heaven and lived on the earth. These were the ten incarnations (*avatárs*) of Vishnu. Siva, the third person of the trinity, appears as both the Destroyer and Reproducer; and thus shows to the eye of faith, that death is but a change of state, and an entry into a new life. Vishnu and Siva, in their diverse male and female shapes, now form the principal gods of the Hindus.

Bráhman Philosophy.—The Bráhmans thus built up a religion for the Indian people. They also worked out a system of philosophy, and arranged its doctrines in six schools—*darsanas*, literally *mirrors* of knowledge—at least 500 years before Christ. They had moreover a circle of sciences of their own. The Sanskrit grammar of Pánini, compiled about 350 B.C., is still the foundation of the study of Aryan language. In this subject the Bráhmans were far before the Greeks or Romans, or indeed any European nation down to the present century. Their Sanskrit, or '*perfected* speech,' succeeded after a long interval to the earlier language of the Veda. But Sanskrit seems to have been used only, or chiefly, by the learned. The people spoke a simpler form of the same language, called Prákrit. From this old Prákrit the modern dialects of India descend. The Bráhmans, however, always wrote in Sanskrit, which sunk in time into a dead language unknown to the people. The Bráhmans alone, therefore, could read the sacred books or write new ones; and in this way they became the only men of learning in India.

Indian Literature.—As early as 250 B.C. two alphabets, or written characters, were used in India. But the Bráhmans preferred to hand down their holy learning by memory, rather than to write it out. Good Bráhmans had to learn the Veda by heart, besides many other books. This was the easier, as almost all their literature was in verse (*slokas*). In the very ancient times, just after the Vedic hymns, a pure style of prose, simple and compact, had grown up. But during more than 2000 years the Bráhmans have composed almost entirely in verse; and prose-writing was for long almost a lost art in India.

Bráhman Astronomy.—The Bráhmans studied the movements of the heavenly bodies, so as to fix the proper dates for the annual sacrifices. More than 3000 years ago, the Vedic poets had worked out a fairly correct calculation of the solar year, which they divided into 360 days, with an extra month every five years to make up for the odd $5\frac{1}{4}$ days *per annum*. They were also acquainted with the phases of the moon, the motions of the planets, and the signs of the zodiac. The Bráhmans had advanced far in astronomy before the Greeks arrived in India in 327 B.C. They were not, however, ashamed to learn from the new-comers; and one of the five systems of Bráhman astronomy is called the Romaka or Greek science. But in time the Hindus surpassed the Greeks in this matter. The fame of the Bráhman astronomers spread westward, and their works were translated by the Arabs about 800 A.D., and so reached Europe. After the Muhammadans began to ravage India in 1000 A.D., Bráhman science declined. But Hindu astronomers arose from time to time, and their observatories may still be seen at Benares and elsewhere. An Indian astronomer, the Rájá Jai Singh, was able to correct the list of stars published by the celebrated French astronomer De la Hire, in 1702.

Bráhman Medicine.—The Bráhmans also worked out a system of medicine for themselves. As they had to study the heavenly bodies in order to fix the dates of their yearly festivals, so they made their first steps in anatomy, by cutting up the animals at the sacrifice, with a view to offering the different parts to the proper gods. They ranked medical science as an Upa-Veda, or later revelation from heaven. The ancient Bráhmans did not shrink from dissecting the dead bodies of animals. They also trained their students by means of operations performed on wax spread over a board, instead of flesh, and on the stems of plants. The hospitals which the Buddhist princes set up throughout India for man and beast, gave great opportunities for the study and treatment of disease.

In medicine the Bráhmans learned nothing from the Greeks, but taught them much. Arab medicine was founded on translations from Sanskrit works about 800 A.D. Mediaeval European medicine, in its turn, down to the seventeenth century, was, in many important respects, based upon the Arabic. The Indian physician Charaka was quoted in European books of medicine written in the middle ages.

Decline of Hindu Medicine.—As Buddhism passed into modern Hinduism (600–1000 A.D.), and the shackles of caste were imposed with an iron rigour, the Bráhmans more scrupulously avoided contact with blood or diseased matter. They left the medical profession to the Vaidyas, a lower caste, sprung from a Bráhman father and a mother of the Vaisya or cultivating class. These in their turn shrank more and more from touching dead bodies, and from those ancient operations on 'the carcase of a bullock,' &c., by which alone surgical skill could be acquired. The abolition of the public hospitals, on the downfall of Buddhism, must also have proved a great loss to Indian medicine. The Muhammadan conquests, commencing in 1000 A.D., brought in a new school of foreign physicians, who derived their knowledge from the Arabic translations of the Sanskrit medical works of the best period. These Musalmán doctors or *hakíms* monopolized the patronage of the Muhammadan princes and nobles of India. The decline of Hindu medicine continued until it sank into the hands of the village *kabiráj*, whose knowledge consists of a jumble of Sanskrit texts, useful lists of drugs, aided by spells, fasts, and quackery. But Hindu students now flock to the medical colleges established by the British Government, and in this way the science is again reviving in India.

Indian Music.—The Bráhmans had also an art of music of their own. The seven notes which they invented, at least four centuries before Christ, passed through the Persians to Arabia, and were thence introduced into European music in the eleventh century A.D. Hindu music declined under the Muhammadan rule. Its complex divisions or modes and numerous sub-tones prevent it from pleasing the modern European ear, which has been trained on a different system; but it is highly original and interesting from a scientific point of view. A great revival of Indian music has been brought about by patriotic native gentlemen in our own days, and its strains give delight to millions of our Indian fellow-subjects.

Bráhman Law.—The Bráhmans made law a part of their religion. Their earliest legal works were the Household Maxims (*Grihyá Sútras*), some of them perhaps as early as 500 B.C. The customs of the Bráhmans in Northern India were collected into the Code of Manu, composed in its present final form between 100 and 500 A.D. Another famous compilation, known as the Code of Yájnavalkya, was drawn up later; apparently in the sixth or seventh century A.D. These codes, and the commentaries written upon them, still rule the family life of the Hindus. They set forth the law in three branches,—namely, (1) domestic and civil rights and duties; (2) the administration of justice; (3) religious purifications and penance. They contain many rules about marriage, inheritance, and food. They keep the castes apart, by forbidding them to intermarry or to eat together. They were accepted as almost divine laws by the Hindus; and the spread of these codes was the work of the Bráhmans as the civilizers of India. But they really record only the customs of the Bráhman kingdoms in the north, and do not truly apply to all the Indian races. The greatest Hindu lawgivers agree that the usages of each different country in India are to be respected; and in this way they make allowance for the laws or customs of the non-Aryan tribes. Thus among the Bráhmans it would be disgraceful for a woman to have two husbands. But among the Nairs of Southern India and other non-Aryan races it is the custom; therefore it is legal for such races, and all the laws of inheritance among these peoples are regulated accordingly.

Bráhman Poetry.—The Bráhmans were not merely the composers and keepers of the sacred books, the philosophers, the men of science, and the law-makers of the Hindu people—they were also its poets. They did not write history; but they told the ancient wars and the lives of the Aryan heroes in epic poems. The two most famous of these are the Mahábhárata, or chronicles of the Delhi kings, and the

Rámáyana, or story of the Aryan advance into Southern India.

The Mahábhárata.—The Mahábhárata is a great collection of Indian legends in verse, some of them as old as the Vedic hymns. The main story deals with a period not later than 1200 B.C. But it was not put together in its present shape till more than a thousand years later. An idea of the extent of the Mahábhárata may be gained from the fact that it contains 220,000 lines; while the *Iliad* of Homer does not amount to 16,000 lines, and Virgil's *Aeneid* contains less than 10,000.

Its Central Story.—The central story of the Mahábhárata occupies scarcely one-fourth of the whole, or about 50,000 lines. It narrates a struggle between two families of the ruling Lunar race for a patch of country near Delhi. These families, alike descended from the Royal Bharata, consisted of two brotherhoods, cousins to each other, and both brought up under the same roof. The five Pándavas were the sons of King Pándu, who, smitten by a curse, resigned the sovereignty to his brother Dhrita-ráshtra, and retired to a hermitage in the Himálayas, where he died. The ruins of his capital, Hastinápura, or the 'Elephant City,' are pointed out beside a deserted bed of the Ganges, 57 miles north-east of Delhi, at this day. His brother Dhrita-ráshtra ruled in his stead; and to him one hundred sons were born, who took the name of the Kauravas from an ancestor, Kuru. Dhrita-ráshtra acted as a faithful guardian to his five nephews, the Pándavas, and chose the eldest of them as heir to the family kingdom. His own sons resented this act of supercession; and so arose the quarrel between the hundred Kauravas and the five Pándavas, which forms the main story of the Mahábhárata.

Its Outline.—The hundred Kauravas forced their father to send away their five Pándava cousins into the forest, and there they treacherously burned down the hut in which the five Pándavas dwelt. The Pándavas escaped, and wandered in the disguise of Bráhmans to the court of King Draupada, who had proclaimed a *swayam-vara*, or maiden's 'own-choice.' This was a contest of arms, or with the bow, among the chiefs, at which the king's daughter would take the victor as her husband.

Arjuna, one of the five Pándavas, bent the mighty bow which had defied the strength of all the rival chiefs, and so obtained the fair princess, Draupadí, who became the common wife of the five brethren. Their uncle, the good Dhrita-ráshtra, recalled them to his capital, and gave them one half of the family territory, reserving the other half for his own sons. The Pándava brethren hived off to a new settlement, Indra-prastha, afterwards Delhi; clearing the jungle, and driving out the Nágas or forest-races.

For a time peace reigned. But the Kauravas tempted Yudhishthira, 'firm in fight,' the eldest of the Pándavas, to a gambling match, at which he lost his kingdom, his brothers, himself, and last of all his wife. Their father, however, forced his sons to restore their wicked gains to their cousins. But Yudhishthira was again seduced by the Kauravas to stake his kingdom at dice, again lost it, and had to retire with his wife and brethren into exile for twelve years. Their banishment ended, the five Pándavas returned at the head of an army to win back their kingdom. Many battles followed, gods and divine heroes joined in the struggle, until at last all the hundred Kauravas were slain, and of the friends and kindred of the Pándavas only the five brethren remained. Their uncle, Dhrita-ráshtra, made over to them the whole kingdom. For a long time the Pándavas ruled gloriously, celebrating the *asva-medha*, or 'great horse sacrifice,' in token of their holding imperial sway. But their uncle, old and blind, ever taunted them with the slaughter of his hundred sons, until at last he crept away, with his few surviving ministers, his aged wife, and his sister-in-law, the mother of the Pándavas, to a hermitage, where the worn-out band perished in a forest fire. The five brethren, smitten by remorse, gave up their kingdom; and, taking their wife, Draupadí, and a faithful dog, they departed to the Himálayas to seek the heaven of Indra on Mount Meru. One by one the sorrowful pilgrims died upon the road, until only the eldest brother, Yudhishthira, and the dog reached the gate of heaven. Indra invited him to enter, but he refused if his lost wife and brethren were not also admitted. The prayer was granted; but he still declined unless his faithful dog might come in with him. This could not be allowed; and Yudhishthira, after a glimpse of heaven, was thrust down to hell, where he found many of his old comrades in anguish. He resolved to share their sufferings rather than to enjoy paradise alone. But, having triumphed in this crowning trial, the whole scene was revealed to him to be *máyá* or illusion, and the reunited band entered into heaven, where they rest for ever with Indra.

Remainder of the Mahábhárata.—The struggle for the kingdom of Hastinápur forms, however, only a fourth of the Mahábhárata. The remainder is made up of other early legends, stories of the gods, and religious discourses, intended to teach the military caste its duties, especially its duty of reverence to the Bráhmans. Taken as a whole, the Mahábhárata may be said to form the cyclopaedia of the Heroic Age in Northern India.

The Rámáyana.—The second great Indian epic, the Rámáyana, recounts the advance of the Aryans into Southern India. It is said to have been composed by the poet Válmíki; and its main story refers to a period loosely estimated at about 1000 B.C. But the Rámáyana could not have been put together in its present shape many centuries, if at all, before the Christian era. Parts of it may be earlier than the Mahábhárata, but the compilation as a whole apparently belongs to a later date. The Rámáyana consists of about 48,000 lines.

Outline of the Rámáyana.—As the Mahábhárata celebrates the Lunar race of Delhi, so the Rámáyana forms the epic (or poetic history) of the Solar race of Ayodhya, the capital of the modern province of Oudh. The two poems thus preserve the legends of the two most famous Aryan kingdoms at the two opposite, or eastern and western, borders of the old Middle Land of Hindustán (Madhya-desa). The opening books of the Rámáyana recount the wondrous birth and boyhood of Ráma, eldest son of Dasaratha, King of Ayodhya or Oudh; his marriage with the princess Sítá, after he proved himself the victor at her 'own choice' of a husband (*swayam-vara*), by bending the mighty bow of Siva in the contest of chiefs; and his selection as heir-apparent to his father's kingdom. A *zanána* intrigue ends in the youngest wife of Dasaratha (Ráma's father) obtaining the succession for her own son, Bharata, and in the exile of Ráma, with his bride Sítá, for fourteen years to the forest. The banished pair wander south to Prayág, the modern Allahábád, already a place of sanctity, and thence across the river to the hermitage of Válmíki, among the jungles of Bundelkhand, where a hill is still pointed out as the scene of their abode. Meanwhile Ráma's father dies; and the loyal younger brother, Bharata, although declared the lawful successor, refuses to enter on the inheritance, and goes in search of Ráma to bring him back as rightful heir. A contest of fraternal affection takes place; Bharata at length returning to rule the family kingdom in the name of Ráma, until the latter should come to claim it at the end of his fourteen years of banishment.

The Aryans advance Southwards.—So far, the Rámáyana merely narrates the local annals of the court of Ayodhya. In the third book the main story begins. Rávana, the demon or aboriginal king of the far south, smitten by the fame of Sítá's beauty, seizes her at the hermitage while her husband Ráma is away in the jungle, and flies off with her in a magic chariot through the air to Ceylon. The next three books (4th, 5th, 6th) recount the expedition of the bereaved Ráma for her recovery. He allies himself with the aboriginal tribes of Southern India, who bear the names of monkeys and bears, and raises among them a great army. The Monkey general, Hanumán, jumps across the straits between India and Ceylon, discovers the princess in captivity, and leaps back with the news to Ráma. The monkey troops then build a causeway across the narrow sea,—the Adam's Bridge of modern geography,—by which Ráma marches across, and, after slaying the monster Rávana, delivers Sítá. The rescued wife proves her faithfulness to him, during her stay in the palace of Rávana, by the ancient ordeal of fire. Agni, the god of that element, himself conducts her out of the burning pile to her husband; and, the fourteen years of banishment being over, Ráma and Sítá return in triumph to Ayodhya. There they reigned gloriously; and Ráma celebrated the great horse sacrifice (*asva-medha*) as a token of his imperial sway over India. But a famine having smitten the land, Ráma regards it as a punishment sent by God for some crime committed in the royal family. Doubts arise in his heart as to his wife's purity while in her captor's power at Ceylon. He accordingly banishes the faithful Sítá, who wanders forth again to Válmíki's hermitage, where she gives birth to Ráma's two sons. After sixteen years of exile, she is reconciled to her repentant husband, and Ráma and Sítá and their children are at last reunited.

Later Sanskrit Epics.—The Mahábhárata and the Rámáyana, however overlaid with fable, form the chronicles of the kings of the Middle Land of Hindustán (Madhya-desa), their family feuds, and their national enterprises. In the later Sanskrit epics, the stories of the heroes give place more and more to legends of the gods. Among them the Raghu-vansa and the Kumára sambhava, both assigned to Kálidása, take the first rank. The Raghu-vansa celebrates the Solar line of Raghu, King of Ayodhya, and especially his descendant Ráma. The Kumára-sambhava recounts the Birth of the War-god. These two poems could not have been composed in their present shape before 350 A.D.

The Sanskrit Drama.—In India, as in Greece and Rome, scenic representations seem to have taken their rise in the rude pantomime of a very early age, possibly as far back as the Vedic ritual; and the Sanskrit word for the drama, *nátaka*, is derived from *nata*, a dancer. But the Sanskrit plays of the classical age which have come down to us probably belong to the period between the first century B.C. and the eighth century A.D. The father of the Sanskrit drama is Kálidása, already mentioned as the composer of the two later Sanskrit epics. According to Hindu tradition, he was one of the 'Nine Gems,' or distinguished men at the court of Vikramáditya, King of Ujjain, in 57 B.C. But as a matter of fact there were several king Vikramádityas, and the one under whom Kálidása flourished appears to have ruled over Málwá in the sixth century A.D.

Sakuntalá.—The most famous drama of Kálidása is Sakuntalá, or the Lost Ring. Like the ancient Sanskrit epics, it divides its action between the court of the king and the hermitage in the forest. Prince Dushyanta, an ancestor of the noble Lunar race, weds a beautiful Bráhman girl, Sakuntalá, at her father's retreat in the jungle. Before returning to his capital, he gives his bride a ring as a pledge of his love; but, smitten by a curse from a Bráhman, she loses the ring, and cannot be recognized by her husband till it is found. Sakuntalá bears a son in her loneliness, and sets out to claim recognition for herself and child at her husband's court. But she is as one unknown to the prince, till, after many sorrows and trials, the ring comes to light. She is then happily reunited with her husband, and her son grows up to be the noble Bharata, the chief founder of the Lunar dynasty, whose achievements form the theme of the Mahábhárata. Sakuntalá, like Sítá, is a type of the chaste and faithful Hindu wife; and her love and sorrow, after forming the favourite romance of the Indian people for perhaps eighteen hundred years, supplied a theme for Goethe, the greatest European poet of our age.

Other Dramas.—Among other Hindu dramas may be mentioned the Mrichchhakatí, or Toy Cart, in ten acts, on the old theme of the innocent cleared and the guilty punished; and the poem of Nala and Damayantí, or the Royal Gambler and the Faithful Wife. Many plays, often founded upon some story in the Mahábhárata or Rámáyana, issue every year from the Indian press.

Beast Stories.—Fables of animals have from old been favourites in India. The Sanskrit Pancha-tantra, or Book of Beast Tales, was translated into Persian as early as the sixth century A.D.; and thence found its way to Europe. The animal fables of ancient India are the familiar nursery stories of England and America at the present day.

Lyric Poetry.—Besides the epic chronicles of their gods and heroes, the Bráhmans composed many religious poems. One of the most beautiful is the Gíta Govinda, or Song of the Divine Herdsman, written by Jayadeva about 1200 A.D. The Puránas are an enormous collection of religious discourses in verse; they will be described hereafter at p. 103.

Bráhman Influence.—In order to understand the long rule of the Bráhmans, and the influence which they still wield, it is necessary ever to keep in mind their position as the great literary caste. Their priestly supremacy has been repeatedly assailed, and during a space of nearly a thousand years it was overborne by the Buddhists. But throughout twenty-five centuries the Bráhmans have been the writers and thinkers of India, the counsellors of Hindu princes and the teachers of the Hindu people. The education and learning which so long gave them their power, have ceased to be the monopoly of their caste; and may now be acquired by all races and all classes of His Majesty's Indian subjects.

Materials for Reference.

The literature on ancient India is so copious that it must suffice to name a few of the most useful and most easily available works. Weber's *History of Indian Literature* is perhaps the most compendious; a new edition of Max Müller's *History of Ancient Sanskrit Literature* (1859) would be a boon to the student, and his *Chips from a German Workshop* are delightful. Among standard treatises may be mentioned John Muir's valuable translations of *Sanskrit Texts* (5 vols. 2nd ed. 1868–73); Max Duncker's *Ancient History of India*; Lassen's *Indische Alterthumskunde*; James Prinsep's *Essays on Indian Antiquities*; Horace Hayman Wilson's *Collected Works*; and the writings of Roth, Benfey, K. M. Banarji, General Cunningham, Hoernle, Bühler, and Burnell. Some of the most valuable original Sanskrit texts are now rendered available to the English student in Max Müller's magnificent series of *Sacred Books of the East*. His new edition of the *Rig-Veda-Samhita* forms a splendid monument alike to the Indian prince who provided the cost of the work, and to the European scholar who has executed it.

CHAPTER V.

Buddhism—543 B.C. to 1000 A.D.

Rise of Buddhism, 543 B.C.*—The Bráhmans had firmly established their power 600 years before Christ. But after that date a new religion arose in India, called Buddhism, from the name of its founder, Gautama Buddha. This new religion was a rival to Bráhmanism during more than a thousand years. About the ninth century A.D. Buddhism was driven out of India. But it is still professed by 500 millions of people in Asia, and has more followers than any other religion in the world.

The Legend of Buddha: his Early Life.—Gautama, afterwards named BUDDHA, 'The Enlightened,' was the only son of Suddhodana, King of Kapilavastu. This prince ruled over the Sakya people, about 100 miles north of Benares, and within sight of the snow-topped Himálayas. The king wished to see his son grow up into a warrior like himself. But the young prince shunned the sports of his playmates, and spent his time alone in nooks of the palace garden. When he reached manhood, however, he showed himself brave and skilful with his weapons. He won his wife by a contest at arms over all rival chiefs. For a time he forgot the religious thoughts of his boyhood in the enjoyment of the world. But in his drives through the city he was struck by the sights of old age, disease, and death which met his eye; and he envied the calm of a holy man, who seemed to have raised his soul above the changes and sorrows of this life. After ten years, his wife bore to him an only son; and Gautama, fearing lest this new tie should bind him too closely to the things of earth, retired about the age of thirty to a cave in the jungles. The story is told how he turned away from the door of his wife's lamp-lit chamber, denying himself even a parting caress of his new-born babe, lest he should wake the sleeping mother, and galloped off into the

* The Nirvána or death of Buddha is assigned to 543 or to 478 B.C.

darkness. After a gloomy night ride, he sent back his one companion, the faithful charioteer, with his horse and jewels to his father. Having cut off his long warrior hair, and exchanged his princely raiment for the rags of a poor passer-by, he went on alone a homeless beggar. This giving up of princely pomp, and of loved wife and new-born son, is the Great Renunciation which forms a favourite theme of the Buddhist Scriptures.

Legend of Buddha's Forest Life, æt. 30 to 36.—For a time Gautama studied under two Bráhman hermits, in Patná District. They taught him that the peace of the soul was to be reached only by mortifying the body. He then buried himself deeper in the jungles near Gayá, and during six years wasted himself by austerities in company with five disciples. The temple of Buddha-Gayá marks the site of his long penance. But instead of earning peace of mind by fasting and self-torture, he sank into a religious despair, during which the Buddhist Scriptures affirm that the enemy of mankind, Mára, wrestled with him in bodily shape. Torn with doubts as to whether all his penance availed anything, the haggard hermit fell senseless to the earth. When he recovered, the mental agony had passed. He felt that the path to salvation lay not in self-torture in mountain-jungles or caves, but in preaching a higher life to his fellow-men. He gave up penance. His five disciples, shocked by this, forsook him; and he was left alone in the forest. The Buddhist Scriptures depict him as sitting serene under a fig-tree, while demons whirled round him with flaming weapons. From this temptation in the wilderness he came forth with his doubts for ever laid at rest, seeing his way clear, and henceforth to be known as Buddha, literally 'The Enlightened.'

Public Teaching of Buddha, æt. 36 to 80.—Buddha began his public teaching in the Deer-Forest, near the great city of Benares. Unlike the Bráhmans, he preached, not to one or two disciples of the sacred caste, but to the people. His first converts were common men, and among the earliest were women. After three months he had gathered around him sixty disciples, whom he sent forth to the neighbouring countries with these words: 'Go ye now, and preach the most excellent law.' Two-thirds of each year he spent as a wandering preacher. The remaining four months, or the rainy season, he abode at some fixed place, teaching the people who flocked around his little dwelling in the bamboo grove. His five old disciples, who had forsaken him in the time of his sore temptation in the wilderness, now came back to their master. Princes, merchants, artisans, Bráhmans and hermits, husbandmen and serfs, noble ladies and repentant women who had sinned, were added to those who believed. Buddha preached throughout Behar, Oudh, and the adjacent districts in the North-Western Provinces. He had ridden forth from his father's palace as a brilliant young prince. He now returned to it as a wandering preacher, in dingy yellow robes, with shaven head and the begging bowl in his hand. The old king heard him with reverence. The son, whom Buddha had left as a new-born babe, was converted to the faith; and his beloved wife, from the threshold of whose chamber he had ridden away into the darkness, became one of the first of Buddhist nuns.

Legend of Buddha's Death and Last Words.—Buddha's Great Renunciation took place in his thirtieth year. After long self-preparation, his public teaching began when he was about thirty-six, and during forty-four years he preached to the people. In foretelling his death, he said to his followers: 'Be earnest, be thoughtful, be holy, Keep steadfast watch over your own hearts. He who holds fast to the law and discipline, and faints not, he shall cross the ocean of life and make an end of sorrow.' 'The world is fast bound in fetters,' he added; 'I now give it deliverance, as a physician who brings heavenly medicine. Keep your mind on my teaching: all other things change, this changes not. No more shall I speak to you. I desire to depart. I desire the eternal rest (*Nirvána*).' He spent the night in preaching, and in comforting a weeping disciple. His latest words, according to one account, were, 'Work out your salvation with diligence.' He died calmly, at the age of eighty, under the shadow of a fig-tree, according to the commonly received tradition in 543 B.C.; or according to later criticism in 478 B.C.

The Law of Karma.—The secret of Buddha's success was,

that he brought spiritual deliverance to the people. He preached that salvation was equally open to all men, and that it must be earned, not by propitiating imaginary deities, but by our own conduct. He thus did away with sacrifices, and with the priestly claims of the Bráhmans as mediators between God and man. He taught that the state of a man in this life, in all previous and in all future lives, is the result of his own acts (*Karma*). What a man sows, that he must reap. As no evil remains without punishment, and no good deed without reward, it follows that neither priest nor God can prevent each act from bringing about its own consequences. Misery or happiness in this life is the unavoidable result of our conduct in a past life; and our actions here will determine our happiness or misery in the life to come. When any creature dies, he is born again in some higher or lower state of existence, according to his merit or demerit. His merit or demerit consists of the sum total of his actions in all previous lives. A system like this, in which our whole well-being—past, present, and to come—depends on ourselves, leaves little room for a personal God.

The Liberation of the Soul.—Life, according to Buddha, must always be more or less painful; and the object of every good man is to get rid of the evils of existence by merging his individual soul into the universal soul. This is *Nirvána*, literally 'cessation.' Some scholars explain it to mean that the soul is blown out like the flame of a lamp. Others hold that it is the extinction of the sins, sorrows, and selfishness of a man's individual life—the final rest of the soul. The pious Buddhist strives to reach a state of holy meditation in this world, and he looks forward to an eternal calm in a world to come. Buddha taught that this end could only be reached by leading a good life. Instead of the Bráhman sacrifices, he laid down three great duties, namely, control over self, kindness to other men, and reverence for the life of all living creatures.

Missionary Aspects of Buddhism.—He urged on his disciples that they must not only follow the true path themselves, but that they should preach it to all mankind. Buddhism has from the first been a missionary religion. One of the earliest acts of Buddha's public ministry was to send forth the Sixty Disciples. He also formed a religious order, whose duty it was to go forth unpaid and preach to all nations. While, therefore, the Bráhmans kept their ritual for the Twice-born Aryan castes, Buddhism addressed itself not only to those castes and to the lower mass of the people, but to all the non-Aryan races throughout India, and eventually to the whole Asiatic world.

The First and Second Councils.—On the death of Buddha in 543 B.C., five hundred of his disciples met in a vast cave near Patná, to gather together his sayings. This was the first Council. They chanted the lessons of their master in three great divisions,—the words of Buddha to his disciples; his code of discipline; and his system of doctrine. These became the Three Collections of Buddha's teaching; and the word for a Buddhist Council means literally 'a singing together.'

A century afterwards, a Second Council, of seven hundred, was held in 443 B.C., to settle disputes between the more and the less strict followers of Buddhism.

Asoka.—During the next two hundred years Buddhism spread over Northern India. About 257 B.C., Asoka, the King of Magadha or Behar, became a zealous convert to the faith. He was grandson of Chandra Gupta, whom we shall afterwards hear of in Alexander's camp. Asoka is said to have supported 64,000 Buddhist priests; he founded many religious houses; and his kingdom is called the Land of the Monasteries (Vihára or Behar) to this day. Asoka did for Buddhism what the Emperor Constantine afterwards effected for Christianity—he made it a State religion. This he accomplished by five means,—(1) by a Council to settle the faith; (2) by Edicts setting forth its principles; (3) by a State Department to watch over its purity; (4) by Missionaries to spread its doctrines; and (5) by an Authoritative Revision or Canon of the Buddhist Scriptures.

The Work of Asoka.—In 244 B.C., Asoka convened at Patná the Third Buddhist Council, of one thousand elders. Evil men, taking on them the yellow robe of the Buddhist order, had given forth their own opinions as the teaching of Buddha. Such heresies were now corrected; and the Buddhism of

Southern Asia practically dates from Asoka's Council. In a number of edicts, both before and after that Council, he published throughout his empire the grand principles of the faith. Forty of these royal sermons are still found graven upon pillars, caves, and rocks throughout India. Asoka also founded a State department, with a Minister of Justice and Religion at its head, to watch over the purity, and to direct the spread, of the faith. Wells were to be dug and trees planted along the roads for the wearied wayfarers. Hospitals were established for man and beast. Officers were appointed to watch over family life and the morals of the people, and to promote instruction among the women as well as the youth. Asoka thought it his duty to convert all mankind to Buddhism. His rock inscriptions record how he sent forth missionaries 'to the utmost limits of the barbarian countries,' to 'intermingle among all unbelievers' for the spread of religion. They were to mix equally with soldiers, Bráhmans, and beggars, with the dreaded and the despised, both within the kingdom 'and in foreign countries, teaching better things.' But conversion was to be effected by persuasion, not by the sword. Buddhism was at once the most intensely missionary religion in the world, and the most tolerant. Asoka, however, not only laboured to spread his religion—he also took steps to keep its doctrines pure. He collected the Buddhist sacred books into an authoritative version, in the Magadhi language of his central kingdom in Behar,—a version which for two thousand years has formed the Southern Canon of the Buddhist Scriptures.

Kanishka.—The fourth and last of the great Buddhist Councils was held under the Scythian King Kanishka, who ruled in North-Western India about 40 A.D. He again revised the sacred books, and his version has supplied the Northern Canon to the Buddhists of Tibet, Tartary, and China. Meanwhile Buddhist missionaries were preaching all over Asia. About 244 B.C., Asoka's son is said to have carried his father's Southern Canon of the sacred books to Ceylon, whence it spread in later times to Burma and the Eastern Archipelago. The Northern Canon of Buddhism, as laid down at the Council of Kanishka, became one of the State religions of China in 65 A.D.;

and it is still professed by the northern Buddhists from Tibet to Japan. The Buddhist ritual and doctrines also spread westwards, and exercised an influence upon early Christianity.

Buddhism as a National Religion.—Buddhism was thus formed into a State religion by the Councils of Asoka and Kanishka. It did not abolish caste. On the contrary, reverence to Bráhmans and to the spiritual guide ranked as one of the three great duties, along with obedience to parents and acts of kindness to all men and animals. Buddha, however, divided mankind not by their caste, but according to their religious merit. He told his hearers to live good lives, not to offer victims to the gods. The public worship in Buddhist countries consists, therefore, in doing honour to the relics of holy men who are dead, instead of sacrifices. Its sacred buildings were, originally, not temples to the gods, but monasteries for the monks and nuns, with their bells and rosaries; or memorial shrines, reared over a tooth or bone of the founder of the faith.

Buddha's personality denied.—While, on the one hand, many miraculous stories have grown up around Buddha's life and death, it has been denied, on the other hand, that such a person as Buddha ever existed. The date of his birth cannot be fixed with certainty; the dates which I have given for his life are those of the received Indian tradition. Some scholars hold that Buddhism is merely a religion based on the Bráhmanical or Sánkhya philosophy of Kapila. They argue that Buddha's birth is placed at a purely allegorical town, Kapila-Vastu, 'the abode of Kapila'; that his mother is called Máyá-deví, in referance to the Máyá or 'illusion' doctrine of Kapila's system; and that the very name of Buddha is not that of any real person, but merely means 'The Enlightened.' This theory is so far true, that Buddhism was not a sudden invention of any single mind, but was worked out from the Bráhman philosophy and religion which preceded it. But such a view leaves out of sight the two great traditional features of Buddhism, namely, the preacher's appeal to the people, and the undying influence of his own beautiful life.

Bráhmanism never crushed.—Buddhism never drove Bráhmanism out of India. The two religions lived together during more than a thousand years, from before 250 B.C. to about 900 A.D. Modern Hinduism is the joint product of both. In certain kingdoms of India, and at certain periods, Buddhism prevailed. But Bráhmanism was at no time crushed; and the Bráhmans in the end claimed Buddha as the ninth incarnation of their own god, Vishnu. The Chinese Pilgrims to India in 400 and 630 A.D. found Buddhist monasteries and Bráhman temples side by side.

Council of Síláditya, 634 A.D.—In Northern India, for example, a famous Buddhist king, Síláditya, ruled at the latter date. He seems to have been an Asoka of the seventh century A.D.; and he strictly carried out the two great Buddhist duties of charity and spreading the faith. He tried to extend Buddhism by means of a General Council in 634 A.D. Twenty-one tributary sovereigns attended, together with the most learned Buddhist monks and Bráhmans of their kingdoms. But the object of the Council was not merely to assert the Buddhist faith. It dealt with the two religions of India at that time. First, a discussion took place between the Buddhists and the Bráhmans; second, a dispute between the two Buddhist sects who followed respectively the Northern Scriptures or Canon of Kanishka and the Southern Scriptures or Canon of Asoka. The rites of the populace were as mixed as the doctrines of their teachers. On the first day of the Council, a statue of Buddha was installed with great pomp; on the second, an image of the Bráhman Sun-god; on the third, an idol of the Hindu Siva.

Síláditya's Charity.—Síláditya held a solemn distribution of his royal treasures every five years. The Chinese Pilgrim Hiuen Tsiang describes how, on the plain where the Ganges and the Jumna unite their waters, near Allahábád, all the kings of the empire, and a multitude of people, were feasted for seventy-five days. Síláditya brought forth the stores of his palace, and gave them away to Bráhmans and Buddhists, monks and heretics, without distinction. At the end of the festival he stripped off his jewels and royal raiment, handed them to the bystanders, and, like Buddha of old, put on the rags of a beggar. By this ceremony the king commemorated the Great Renunciation of Buddha, and also practised the highest duty laid down by the Bráhmans, namely, almsgiving.

Monastery of Nalanda.—The vast Buddhist monastery of Nalanda, near Gayá, formed a seat of learning which recalls the Christian abbeys and universities of mediaeval Europe. Ten thousand monks and novices of the eighteen Buddhist schools here studied theology, philosophy, law, science, especially medicine, and practised their devotions. They lived in learned ease, fed by the royal bounty. But even this stronghold of Buddhism is a proof that Buddhism was only one of two hostile creeds in India. During one short period (about 640 A.D.) it was three times destroyed by the enemies of the Buddhist faith.

Victory of Bráhmanism, 700 to 900 A.D.—Between 700 and 900 A.D. there arose various great reformers of the Bráhman faith. After 800 A.D. Bráhmanism gradually became the ruling religion. Legends dimly tell of persecutions stirred up by Bráhman reformers. But although there were severe local persecutions of Buddhists, the downfall of Buddhism seems to have resulted partly from its own decay, and from new movements of religious thought, rather than from any general suppression by the sword. In the tenth century, only outlying states, such as Kashmír and Orissa, remained faithful; and before the Muhammadans fairly came upon the scene, Buddhism as a popular faith had almost disappeared from India.

Buddhism an Exiled Religion, 900 A.D.—During the last thousand years Buddhism has been a banished religion from its native Indian home. But it has won greater triumphs in its exile than it could have ever achieved in the land of its birth. It created a literature and a religion for nearly one-half of the human race; and it is supposed, by its influence on early Christianity, to have affected the beliefs of a large part of the other half. Five hundred millions of men, or forty per cent. of the inhabitants of the world, still follow the teaching of Buddha. Afghánistán, Nepál, Eastern Turkistán, Tibet, Mongolia, Manchuria, China, Japan, the Eastern Archipelago, Siam, Burma, Ceylon, and India, at one time or another marked the magnificent circle of its conquests. Its shrines and monasteries stretched from what are now provinces of the Russian empire, to Japan and the islands of the Malay Sea. During twenty-four centuries, Buddhism has encountered and outlived a series of rival faiths. At this day it forms, with Christianity and Islám, one of the three great religions of the world; and the most numerously followed of the three.

The Jains.—Even in India Buddhism did not altogether die. Many of its doctrines still live in Hinduism. It also left behind a special sect, the Jains, who number over 1¼ millions in India. Like the Buddhists, they deny the authority of the Veda, except in so far as it agrees with their own tenets; disregard sacrifice; practise a strict morality; believe that their past and future states depend upon their own actions rather than on any external deity; and refuse to kill either man or beast. The Jains divide time into three eras; and adore twenty-four *Jinas*, or just men made perfect, in the past age, twenty-four in the present, and twenty-four in the era to come. The colossal statues of this great company of saints stand in their temples. They choose wooded mountains and the most lovely retreats of nature for their places of pilgrimage, and cover them with exquisitely carved shrines in white marble or dazzling stucco. The Jains of India are usually merchants or bankers. Their charity is boundless; and they form the chief supporters of the beast hospitals, which the old Buddhistic tenderness for animals has left in many of the cities of India. They claim, not without evidence, that the Jain religion is even older than Buddhism; and that the teaching of Buddha was based on the Jain faith.

The Present Influence of Buddhism in India.—Buddhism is still the religion of Burma, and has there over nine millions of followers, or nine-tenths of the population. The Buddhist monasteries have from ancient times been schools for the young as well as religious houses for the monks; and they now form the basis of the British system of Public Instruction throughout Burma. In all the rest of British India there are only about 227,000 pure Buddhists, chiefly in the Bengal Districts adjacent to Burma, and in the remote valleys of the Himálayan ranges. From time to time Buddhism seems to take a new start in Lower Bengal, and Buddhist journals are published in Calcutta and elsewhere. The Jain faith, an allied religion to Indian Buddhism, has been described in the last paragraph. But the noblest survivals of Buddhism in India are to be found not among any peculiar body, but in the religion of the whole Hindu people; in that principle of the brotherhood of man, with the re-assertion of which each new revival of Hinduism starts; in the asylum which the great Hindu sect of Vaishnavs affords to women who have fallen victims to caste rules, to the widow and the outcast; in that gentleness and charity to all men, which take the place of a poor-law in India, and give a high significance to the half-satirical epithet of the 'mild' Hindu.

Materials for Reference.

The most convenient English summary of this subject will be found in Professor Rhys Davids' *Buddhism*, his *Buddhist Birth-Stories*, and *Hibbert Lectures*. Among many other works may be mentioned Bishop Bigandet's *Life and Legend of Buddha* (London edition, 1880); Spence Hardy's *Manual of Buddhism* (modern), and his *Eastern Monachism*; Oldenberg's *Buddha, sein Leben* (and English translation by Hoey, 1882, an admirable work); Rockhill's *Life of the Buddha* (from Tibetan sources); Copleston's *Buddhism Primitive and Present in Magadha and in Ceylon*; Senart's *Essai sur la Légende du Bouddha*; Beale's *Catena of Buddhist Scriptures from the Chinese*; Edkin's *Chinese Buddhism*; Childers' *Dictionary of the Páli Language* (s. v. Buddho, &c.); General Maisey's *Sánchi and its remains*; General Cunningham's *Ancient Geography of India*, his *Corpus Inscriptionum Indicarum*, and his other archaeological writings, of which the latest is the *Mahábodhi, or the Great Buddhist Temple at Buddha-Gaya* (1892). An interesting Buddhist magazine, entitled *The Journal of the Mahábodhi Society*, is published monthly in Calcutta (1892).

CHAPTER VI.

The Greeks in India, 327 to 161 B.C.

External Sources of the History of India.—The external history of India commences with the Greek invasion in 327 B.C. Some indirect trade between India and the Mediterranean seems to have existed from very ancient times. Homer was acquainted with tin, and other articles of Indian merchandise, by their Sanskrit names; and a long list has been made of Indian products mentioned in the Hebrew Bible. The first Greek historian who speaks clearly of India is Hekataios of Miletos (549–486 B.C.); the knowledge of Herodotos (450 B.C.) ended at the Indus; and Ktesias, the physician (401 B.C.), brought back from his residence in Persia only a few facts about the products of India, its dyes and fabrics, monkeys and parrots. India to the east of the Indus was first made known to Europe by the historians and men of science who accompanied Alexander the Great, King of Macedon, in 327 B.C.

Alexander's Expedition.—Alexander the Great entered India early in 327 B.C.; crossed the Indus above Attock, and advanced, without a struggle, over the intervening territory of the Taxiles to the Jehlam (Hydaspes). He found the Punjab divided into petty kingdoms jealous of each other, and many of them inclined to join an invader rather than to oppose him. One of these local monarchs, Porus, disputed the passage of the Jehlam with a force which, substituting chariots for guns, about equalled the army of Ranjít Singh, the ruler of the Punjab in the present century. Plutarch gives a vivid description of the battle from Alexander's own letters. Having drawn up his troops at a bend of the Jehlam, about 14 miles west of the modern field of Chilianwála, the Greek king crossed under shelter of a tempestuous night. The chariots hurried out by Porus stuck in the muddy bank of the river. In the engagement which followed, the elephants of the Indian prince refused to face the Greeks, and, wheeling round, trampled Porus' own army under foot. His son fell early in the onset; Porus himself fled wounded;

but, on tendering his submission, he was confirmed in his kingdom, and became Alexander's trusted friend. Alexander built two memorial cities on the site of his victory—Bucephala, on the west bank of the Jehlam (near the modern Jalálpur), named after his beloved charger slain in the battle; and Nikaia, the present Mong, on the east side of the river.

Alexander in the Punjab.—Alexander advanced south-east through the kingdom of the younger Porus to Amritsar, and, after a sharp bend backward to the west to fight the Kathaei at Sangala, he reached the Beas (Hyphasis). Here, at a spot not far from the modern battle-field of Sobráon, he halted his victorious standards. He had resolved to march to the Ganges; but his troops were worn out by the heats of the Punjab summer, and broken in spirit by the hurricanes of the south-west monsoon. The native tribes had already risen in his rear; and the Conqueror of the World was forced to turn back before he had crossed even the frontier Province of India. The Sutlej, the eastern Districts of the Punjab, and the mighty Jumna still lay between him and the Ganges. A single defeat might have been fatal to his army; if the battle on the Jehlam had gone against him, not a Greek would probably have reached the Afghán side of the passes. Yielding at length to the clamour of his men, he led them back to the Jehlam. He there embarked 8000 of his troops in boats, and floated them down the river through the Southern Punjab to Sind; the remainder of his army marched in two divisions along the banks.

Alexander in Sind.—The country was hostile, and the Greeks held only the land on which they encamped. At Múltán, then as now the capital of the Southern Punjab, Alexander had to fight a pitched battle with the Malli, and was severely wounded in taking the city. His enraged troops put every soul within it to the sword. Farther down, near the confluence of the Five Rivers of the Punjab, he made a long halt, built a town, Alexandria,—the modern Uchh,—and received the submission of the neighbouring states. A Greek garrison and satrap, whom he here left behind, laid the foundation of a lasting Greek influence. Having constructed a new fleet, suitable for the greater rivers on which he was now to embark, Alexander proceeded southwards through Sind, and followed the course of the Indus until he reached the ocean. In the apex of the delta, he founded or refounded a city—Patala—which survives to this day as Haidarábád, the native capital of Sind. At the mouth of the Indus, Alexander beheld for the first time the majestic phenomenon of the tides. One part of his army he shipped off under the command of Nearchus to coast along the Persian Gulf; the remainder he himself led through Southern Balúchistán and Persia to Susa, where, after terrible losses from want of water and famine on the march, he arrived in 325 B.C.

Results of Alexander the Great's Expedition.—During his two years' campaign in the Punjab and Sind, Alexander subjugated no Province; but he made alliances, founded cities, and planted Greek garrisons. He had given much territory to Indian chiefs devoted to his cause; every petty Indian court had its Greek faction; and the troops which he left behind at many points, from the Afghán frontier on the west to the Beas river on the east, and as far south as the Sind delta, seemed visible pledges of his return. A large part of his army remained in Bactria; and in the partition of the empire after Alexander's death in 323 B.C., Bactria and India fell to Seleukos Nikator, the founder of the Syrian monarchy.

Chandra Gupta.—Meanwhile a new power had arisen in India. Among the Indian adventurers who thronged Alexander's camp in the Punjab, each with his plot for winning a kingdom or crushing a rival, Chandra Gupta, an exile from the Gangetic valley, seems to have played a somewhat ignominious part. He tried to tempt the wearied Greeks on the banks of the Beas with schemes of conquest in the rich Provinces of Hindustán to the south-east; but, having personally offended Alexander, he had to fly the camp (326 B.C.). In the confused years which followed, he managed, with the aid of plundering hordes, to found a kingdom on the ruins of the Nanda dynasty in Magadha, or Behar (316 B.C.). He seized their capital, Pataliputra, the modern Patná; established himself firmly in the Gangetic valley, and compelled the north-western principalities, Greek garrisons and Indian princes alike, to acknowledge his suzerainty. While the Greek general Seleukos was winning his way to the Syrian monarchy during the eleven years which followed Alexander's death, Chandra Gupta was building up an empire in Northern India. Seleukos reigned in Syria from 312 to 280 B.C.; Chandra Gupta in the Gangetic valley from 316 to 292 B.C. In 312 B.C. these two monarchs advanced their kingdoms to each other's frontier; they had to decide whether they were to live in peace or at war. Seleukos in the end sold the Greek conquests in the Kábul valley and the Punjab to Chandra Gupta, and gave his daughter in marriage to the Indian king. He also stationed a Greek ambassador at Chandra Gupta's court from 306 to 298 B.C.

Megasthenes' Account of India.—This ambassador was the famous Megasthenes. His description of India is perhaps the best that reached Europe during two thousand years, from 300 B.C. to 1700 A.D. He says that the people were divided into seven castes instead of four—namely, philosophers, husbandmen, shepherds, artisans, soldiers, inspectors, and the counsellors of the king. The philosophers were the Bráhmans, and the prescribed stages of their religious life are indicated. Megasthenes draws a distinction between the Bráhmans (*Brachmanes*) and the Sramans (*Sarmanai*), from which some scholars infer that the Buddhist Sramanas or monks were a recognized order fifty years before the Council of Asoka. But the Sarmanai of Megasthenes probably also include Bráhmans in the first and third stages of their life, as students and forest recluses. The inspectors, or sixth class of Megasthenes, have been identified with the Buddhist supervisors of morals. Arrian's name for them, *episkopoi*, is the Greek word which has become our modern Bishop or *overseer* of souls.

Indian Society, 300 B.C.—The Greek ambassador observed with admiration the absence of slavery in India, the chastity of the women, and the courage of the men. In valour, he says, they excelled all other Asiatics; they required no locks to their doors; above all, no Indian was ever known to tell a lie. Sober and industrious, good farmers, and skilful artisans, they scarcely ever had recourse to a lawsuit, and lived peaceably under their native chiefs. The kingly government is portrayed almost as described in the Code of Manu. Megasthenes mentions that India was divided into 118 kingdoms; some of which, as the Prasii under Chandra Gupta, exercised suzerain powers over other kings or dependent princes. The Indian village system is well described, each of the village communities seeming to the Greek an independent republic. Megasthenes remarked the exemption of the husbandmen (Vaisyas) from war and public services; and enumerates the dyes, fibres, fabrics, and products (animal, vegetable, and mineral) of India. Husbandry then as now depended on the periodical rains; and forecasts of the weather, with a view to 'make adequate provision against a coming deficiency,' formed a special duty of the Bráhmans. 'The philosopher,' he says, 'who errs in his predictions observes silence for the rest of his life.'

Later Greek Invasions.—After the time of Alexander the Great the Greeks made no important conquests in India. Antiochos, the grandson of Seleukos, entered into a treaty with the famous Buddhist king, Asoka, the grandson of Chandra Gupta, in 256 B.C. The Greeks had founded a powerful kingdom in Bactria, to the north-west of the Himálayas. During the hundred years after the Indo-Greek treaty of 256 B.C. the Greco-Bactrian kings sent invading hosts into the Punjab; some of whom reached eastwards as far as Muttra, or even Oudh, and southwards to Sind and Cutch, between 181 and 161 B.C. But they founded no kingdoms; and the only traces which the Greeks left in India were their science of astronomy, their beautiful sculptures, and their coins. Some of the early Buddhist statues, after 250 B.C., have exquisite Greek faces; and the same type is preserved in the most ancient carvings on the Hindu temples. By degrees even this trace of Greek influence faded away; but specimens of Indo-Greek sculptures may still be found in the museums of India.

Materials for Reference.

The works most easily available to the English reader are Mr. McCrindle's admirable series of translations of the Greek writers, and fragments dealing with India, especially his *Commerce and Navigation of the Erythræan Sea*; General Cunningham's *Ancient Geography of India*; Weber's *History of Indian Literature*; and the *Reports of the Archæological Survey of India*, especially of Western India. Mr. McCrindle's translations are about to be republished by Mr. Constable under the title of *The Invasion of India by Alexander the Great as described by Arrian, Quintus Curtius, Diodoros, Plutarch, and Justin* (1892).

CHAPTER VII.

The Scythic Inroads, from about 100 B.C. to 500 A.D.

The Scythians in Central Asia.—The Greek or Bactrian expeditions into India ended more than a century before Christ; but a new set of invaders soon began to pour into India from the north. These came from Central Asia, and, for want of a more exact name, have been called the Scythians. They belonged to many tribes, and they form a connecting link between Indian and Chinese history. As the Aryan race in the west of Asia had, perhaps 3000 years before Christ, sent off branches to Europe on the one hand, and to India on the other; so the Scythians, who dwelt to the east of the old Aryan camping-ground in Asia, swarmed forth into India and to China. These Scythic inroads went on during a great period of time. Buddha himself is said by some to have been a Scythian. But they took place in very great force during the century preceding the birth of Christ. They were the forerunners of a long series of inroads which devastated Northern India more than a thousand years later, under such leaders as Changíz Khán and Timúr, and which in the end founded the Mughal empire.

Scythic Kingdoms in Northern India.—About the year 126 B.C., the Tartar or Scythian tribe of Su are said to have driven out the Greek dynasty from the Bactrian kingdom, on the north-west of the Himálayas. Soon afterwards the Scythians rushed through the Himálayan passes and conquered the Greco-Bactrian settlements in the Punjab. About the beginning of the Christian era, they had founded a strong monarchy in Northern India and in the countries just beyond. Their most famous king was Kanishka, who summoned the Fourth Buddhist Council about 40 A.D. King Kanishka held his court in Kashmír; but his suzerainty extended from Agra and Sind in the south, to Yarkand and Khokand on the north of the Himálayas. He seems to have carried on successful wars as far as China. Six hundred years afterwards, in 630 A.D., a town called China-pati in the Punjab was pointed out as the place where King Kanishka kept his Chinese hostages. The Scythian monarchies of Northern India came in contact with the Buddhist kingdom under the successors of Asoka in Hindustán. The Scythians themselves became Buddhists; but they made changes in that faith. The result was, as we have seen, that while the countries to the south of India had adopted the Buddhist religion as settled by Asoka's Council in 244 B.C., the Buddhist religion as settled by Kanishka's Council in 40 A.D. became the faith of the Scythian nations to the north of India, from Central Asia to Japan (*ante*, p. 79).

Scythic Races still in India.—Kanishka was the most famous of the Scythian kings in India, but there were many other Scythian settlements. Indeed, the Scythians are believed to have poured into India in such numbers as to make up a large proportion of the population in the north-western frontier Provinces at the present day. For example, two old Scythian tribes, the Getae and the Dahae, are said to have dwelt side by side in Central Asia, and perhaps advanced together into India. Some writers hold that the Játs, who form nearly one-half of the inhabitants of the Punjab, are descended from these ancient Getae; and that a great subdivision of the Játs, called the Dhe, in like manner sprang from the Dahae. Other scholars try to show that certain of the Rájput tribes are of Scythian origin. However this may be, it is clear that many Scythian inroads took place into India from the first century B.C. to the fifth century A.D.

King Vikramáditya, 57 B.C.—During that long period several Indian monarchs won fame by attempting to drive out the Scythians. The best known of these is Vikramáditya, King of Ujjain in Málwá, in honour of whose victories one of the great eras in India, or systems of reckoning historical dates, is supposed to have been founded. It is called the *Samvat* era, and begins in 57 B.C. Its reputed founder is still known as Vikramáditya Sakári, or Vikramáditya the enemy of the Scythians. According to the Indian tradition, he was a learned as well as a valiant monarch, and he gathered round him the poets and philosophers of his time. The chief of these were called 'The Nine Jewels' of the court of Vikramáditya. They became so famous, that in after times a great many of the best Sanskrit poems or dramas, and works of philosophy or science, were ascribed to them; although the style and contents of the works prove that they must have been written at widely different periods. The truth is that the name Vikramáditya is merely a royal title, meaning 'A very Sun in Prowess,' which has been borne by several kings in Indian history. But the Vikramáditya of the first century before Christ was the most famous of them—famous alike as a defender of his country against the Scythian hordes, as a patron of men of learning, and as a good ruler of his subjects.

King Sáliváhana, 78 A.D.—About a hundred years later, another valiant Indian king arose against the Scythians. His name was Sáliváhana; and a new era, called the *Sáka* or Scythian, was founded in his honour in 78 A.D. These two eras—the *Samvat*, beginning in 57 B.C., and the *Sáka*, commencing in 78 A.D.—still form two well-known systems of reckoning historical dates in India.

Later Opponents of the Scythians.—During the next five centuries, three great Indian dynasties maintained the struggle against the Scythians. The Sáh kings reigned in the north-west of Bombay from 60 to 235 A.D. The Gupta kings reigned in Oudh and Northern India from 319 to 470 A.D., when they seem to have been overpowered by fresh hosts of Huns or Scythians. The Valabhí kings ruled over Cutch, Málwá, and the north-western districts of Bombay from 480 to after 722 A.D. The Greek traders in the Red Sea heard of the Huns as a powerful nation of Northern India about 535 A.D. The Chinese Pilgrim, Hiuen Tsiang, gives a full account of the court and people of Valabhí (630–640 A.D.). His description shows that Buddhism was the State religion; but heretics (i.e. Bráhmans) abounded; and the Buddhists themselves were divided between the northern school of the

Scythian dynasties, and the southern or Indian school of Asoka. The Valabhí dynasty seems to have been overthrown by the early Arab invaders of Sind in the eighth century A.D.

Materials for Reference.

The leading sources for this obscure and confused period are the *Reports of the Archæological Survey of Western India*; the coins and inscriptions of the Gupta, Sáh, and other dynasties; Rockhill's *Life of the Buddha*; the Gazetteers or District Statistical Surveys of Northern and Western India and of the Central Provinces; articles contributed to the *Indian Antiquary*; Colonel Tod's not always trustworthy *Annals and Antiquities of Rájásthán*; the magnificent volumes of the *Corpus Inscriptionum Indicarum*; and various papers in the *Royal Asiatic Society's Journal* by Dr. James Fergusson and other polemical scholars.

CHAPTER VIII.

Growth of Hinduism, 700 to 1500 A.D.

The Three Sources of the Indian People.—We have now got a view of the three races which make up the Indian people. These were, first, the non-Aryans, or the earliest inhabitants of the country, sometimes called the aborigines. Second, the Aryan race, who came to India from Central Asia in prehistoric times. Third, the Scythians or Tartars, who had also begun to move into India before the dawn of history, and whose later hordes came in great force between the first century B.C. and the fifth century after Christ. Each of these races had their own customs, their own religion, and their own speech.

The Aryans and the non-Aryans.—The non-Aryans were hunting tribes. In their family life, some of them kept up the early form of marriage, according to which a woman was the wife of several brethren, and a man's property descended, not to his own, but to his sister's children. In their religion, the non-Aryans worshipped demons, and tried by bloody sacrifices or human victims to avert the wrath of the malignant spirits whom they called gods. **The Aryans** early advanced beyond the rude existence of the hunter to the semi-settled industry of the cattle-breeder and tiller of the soil. In their family life, a woman had only one husband, and their customs and laws of inheritance were nearly the same as those which now prevail in India. In their religion, they worshipped bright and friendly gods.

The Scythians.—The third race, or the Scythians, held a position between the other two. The early Scythians, indeed, who arrived in prehistoric times, may have been as wild as the non-Aryans, and they probably supplied a section of what we call the aborigines of India. But the Scythian hordes, who poured into India from 126 B.C. to 400 A.D., were neither hunters like the Indian non-Aryan tribes, nor half-cultivators like the Aryans. They were shepherds or herdsmen, who roamed across the plains of Central Asia with their cattle, and whose one talent was for war.

The Aryan Work of Civilization.—The Aryans supplied, therefore, the civilizing power in India. One of their divisions or castes, the Vaisyas, brought the soil under the plough; another caste, the Kshattriyas, conquered the rude non-Aryan peoples; their third caste, the Bráhmans, created a religion and a literature. The early Bráhman religion made no account of the lower races; but, as we have seen, about 500 B.C. a wider creed, called the Buddhist, was based upon it. This new faith did much to bring the early non-Aryan tribes under the influence of the higher Aryan race, and it was accepted by the later Scythian hordes who came into India from 126 B.C. to 400 A.D. Buddhism was therefore the first great bond of union among the Indian races. It did something to combine the non-Aryans, the Aryans, and the Scythians into a people with similar customs and a common faith. But it was driven out of India before it finished its work.

The Bráhmans.—The work was continued by the Bráhmans. This ancient caste, which had held a high place even during the triumph of the Buddhist religion, became all-powerful upon the decay of that faith. The Chinese Pilgrim to India in 640 A.D. relates how the Bráhmans, or, as he calls them, the heretics, were again establishing their power. The Buddhist monasteries had, even at that time, a struggle to hold their own against the Bráhman temples. During the next two centuries the Bráhmans gradually got the upper hand. The conflict between the two religions brought forth a great line of Bráhman apostles, some of whose lives are almost as beautiful as that of Buddha himself. The first of these, Kumárila, a holy Bráhman of Behar, began his preaching in the eighth century A.D. He taught the old Vedic doctrine of a personal Creator and God. The Buddhists had no personal God. According to a later legend, Kumárila not only preached against the Buddhists, but persuaded a king of Southern India to persecute them. This prince, it is said, 'commanded his servants to put to death the old men and the young children of the Buddhists, from the southernmost point of India to the Snowy

Mountain. Let him who slays not, be slain.' At that time, however, there was no king in India whose power to persecute reached from the Himálayas to Cape Comorin. The story is probably an exaggerated account of a local persecution by one of the many princes of Southern India. The Bráhmans gained the victory partly because Buddhism was itself decaying, and partly because they offered a new bond of union to the Indian races. This new bond of union was Hinduism.

Twofold Basis of Hinduism.—Hinduism is a social league and a religious alliance. As a social league, it rests upon caste, and has its roots deep down in the race elements of the Indian people. As a religious alliance, it represents the union of the Vedic faith of the Bráhmans with Buddhism on the one hand, and with the ruder rites of the non-Aryan peoples on the other. We must get a clear view of both these aspects of Hinduism —as a social league, and as a religious alliance.

Caste Basis of Hinduism.—As a social league, Hinduism arranged the people into the old division of the 'Twice-born' Aryan castes, namely the Bráhmans, Kshattriyas, Vaisyas; and the 'Once-born' castes, consisting of the non-Aryan Súdras, and the classes of mixed descent. This arrangement of the Indian races remains to the present day. The 'Twice-born' castes still wear the sacred thread, and claim a joint, although an unequal, inheritance in the holy books of the Veda. The 'Once-born' castes are still denied the sacred thread; and they were not allowed to study the holy books, until the English set up schools in India for all classes of the people. But while caste is thus founded on the distinctions of race, it has been influenced by two other systems of division, namely, the employments of the people, and the localities in which they live. Even in the oldest times, the castes had separate occupations assigned to them. They could be divided either into Bráhmans, Kshattriyas, Vaisyas, and Súdras; or into priests, warriors, husbandmen, and serfs. They are also divided according to the parts of India in which they live. Even the Bráhmans have among themselves ten distinct classes, or rather nations. Five of these classes or Bráhman nations live to the north of the Vindhya mountains; five of them live to the south. Each of the ten feels itself to be quite apart from the rest; and they have among themselves no fewer than 1886 subdivisions or separate Bráhmanical tribes. In like manner, the Kshattriyas or Rájputs number 590 separate tribes in different parts of India.

Complexity of Caste.—While, therefore, Indian caste seems at first a very simple arrangement of the people into four classes, it is in reality a very complex one. For it rests upon three distinct systems of division; namely, upon race, occupation, and geographical position. It is very difficult even to guess at the number of the Indian castes. But there are not fewer than 3000 of them which have separate names, and which regard themselves as separate classes. The different castes cannot intermarry with each other, and most of them cannot eat together. The ordinary rule is that no Hindu of good caste can touch food cooked by a man of inferior caste. By rights, too, each caste should keep to its own occupation. Indeed, there has been a tendency to erect every separate kind of employment or handicraft in each separate Province into a distinct caste. But, as a matter of practice, the castes often change their occupation, and the lower ones sometimes raise themselves in the social scale. Thus the Vaisya caste were in ancient times the tillers of the soil. They have in most Provinces given up this toilsome occupation, and the Vaisyas are now the great merchants and bankers of India. Their fair skins, intelligent faces, and polite bearing, must have altered since the days when their forefathers ploughed, sowed, and reaped under the hot sun. Such changes of employment still occur on a smaller scale throughout India.

Caste as a System of Trade-guilds.—The system of caste exercises a great influence upon the industries of the people. Each caste is, in the first place, a trade-guild. It ensures the proper training of the youth of its own special craft; it makes rules for the conduct of the caste-trade; it promotes good feeling by feasts or social gatherings. The famous manufactures of mediæval India, its muslins, silks, cloth of gold, inlaid weapons, and exquisite work in precious stones—were brought to perfection under the care of the castes or trade-guilds. Such guilds may still be found in full work in many parts of India.

Thus, in the North-Western Districts of Bombay, all heads of artisan families are ranged under their proper trade-guild. The trade-guild or caste prevents undue competition among the members, and upholds the interest of its own body in any dispute arising with other craftsmen.

In 1873, for example, a number of the bricklayers in Ahmadábád could not find work. Men of this class sometimes added to their daily wages by rising very early in the morning, and working overtime. But when several families complained that they could not get employment, the bricklayers' guild met, and decided that as there was not enough work for all, no member should be allowed to work in extra hours. In the same city, the clothdealers in 1872 tried to cut down the wages of the sizers or men who dress the cotton cloth. The sizers' guild refused to work at lower rates, and remained six weeks on strike. At length they arranged their dispute, and both the trade-guilds signed a stamped agreement fixing the rates for the future. Each of the higher castes or trade-guilds in Ahmadábád receives a fee from young men on entering their business. The revenue derived from these fees, and from fines upon members who break caste rules, is spent in feasts to the brethren of the guild, and in helping the poorer craftsmen or their orphans. A favourite plan of raising money in Surat is for the members of the trade to keep a certain day as a holiday, and to shut up all their shops except one. The right to keep open this one shop is put up to auction, and the amount bid is expended on a feast. The trade-guild or caste allows none of its members to starve. It thus acts as a mutual assurance society and takes the place of a poor law in India. The severest social penalty which can be inflicted upon a Hindu is to be put out of his caste.

The Religious Basis of Hinduism.—Hinduism is, however, not only a social league resting upon caste—it is also a religious alliance based upon worship. As the various race elements of the Indian people have been welded into caste, so the simple old beliefs of the Veda, the mild doctrines of Buddha, and the fierce rites of the non-Aryan tribes, have been thrown into the melting-pot, and poured out thence as a mixture of precious metal and dross, to be worked up into the complex worship of the Hindu gods.

Buddhist Influences.—Buddhism not only inspired Hinduism with its noble spirit of charity, but also bequeathed to it many of its institutions. The Hindu monasteries in Orissa in our own day recall the Buddhist convents of King Síláditya eleven hundred years ago. At the present time, the bankers' guild of Surat devotes a part of the fees which it levies on bills of exchange to maintain a hospital for sick animals—a true survival of the system of medical aid for man and beast which King Asoka founded in 244 B.C. The religious life of the Hindu Vishnuite sect is governed by the old rules laid down by Buddha himself. The great Bengal scholar, Rájendra Lálá Mitra, himself a Vishnuite, believed that the car festival of Jagannáth is a relic of a Buddhist procession.

Non-Aryan Influences.—Hinduism also drew much of its strength, and many of its rites, from the non-Aryan peoples of India. To them is due the worship of stumps of wood, of rude stones, and of trees, which makes up the religion of the villagers of Bengal. Each hamlet has usually its local god, which it adores in the form either of an unhewn stone, or a stump, or a tree marked with red-lead. Sometimes a lump of clay placed under a tree does service for a deity. Serpent-worship, and the honour paid by certain sects of Hindus to the *linga*, or symbol of male creative energy, may probably be traced back to the Scythian tribes who came to India, in very early times, from Central Asia.

The Hindu Book of Saints.—Hinduism boasts a line of religious founders stretching from about 700 A.D. to the present day. The lives of the mediæval saints and their wondrous works are recorded in the Bhakta-Málá, or The Garland of the Faithful, compiled by Nábhájí about three centuries ago. It is the Book of Saints and Golden Legend of Hinduism. The same wonders are not recorded of each of its apostles, but miracles abound in the life of all. The greater ones rank as divine incarnations prophesied of old. According to the Hindu stories, some were born of virgins; others overcame lions; raised the dead; their hands and feet when cut off sprouted afresh; prisons were opened to them; the sea received them and returned them to the land unhurt, while the earth opened and swallowed up their slanderers. Their lives were marvellous, and the deaths of the greatest of them a solemn mystery.

Sankara Achárya, Ninth Century A.D.—The first in the line of apostles was Kumárila, a Bráhman of Behar, who has been already referred to as having stirred up a legendary persecution of Buddhism throughout India in the eighth century A.D. His yet more famous disciple was Sankara Achárya, with whom we reach historical ground. Sankara was born in Malabar, wandered as an itinerant preacher over India as far as Kashmír, and died at Kedarnáth in the Himálayas, aged 32. He moulded the Vedánta philosophy of the Bráhmans into its final form, and popularized it into a national religion. It is scarcely too much to say, that since his short life in the eighth or ninth century every new Hindu sect has had to start with a personal God. He addressed himself to the high-caste philosophers on the one hand, and to the low-caste multitude on the other. He left behind, as the twofold results of his life's work, a compact Bráhman sect and a popular religion.

Forms of Siva and his Wife.—In the hands of Sankara's followers and apostolic successors, Siva-worship became one of the two chief religions of India. Siva, at once the Destroyer and Reproducer, represented profound philosophical doctrines, and was early recognized as being in a special sense the god of the Bráhmans. To them he was the symbol of death as merely a change of life. On the other hand, his terrible aspects, preserved in his long list of names, from the Roarer (Rudra) of the Veda, to the Dread One (Bhíma) of the modern Hindu pantheon, well adapted him to the religion of fear prevalent among the ruder non-Aryan races. Siva, in his twofold character, thus became the deity alike of the highest and of the lowest castes. He is the Mahá-deva, or Great God of modern Hinduism; his wife is Deví, literally and pre-eminently THE Goddess. His symbol of worship is the *linga*, or emblem of male reproduction; his sacred beast, the bull, is connected with the same idea; a trident tops his temples. His images partake of his double nature. The Bráhmanical conception of Siva is represented by his attitude as a fair-skinned man, seated in profound thought, the symbol of the fertilizing Ganges above his head, and the bull (emblem alike of procreation and of Aryan plough-tillage) near at hand. The wilder non-Aryan aspects of his character are signified by his necklace of skulls, his collar of twining serpents, his tiger-skin, and his club with a human head at the end. Siva has five faces and four arms. His wife Deví, in like manner, appears in her Aryan or Bráhmanical form as Umá, 'Light,' a gentle goddess and the type of high-born loveliness; in her composite character as Durgá, a golden-coloured woman, beautiful but menacing, riding on a tiger; and in her terrible non-Aryan aspects as Kálí, a black fury, of a hideous countenance, dripping with blood, crowned with snakes, and hung round with skulls.

Twofold Aspects of Siva-worship.—The ritual of Siva-worship preserves, in an even more striking way, the traces of its double origin. The higher minds still adore the godhead by silent contemplation, as prescribed by Sankara, without the aid of external rites. The ordinary Bráhman hangs a wreath of flowers around the phallic *linga*, or places before it harmless offerings of rice. But the low-castes pour out the lives of countless goats at the feet of the terrible Kálí, the wife of Siva; and until lately, in time of pestilence and famine, tried in their despair to appease that relentless goddess by human blood. During the famine of 1866, in a temple of Kálí, a boy was found with his neck cut, the eyes staring open, and the stiff clotted tongue thrust out between the teeth. In another temple at Húglí (a railway station only twenty-four miles from Calcutta), a head was left before the idol, decked with flowers. Such cases are true survivals of the regular system of human sacrifices which we have seen among the non-Aryan tribes. They have nothing to do with the old mystic *purusha-medha*, or man-offering, whether real or symbolical, of the ancient Aryan faith, but form a part of the non-Aryan religion of terror, which demands that the greater the need, the greater shall be the propitiation.

The Thirteen Sivaite Sects.—The thirteen chief sects of

Siva-worshippers faithfully represent the composite character of their god. The *Smárta* Bráhmans, the lineal successors of Sankara's disciples, still maintain their life of calm monastic piety in Southern India. The *Dandís*, or ascetics, divide their time between begging and meditation. Some of them adore, without rites, Siva as the third person of the Aryan trinity. Others practise an apparently non-Aryan ceremony of initiation, by drawing blood from the inner part of the novice's knee as an offering to the god in his more terrible form, Bhairava. The *Dandís* follow the non-Aryan custom of burying their dead, or commit the body to a sacred stream. The *Yogís* include every class of devotee, from the speechless mystic, who by long suppressions of the breath has lost the consciousness of existence in an ecstatic union with Siva, to the impostor who pretends that he can sit upon air, and the juggler who travels with a performing goat. The Sivaite sects descend, through various gradations of self-mortification and abstraction, to the *Aghorís*, who eat carrion and gash their bodies with knives. The lowest sects follow non-Aryan rather than Aryan types, alike as regards their use of animal food and their bloody sacrifices.

Vishnu-worship.—Vishnu had always been a very human god, from the time when he makes his appearance in the Veda as a solar myth, the 'Unconquerable Preserver,' striding across the universe in three steps. His later incarnations or *avatárs* made him the familiar friend of man. Of these incarnations or 'descents' on earth, which vary according to tradition from ten or twenty-two in number, Vishnu-worship, with the unerring instinct of a popular religion, chose the two most beautiful for adoration. In his two human forms as Ráma and Krishna, the god Vishnu attracted to himself innumerable loving legends. Ráma, his seventh incarnation, is the hero of the Sanskrit epic, the Rámáyana. In his eighth incarnation, as Krishna, Vishnu appears as a high-souled prince in the other epic, the Mahábhárata. As Krishna, also, he afterwards grew into the central figure of Indian pastoral poetry; was spiritualized into the supreme god of the Vishnuite Puránas; and now flourishes as the most popular deity of the Hindus. Under his title of Jagannáth, 'The Lord of the World,' Vishnu is especially worshipped at Purí, whence his fame has spread through the civilized world. But nothing can be more unjust than the vulgar story which associates his car festival with the wholesale self-murder of his worshippers. Vishnu is essentially a bright and friendly god, who asks no offerings but flowers, and to whom the shedding of blood is a pollution. The official records, and an accurate examination on the spot, disprove the calumnies of some English writers on this subject. Fatal accidents frequently happened amid an excited crowd. Suicides on occasions have taken place. But the stories of wholesale bloodshed at one time told about Jagannáth, were merely ignorant libels on a gentle and peaceful god, to whom no sacrifice which cost the life even of a kid could be offered. The Vishnu sects are called Vaishnavas.

The Vishnu Purána, circ. 1045 A.D.—In the eleventh century the Vishnuite doctrines were gathered into a religious treatise. The *Vishnu Purána* dates from about 1045 A.D., and probably represents, as indeed its name implies, 'ancient' traditions of Vishnu which had co-existed with Sivaism and Buddhism for centuries. It derived its doctrines from the Vedas, not, however, in a direct channel, but filtered through the two great epic poems. It forms one of the eighteen Puránas or Sanskrit theological works, in which the Bráhman moulders of Vishnuism and Sivaism embodied their rival systems. These works especially extol the second and third members of the Hindu triad, now claiming the pre-eminence for Vishnu as the sole deity, and now for Siva; but in their higher flights rising to a recognition that both are but forms for representing the one eternal God. They are said to contain 1½ million lines. But they exhibit only the Bráhmanical aspect of Vishnu-worship and Siva-worship, and are devoid of any genuine sympathy for the lower castes.

Vishnuite Apostles—Rámánuja, 1150 A.D.—The first of the line of Vishnuite reformers was Rámánuja, a Bráhman of Southern India. In the middle of the twelfth century, he led a movement against the Sivaites, proclaiming the unity of God, under the title of Vishnu, the Cause and the Creator of all things. Persecuted by the Chola king in Southern India, who tried to enforce Sivaite conformity throughout his dominions, Rámánuja fled to the Jain sovereign of Mysore. This Jain prince he converted to the Vishnuite faith by expelling an evil spirit from his daughter. Seven hundred monasteries, of which four still remain, are said to have been erected by his followers before his death.

Rámánand, 1300–1400 A.D.—Rámánand stands fifth in the apostolic succession from Rámánuja, and spread his doctrine through Northern India. He had his headquarters in a monastery at Benares, but wandered from place to place, preaching the one God under the name of Vishnu. He chose twelve disciples, not from the priests or nobles, but among the despised castes. One of them was a leather-dresser, another a barber, and the most distinguished of all was the reputed son of a weaver. Rámánuja had addressed himself chiefly to the pure Aryan castes, and wrote in the Sanskrit language of the Bráhmans. Rámánand appealed to the people, and the literature of his sect is in the dialects familiar to the masses. The Hindí vernacular owes its development into a written language, partly to the folk-songs of the peasantry and the war-ballads of the Rájput court-bards, but chiefly to the literary requirements of the new popular religion of Vishnu.

Kabír, 1380–1420 A.D.—Kabír, one of the twelve disciples of Rámánand, carried his doctrines throughout Bengal. As his master had laboured to gather together all castes of the Hindus into one common faith, so Kabír, seeing that the Hindus were no longer the whole inhabitants of India, tried, about the beginning of the fifteenth century, to build up a religion that should embrace Hindu and Muhammadan alike. The writings of his sect acknowledge that the God of the Hindu is also the God of the Musalmán. His universal name is The Inner, whether he be invoked as the Alí of the Muhammadans, or as the Ráma of the Hindus. 'To Alí and to Ráma we owe our life,' say the scriptures of Kabír's sect, 'and we should show like tenderness to all who live. . . . The Hindu fasts every eleventh day; the Musalmán on the Ramazán. Who formed the remaining months and days, that you should venerate but one? . . . The city of the Hindu God is to the east [Benares], the city of the Musalmán God is to the west [Mecca]; but explore your own heart, for there is the God both of the Musalmáns and of the Hindus. Behold but One in all things. He to whom the world belongs, he is the father of the worshippers alike of Alí and of Ráma. He is my guide, he is my priest.'

Chaitanya, 1485–1527 A.D.—In 1485 Chaitanya was born, and spread the Vishnuite doctrines, with the worship of Jagannáth, throughout the deltas of Bengal and Orissa. Signs and wonders attended Chaitanya through life; and during four centuries he has been worshipped as an incarnation of Vishnu. Extricating ourselves from the halo of legend which surrounds this apostle of Jagannáth, we know little of his private life except that he was the son of a Bráhman settled at Nadiyá in Bengal; that in his youth he married the daughter of a celebrated saint; that at the age of twenty-four he forsook the world, and, renouncing the state of a householder, repaired to Orissa, where he devoted the rest of his days to the propagation of the faith. He disappeared in 1527 A.D. But with regard to his doctrine we have the most ample evidence. He held that all men are alike capable of faith, and that all castes by faith become equally pure. Implicit belief and incessant devotion were his watchwords. Contemplation rather than ritual was his pathway to salvation. Obedience to the religious guide is one of the leading features of his sect; but he warned his disciples to respect their teachers as second fathers, and not as gods. The great end of his system, as of all Indian forms of worship, is the liberation of the soul. He held that such liberation does not mean the annihilation of separate existence. It consists in nothing more than an entire freedom from the stains and the frailties and sinful desires of the body.

The Chaitanya Sect.—The followers of Chaitanya belong to every caste, but they acknowledge the rule of the descendants of the original disciples (*gosáins*). The sect is open alike to the married and unmarried. It has its celibates and wandering mendicants, but its religious teachers are generally married men. They live with their wives and children in clusters of houses around a temple to Krishna (an incarnation of Vishnu). The adoration of the founder, Chaitanya, is thus a sort of family worship in Orissa. The landed gentry worship him with a daily ritual in household chapels dedicated to his name. After his death, a sect arose among his followers, who asserted the spiritual independence of women. In their monastic enclosures, male and female cenobites live in celibacy,—the women shaving their heads, with the exception of a single lock of hair. The two sexes chant the praises of Vishnu and Chaitanya together in hymn and solemn dance. But the really important doctrine of the sect is their recognition of the value of women as instructors of the outside female community. For long they were the only teachers admitted into the *zanánas* of good families in Bengal. Fifty years ago they had effected a change for the better in the state of female education; and the value of such instruction was assigned as the cause of the sect spreading so widely in Calcutta.

Vallabha-Swámí, circ. 1520 A.D.—The death of Chaitanya marked the beginning of a spiritual decline in Vishnu-worship. About 1520, Vallabha-Swámí preached in Northern India that the liberation of the soul did not depend upon the mortification of the body; and that God was to be sought, not in nakedness and hunger and solitude, but amid the enjoyments of this life. An opulent sect had, from an early period, attached itself to the worship of Krishna and his bride Rádhá—a mystic significance being of course assigned to their pastoral loves. Still more popular among Hindu women is the adoration of Krishna as the Bála Gopála, or the Infant Cowherd, perhaps unconsciously affected by the Christian worship of the Divine Child. Another influence of Christianity on Hinduism may possibly be traced in the growing importance assigned by the Krishna sects to *bhakti*, or faith, as an all-sufficient instrument of salvation.

Krishna-worship.—Vallabha-Swámí was the apostle of Vishnuism as a religion of pleasure. The special object of his homage was Vishnu in his pastoral incarnation, in which he took the form of the divine youth Krishna, and led an Arcadian life in the forest. Shady bowers, lovely women, exquisite viands, and everything that appeals to the luscious sensuousness of a tropical race, are mingled in his worship.

His daily ritual consists of eight services, in which Krishna's image, as a beautiful boy, is delicately bathed, anointed with essences, splendidly attired, and sumptuously fed. The followers of the first Vishnuite reformers dwelt together in secluded monasteries, and went about scantily clothed, living upon alms. But the Vallabha-Swámí sect performs its devotions arrayed in costly apparel, anointed with oil, and perfumed with camphor or sandal-wood. It seeks its converts not among weavers, or leather-dressers, or barbers, but among wealthy bankers and merchants, who look upon life as a thing to be enjoyed, and upon pilgrimage as a holiday excursion, or an opportunity for trade.

The Religious Bond of Hinduism.—The worship of Siva and Vishnu acts as a religious bond among the Hindus, in the same way as caste supplies the basis of their social organization. Theoretically, the Hindu religion starts from the Veda, and acknowledges its divine authority. But, practically, we have seen that Hinduism takes its origin from many sources. Vishnu-worship and Sivaite rites represent the two most popular combinations of these various elements. The highly cultivated Bráhman is a pure theist; the less cultivated worships the Divinity under some chosen form, his *ishta-devatá*. The ordinary Bráhman, especially in the south, takes as his 'chosen deity' Siva in his deep philosophical aspects as the fountain of being and of reproduction, the symbol of death deprived of its terrors and welcomed as the entrance into new forms of life. The phallic *linga* serves him as an emblem of the unseen God. The middle classes and the trading community adore some incarnation of Vishnu. The low-castes propitiate Siva the Destroyer, or one of his female manifestations, such as the dread Kálí. But almost every Hindu of education feels that his outward object of homage is merely his *ishta-devatá*, or a 'chosen' form under which to adore the supreme Deity, PARAM-ESWARA.

MATERIALS FOR REFERENCE.

Hinduism is the joint product of Bráhmanism, Buddhism, and the non-Aryan worships, dealt with in Chapters III, IV, and V. But in addition to the works cited at the end of those chapters, the following may be specially noted: Barth's *Religions of India*; H. H. Wilson's *Religion of the Hindus*, and his *Vishnu Purána*; Sir Alfred Lyall's *Asiatic Studies*; Colebrooke's *Essays on the Religion and Philosophy of the Hindus*; Garçin de Tassy's *Histoire de la Littérature Hindouie et Hindoustanie*, and his *Les Auteurs Hindoustanis et leurs Ouvrages*; Graf Björnstjerna's *Die Theogonie Philosophie und Kosmogonie der Hindus*; Fergusson's *History of Indian and Eastern Architecture*, and his *Tree and Serpent Worship*; Trumpp's *Die Religion der Sikhs*, and his *Nanak*; Mozoomdar's *Faith and Progress of the Brahmo-Somaj* (Calcutta, 1882); and Miss Collet's *Brahmo Year-Book*; Sir Monier Williams' *Non-Christian Religious Systems, Hinduism*, and his *Religious Thought and Life in India*; Sir William Hunter's *Orissa*, and his *Rural Bengal*; Dr. J. Wilson's *Indian Caste*, and Sherring's *Hindu Tribes and Castes* (two works of great original value); Steele's *Law and Custom of Hindu Castes* (for Western India); Nelson's *View of Hindu Law*, and Burnell's *Dayavibhága* (for the Madras Presidency). Also again Max Müller's *Hibbert Lectures* and his *Sacred Books of the East*, together with the easily accessible volumes of Trübner's *Oriental Series* and in the *Bibliotheca Indica* too numerous to specify.

CHAPTER IX.

Early Muhammadan Conquerors, 714–1526 A.D.

Muhammadan Influence on Hinduism.—Hinduism was for a time submerged, but never drowned, by the tide of Muhammadan conquest, which set steadily towards India about 1000 A.D. At the present day, the south of India remains almost entirely Hindu. By far the greater number of the Indian Feudatory Chiefs are still under Bráhman influence. But in the north-west, where the first waves of invasion have always broken, about one-third of the population now profess Islám. The upper valley of the Ganges boasts a succession of Musalmán capitals; and in the swamps of Lower Bengal, the bulk of the non-Aryan or aboriginal population have become converts to the Muhammadan religion. The Musalmáns now make 62 millions of the total of 294 millions in India.

Early Muhammadan Dynasties, 714–1526 A.D.—The present chapter is devoted to the early Muhammadan conquerors in the north of India before the rise of the Mughal Empire. But it is convenient to give in this place a chronological list of all the Muhammadan dynasties, whose succession makes up so large a part of the history of mediæval India.

Chronological Summary of Muhammadan Conquerors and Dynasties of India, 1001–1857.

I. House of Ghazni (Túrkí).

1001–1186. Mahmúd of Ghazní to Sultán Khusrú.

II. House of Ghor (Afghán).

1186–1206. Muhammad of Ghor (Shaháb-ud-dín).

III. Slave Kings (chiefly Túrkí).

1206–1290. Kutab-ud-dín to Balban and Kaikubád.

IV. House of Khilji.

1290–1320. Jalál-ud-dín to Násir-ud-dín Khusrú.

V. House of Tughlak (Punjab Túrkí).

1320. Ghiyás-ud-dín Tughlak.

1325. Muhammad Tughlak.

1351. Fíruz Sháh Tughlak.

1414. End of the Tughlak dynasty.

1398. [Irruption of the Mughals under Timúr (Tamerlane) in 1398–99, leaving behind a fifteen years' anarchy under the last of the line of Tughlak, until the accession of the Sayyids in 1414.]

VI. THE SAYYIDS.

1414–1450. Curtailed power of the Delhi Kingdom.

VII. THE LODIS (Afghán).

1450–1526. Feeble reigns; independent States multiply.

VIII. HOUSE OF TIMUR (Mughal).

1526–1530. Báhar.

1530–1556. Humáyún.

[Sher Sháh, the Afghán Governor of Bengal, drives Humáyún out of India in 1542, and his Afghán dynasty rules till 1555.]

1556–1605. Akbar the Great.

1605–1627. Jahángír.

1628–1658. Sháh Jahán; deposed.

1658–1707. Aurangzeb or Alamgír I.

1707–1712. Bahádur Sháh, or Sháh Alam I.

1712. Jahándár Sháh.

1713–1718. Farukhsiyyar.

1719–1748. Muhammad Sháh (after temporary Emperors).

[Irruption of Nádir Sháh the Persian, 1738–1739.]

1748–1754. Death of Muhammad Sháh; and accession of Ahmad Sháh, deposed 1754.

1754–1759. Alamgír II.

[Six invasions of India by Ahmad Sháh Duráni, the Afghán, 1748–1761.]

1759–1806. Sháh Alam II, titular Emperor.

1806–1837. Akbar II, titular Emperor.

1837–1857. Muhammad Bahádur Sháh, titular Emperor; the seventeenth and last Mughal Emperor; gave his sanction to the Mutiny of 1857, and died a State prisoner at Rangoon in 1862.

The Rise of Islám.—While Buddhism was giving place to Hinduism in India, a new faith had arisen in Arabia. Muhammad, born in 570 A.D., created a conquering religion, and died in 632. Within a hundred years after his death, his followers had invaded the countries of Asia as far as the Hindu Kush. Here their progress was stayed; and Islám had to consolidate itself, during three more centuries, before it grew strong enough to grasp the rich prize of India. But almost from the first the Arabs had fixed eager eyes upon that wealthy empire, and several premature inroads foretold the coming storm.

Early Arab Invasions of Sind, 647 to 828 A.D.—About fifteen years after the death of the prophet, Usmán sent a naval expedition to Thána and Broach on the Bombay coast (647?). Other raids towards Sind took place in 662 and 664, with no lasting results. In 711, however, the youthful Kásim advanced into Sind, to claim damages for an Arab ship which had been seized at an Indian port. After a brilliant campaign, he settled himself in the Indus valley; but the further advance of the Musalmáns depended on the personal daring of their leader, and was arrested by his death in 714 A.D. The despairing valour of the Hindus struck the invaders with wonder. One Rájput garrison preferred utter extermination to submission. They raised a huge funeral pile, upon which the women and children first threw themselves. The men having bathed, took a solemn farewell of each other, and, throwing open the gates, rushed upon the weapons of the besiegers, and perished to a man. In 750, the Rájputs are said to have expelled the Muhammadan governor from Sind; but it was not till 828 A.D. that the Hindus regained possession of that province.

India on the Eve of the Muhammadan Conquest.—The armies of Islám had carried the crescent throughout Asia west of the Hindu Kush, and through Africa and Southern Europe, to distant Spain and France, before they obtained a foothold in the Punjab. This long delay was due not only to the daring of the Indian tribes, such as the Sind Rájputs just mentioned, but to the military organization of the Hindu kingdoms. To the north of the Vindhyas, three separate groups of Hindu princes governed the great river-valleys. The Rájputs ruled in the north-west, throughout the Indus plains, and along the upper waters of the Jumna. The ancient Middle Land of Sanskrit times (Madhya-desa) in the valley of the Ganges, was divided among powerful Hindu kingdoms, under the over-lordship of Kanauj. The lower Gangetic valley, from Behar downwards, was still in part governed by Pál or Buddhist dynasties, whose names are found from Benares to jungle-buried hamlets deep in the Bengal Delta. The Vindhya ranges stretched their wall of forest and mountain between the northern and southern halves of India. Their eastern and central regions were peopled by fierce hill tribes. At their western extremity, towards the Bombay coast, lay the Hindu kingdom of Málwá, with its brilliant literary traditions of Vikramáditya, and a vast feudal array of fighting men. India to the south of the Vindhyas was occupied by a number of warlike princes, chiefly of non-Aryan descent, but loosely grouped under three great semi-Hindu or semi-Buddhistic over-lords represented by the Chera, Chola, and Pándya dynasties.

Hindu Power of Resistance.—Each of these groups of kingdoms, alike in the north and in the south, had a certain power of coherence to oppose to a foreign invader; while the large number of the groups and units rendered conquest a very tedious process. For even when the over-lord or central authority was vanquished, the separate groups and units had to be defeated in detail; and each supplied a nucleus for subsequent revolt. We have seen how the brilliant attempt in 711, to found a lasting Muhammadan dynasty in Sind, failed. Three centuries later, the utmost efforts of a series of Musalmán invaders from the north-west only succeeded in annexing a small portion of the frontier Punjab Provinces, between 977 and 1176 A.D. The Hindu power in Southern India was not completely broken till the battle of Tálikot in 1565; and within a hundred years, in 1650, the great Hindu revival had commenced, which, under the form of the Maráthá Confederacy, was destined to break up the Mughal Empire in India. That empire, even in the north of India, was only consolidated by Akbar's policy of incorporating Hindu Chiefs and statesmen into his government (1556-1605). Up to Akbar's time, and during the earlier years of his reign, a series of Hindu or Rájput wars had challenged the Muhammadan supremacy. In less than two centuries after his death, the Mughal successor of Akbar was a puppet and a prisoner in the hands of the Hindu Maráthás at Delhi.

Muhammadan Conquests only Partial and Temporary.—The popular notion that India fell an easy prey to the Musalmáns is opposed to the historical facts. Muhammadan rule in India consists of a series of invasions and partial conquests, during eleven centuries, from Usmán's raid about 647 A.D. to Ahmad Sháh's tempest of devastation in 1761. They represent in Indian history the overflow of the tribes and peoples of Central Asia to the south-east; as the Huns, Túrks, and various Tartar tribes disclose in early European annals the westward movements from the same great breeding-ground of nations. At no time was Islám triumphant throughout all India. Hindu dynasties always ruled over a large area. At the height of the Muhammadan power, the Hindu princes paid tribute, and sent agents to the imperial court. But even this modified supremacy of the Mughal Empire of Delhi did not last for one and a half centuries (1560–1707). Before the end of that brief period, the Hindus had again begun the work of reconquest. The Hindu chivalry of Rájputána was closing in upon Delhi from the south-east; the religious confederation of the Sikhs was growing into a military power on the north-west. The Maráthás, who combined the fighting powers of the Hindu low-castes with the statesmanship of the Bráhmans, had begun to subject the Muhammadan kingdoms in Southern India to tribute. So far as can now be estimated, the advance of the English power in the last century alone saved the Mughal Empire from reverting to the Hindus.

First Túrkí Invasions—Subuktigín, 977 A. D.—The first collision between Hinduism and Islám on the Punjab frontier was the act of the Hindus. In 977, Jaipál, the Hindu Chief of Lahore, annoyed by Afghán raids, led his troops through the mountains against the Muhammadan kingdom of Ghazní, in Afghánistán. Subuktigín, the Ghaznivide prince, after severe fighting, took advantage of a hurricane to cut off the retreat of the Hindus through the pass. He allowed them, however, to return to India, on the surrender of fifty elephants, and the promise of one million *dirhams* (about £25,000). Tradition relates how Jaipál, having regained his capital, was counselled by the Bráhmans standing at his right hand not to disgrace himself by paying ransom to a barbarian; while his nobles and warrior Chiefs, standing at his left, implored him to keep faith. In the end, Subuktigín swept through the hills to enforce his ransom, defeated Jaipál, and stationed an Afghán officer with 10,000 horse to garrison Peshámar (977). Subuktigín was soon afterwards called away to fight in Central Asia, and his Indian raid left behind it only this Peshámar outpost. But henceforth the Afgháns held both ends of the Kháibar pass.

Mahmúd of Ghazní, 1001-1030.—In 997, Subuktigín died, and was succeeded by his son, Mahmúd of Ghazní, aged sixteen. This valiant monarch reigned for thirty-three years, and extended his father's little Afghán kingdom into a great sovereignty stretching from Persia on the west, to far within the Punjab on the east. Having spent four years in consolidating his power in Afghánistán to the west of the Kháibar Pass, Mahmúd led in 1001 A. D. the first of his seventeen invasions of India. Of these, thirteen were directed to the subjugation of the Western Punjab, one was an unsuccessful incursion into Kashmír, and the remaining three were short but furious raids against more distant cities,—Kanauj, Gwalior, and Somnáth. Jaipál, the Hindu frontier Chief of Lahore, was again defeated. According to Hindu custom, a twice-conquered prince was deemed unworthy to reign; and Jaipál, mounting a funeral pile, solemnly made over his kingdom to his son, and burned himself in his regal robes. Another local Chief, rather than yield himself to the victor, fell upon his own sword. In the sixth expedition (1008 A. D.), the Hindu ladies melted their ornaments, while the poorer women spun cotton, to support their husbands in the war. In one great battle the fate of the invaders hung in the balance. Mahmúd, alarmed by a coalition of the Indian kings as far as Oudh and Málwá, entrenched himself near Pesháwar. A sortie which he made was driven back, and the wild Ghakkar tribe burst into the camp and slaughtered nearly 4000 Musalmáns.

The Sack of Somnáth, 1024.—But each expedition ended by further strengthening the Muhammadan foothold in India. Mahmúd carried away enormous booty from the Hindu temples, such as Thaneswar and Nagarkot; and his sixteenth and most famous expedition was directed against the temple of Somnáth in Gujarát (1024 A. D.). After bloody repulses, he took the town. The Hindu garrison, at the end of their gallant defence, left 5000 of their warriors dead, and put out in boats to sea. The famous idol of Somnáth was merely one of the twelve renowned *lingas* or phallic emblems of Siva-worship erected in various parts of India. But Mahmúd, having taken the name of the 'Idol-Smasher,' the modern Persian historians gradually converted the plunder of Somnáth into a legend of his pious zeal. Forgetting the contemporary accounts of the idol as a rude block of stone, Firishta tells how Mahmúd, on entering the temple, was offered an enormous ransom by the priests if he would spare the image. But Mahmúd cried out that he would rather be remembered as the breaker than the seller of idols, and clove the god open with his mace. Forthwith a vast treasure of jewels poured forth from its vitals, which explained the liberal offers of the priests, and rewarded the disinterested piety of the monarch. The growth of this fable can be clearly traced, but it is still repeated. Mahmúd carried off the temple gates, with fragments of the phallic emblem of Siva-worship, to Ghazní, and on the way nearly perished with his army in the Indus desert. But the so-called 'sandal-wood gates of Somnáth,' brought back as a trophy from Ghazní by Lord Ellenborough in 1842, and paraded through Northern India, were as clumsy a forgery as the story of the jewel-bellied idol himself. Mahmúd died at Ghazní in 1030 A.D.

Results of Mahmúd's Invasions.—As the result of seventeen invasions of India, and of twenty-five years' fighting, Mahmúd had reduced the western districts of the Punjab to the control of his Afghán kingdom of Ghazní, and left the remembrance of his raids throughout northern India as far as Kanauj on the east and Gujarát in the south. He never set up as a resident sovereign in India. His expeditions beyond the Punjab were the adventures of a religious knight-errant, with the plunder of a temple-city, or the demolition of an idol, as their object, rather than serious efforts at conquest. But as his father Subuktigín had left Pesháwar as an outpost garrison of Ghazní, so Mahmúd left the Punjab as an outlying Province of that Afghán kingdom.

Stories about Mahmúd.—The Muhammadan chroniclers tell many stories, not only of his valour and piety, but also of his thrift. One day a poor woman complained that her son had been killed by robbers in a distant desert of Irak. Mahmúd said he was very sorry, but that it was difficult to prevent such accidents so far from the capital. The old woman rebuked him with the words, 'Keep no more territory than you can rightly govern'; and the Sultán forthwith rewarded her, and sent troops to guard all caravans passing that way. Mahmúd was an enlightened patron of poets, and his liberality drew the great Ferdousi to his court. The Sultán listened with delight to his *Sháh-námah*, or Book of Kings, and promised him a *dirham*, meaning a golden one, for each verse on its completion. After thirty years of labour, the poet claimed his reward. But the Sultán, finding that the poem had run to 60,000 verses, offered him 60,000 silver *dirhams*, instead of *dirhams* of gold. Ferdousi retired in disgust from the court, and wrote a bitter satire, which to this day tells the story of the alleged base birth of the monarch. Mahmúd forgave the satire, but remembered the great epic, and, repenting of his meanness, sent 100,000 golden *dirhams* to the poet. The bounty came too late; for, according to the legend, as the royal messengers bearing the bags of gold entered one gate of Ferdousi's city, the poet's corpse was being borne out by another.

House of Ghor, 1152-1186.—During a century and a half the Punjab remained under Mahmúd's successors as an Afghán Musalmán Province in India. There had long been a feud between the Afghán towns of Ghor and Ghazní. Mahmúd subdued Ghor in 1010; but about 1051 the Ghor chief captured Ghazní and dragged its principal men to his own capital, where he cut their throats, and used their blood in making mortar for the fortifications. After various reprisals, Ghor finally triumphed over Ghazní in 1152; and Khusrú, the last of Mahmúd's line, fled to Lahore, the capital of his outlying Indian territory. In 1186 this also was wrested from him; and the Ghor prince Shaháb-ud-dín, better known as Muhammad of Ghor, began the conquest of India on his own account. But each of the Hindu principalities fought hard, and some of them still survive, seven centuries after the torrent of Afghán invasion swept over their heads.

Hindu Resistance to Muhammad of Ghor, 1191.—On his first expedition towards Delhi in 1191, Muhammad of Ghor was utterly defeated by the Hindus at Thaneswar in the Punjab, badly wounded, and barely escaped with his life. His scattered hosts were chased for forty miles. But he gathered together the wreck of his army at Lahore, and, aided by new hordes from Afghánistán, again marched into Hindustán in 1193. Family quarrels among the Rájputs prevented a united effort against him. The cities of Delhi and Kanauj stand forth as the centres of rival Hindu monarchies, each of which claimed the first place in Northern India. A Chauhán Rájput prince, ruling over Delhi and Ajmere, bore the proud name of Prithwí Rájá or Suzerain. The Ráhtor Rájput king of Kanauj, whose capital can still be traced across eight square miles of broken bricks and rubbish in Farukhábád District, celebrated a feast, in the spirit of the ancient Hindu Horse-Sacrifice (see pp. 68, 70), to proclaim himself the overlord. At such a feast all menial offices had to be filled by royal vassals; and the Delhi monarch was summoned as a gatekeeper, along with the other princes of Hindustán. During the ceremony, the daughter of the King of Kanauj was to make her *swayam-vara*, or 'own-choice' of a husband, as in the Sanskrit epics (see pp. 67, 69). The Delhi Rájá loved the maiden, but he could not brook to stand at another man's gate. As he did not arrive, the Kanauj king set up a mocking image of him at the door. When the princess entered the hall to make her choice, she looked calmly round the circle of kings, then, stepping proudly past them to the door, threw her bridal garland over the neck of the ill-shapen image. Forthwith, says the story, the Delhi monarch rushed in, sprang with the princess on his horse, and galloped off towards his northern capital. The outraged father led out his Kanauj army against the runaways, and, having, according to the legend, called in the Afgháns to attack Delhi on the other side from the west, brought about the ruin of both the Hindu kingdoms of Delhi and Kanauj.

Distribution of Rájputs, 1193.—The tale serves to record the disputes among the Rájput princes, which prevented a united resistance to Muhammad of Ghor. Muhammad found Delhi occupied by the Tomára clan, Ajmere by the Chauháns, and Kanauj by the Ráhtors. These three Rájput States formed the natural breakwaters against invaders from the north-west. But their feuds are said to have left the King of Delhi and Ajmere, then united under one Chauhán overlord, only 64 survivors out of his 108 warrior Chiefs. In 1193, the Afgháns again swept down on the Punjab. Prithwí Rájá of Delhi and Ajmere was defeated and slain. His heroic queen burned herself on his funeral pile. Muhammad of Ghor, having occupied Delhi, pressed on to Ajmere; and in 1194 overthrew the rival Hindu monarch of Kanauj, whose body was identified on the field of battle by his false teeth. The brave Ráhtor Rájputs of Kanauj, with others of the Rájput clans in Northern India, quitted their homes in large bodies rather than submit to the stranger. They migrated to the regions bordering on the desert of the Indus, and there founded the military kingdoms which bear their name, Rájputána, to this day. History takes her narrative of these events from the matter-of-fact statements of the Persian annalists. But the Hindu court-bard of Prithwí Rájá left behind a patriotic version of the fall of his race. His ballad-chronicle, known as the *Prithwíráj Rásau* of Chánd, is one of the earliest poems in Hindí. It depicts the Musalmán invaders as beaten in all the battles except the last fatal one. Their leader is taken prisoner by the Hindus, and released for a heavy ransom. But the quarrels of the Chiefs ruined the Hindu cause.

Muhammadan Conquest of Bengal, 1203.—Setting aside these patriotic songs, Benares and Gwalior mark the south-western limits of Muhammad of Ghor's own advance. But his general, Bakhtiyár Khiljí, conquered Behar in 1199, and Lower Bengal down to the delta in 1203. On the approach of the Musalmáns, the Bráhmans advised Lakshman Sen, the Hindu King of Bengal, to remove his capital from Nadiyá to some more distant city. But the prince, a religious old man of eighty, could not make up his mind, until the Afghán general had seized his capital, and burst into the palace one day while His Majesty was at dinner. The monarch slipped out by a back door without having time to put on his shoes, and fled to Purí in Orissa, where he spent his remaining days in the service of the god Jagannáth. Meanwhile the Sultán, Muhammad of Ghor, divided his time between campaigns in Afghánistán and Indian invasions. Ghor was his capital, and he had little time to consolidate his Indian conquests. Even in the Punjab, the tribes were defeated rather than subdued. In 1203, the Ghakkars issued from their mountains, took Lahore, and devastated the whole Province. In 1206, a party of the same clan swam the Indus, on the bank of which the Afghán camp was pitched, and stabbed the Sultán while asleep in his tent.

Muhammad of Ghor's Work in India.—Muhammad of Ghor was no religious knight-errant of Islám like Mahmúd of

Ghazní, but a practical conqueror. The objects of his distant expeditions were not temples but Provinces. Subuktigín had left Peshávar as an outpost of Ghazní (977 A. D.); and Mahmúd had reduced the Western Punjab to an outlying Province of the same kingdom (1030 A. D.). That was the net result of the Túrkí invasions of India from Ghazní (977–1186). But Muhammad of Ghor left the whole north of India, from the delta of the Indus to the delta of the Ganges, under skilful Muhammadan generals, who on his death set up as kings on their own account (1206 A. D.).

Kutab-ud-dín, 1206–1210.—His Indian Viceroy, Kutab-ud-dín, proclaimed himself sovereign of India at Delhi, and founded a line which lasted from 1206 to 1290. Kutab claimed the control over all the Muhammadan leaders and soldiers of fortune in India from Sind to Lower Bengal. His name is preserved at his capital by the Kutab Mosque, with its graceful colonnade of richly-sculptured Hindu pillars, and by the Kutab *Minár*, which raises its tapering shaft, encrusted with chapters from the Kurán, high above the ruins of old Hindu Delhi. Kutab-ud-dín had started life as a Túrkí slave, and several of his successors rose by valour or intrigue from the same low condition to the throne. His dynasty is accordingly known as that of the Slave Kings. Under them India became for the first time the seat of resident Muhammadan sovereigns. Kutab-ud-dín died in 1210.

The Slave Dynasty, 1206–1290.—The Slave Dynasty found itself face to face with the three dangers which have beset the Muhammadan rule in India from the outset, and beneath which that rule eventually succumbed. First, rebellions by its own servants—Musalmán generals, or viceroys of Provinces; second, revolts of the Hindus; third, fresh invasions, chiefly by Mughals, from Central Asia.

Altamsh, 1211–1236.—Altamsh, the third and greatest Sultán of the Slave Dynasty, had to reduce the Muhammadan governors of Lower Bengal and Sind, both of whom set up as independent rulers; and he narrowly escaped destruction by a Mughal invasion from Central Asia. The Mughals under Changíz Khán pierced through the Indian passes in pursuit of an Afghán prince;

but their progress was stayed by the Indus, and Delhi remained untouched. Before the death of Altamsh (1236 A. D.), the Hindus had ceased for a time to struggle openly; and the Muhammadan Viceroys of the Slave Dynasty of Delhi ruled all India north of the Vindhya range, including the Punjab, the North-Western Provinces, Oudh, Behar, Lower Bengal, Ajmere, Gwalior, Málwá, and Sind. The Khálif of Baghdad acknowledged India as a separate Muhammadan kingdom during the reign of Altamsh, and coins were struck in recognition of the new Empire of Delhi (1229 A. D.). Altamsh died in 1236.

The Empress Raziyá, 1236–1239.—His daughter Raziyá was the only lady who ever occupied the Muhammadan throne of Delhi. Learned in the Kurán, industrious in public business, firm and energetic in every crisis, she bears in history the masculine name of the *Sultán* Raziyá. But the favour which she showed to her master of the horse, an Abyssinian slave, offended her Afghán generals; and, after a troubled reign of three and a half years, she was deposed and put to death.

Mughal Irruptions and Rájput Revolts.—Mughal irruptions from Central Asia and Hindu revolts within India soon began to undermine the Slave Dynasty. The Mughals are said to have burst through Tibet into North-Eastern Bengal in 1245; and during the next forty-three years they repeatedly marched down the Afghán passes into the Punjab (1245–1288). The wild Indian tribes, such as the Ghakkars and the hillmen of Mewát, ravaged the Muhammadan provinces in the Punjab almost up to the gates of Delhi. Rájput revolts foreshadowed that inextinguishable vitality of the Hindu military races, which was to harass, from first to last, the Muhammadan dynasties, and to outlive them. Under the Slave Kings, even the north of India was only half subdued to the Muhammadan sway. The Hindus rose again and again in Málwá, Rájputána, Bundelkhand, and along the Ganges and the Jumna, as far as Delhi itself.

Balban, 1265–1287.—The last but one of the Slave line, Balban, had not only to fight the Mughals, the wild Indian tribes, and the Rájput clans—he was also compelled to battle with his own viceroys. Having in his youth entered into a compact for mutual support and advancement with forty of his Túrkí fellow-slaves in the palace, he had, when he came to the throne, to break the powerful confederacy thus formed. Some of his provincial governors he publicly scourged; others were beaten to death in his presence; and a general who failed to reduce the rebel Muhammadan Viceroy of Bengal was hanged. Balban himself moved down to the Gangetic delta, and crushed the Bengal revolt with merciless skill. His severity against Hindu rebels knew no bounds. He nearly exterminated the Rájputs of Mewát, south of Delhi, putting 100,000 of them to the sword. He then cut down the forests which formed their retreats, and opened up the country to tillage. The miseries caused by the Mughal hordes at that time in Central Asia drove a crowd of princes and poets from Afghánistán and other Muhammadan countries to seek shelter at the Indian court. Balban boasted that no fewer than fifteen once independent sovereigns had fed on his bounty, and he called the streets of Delhi by the names of their late kingdoms, such as Baghdad, Kharizm, and Ghor. He died in 1287 A.D. His successor was poisoned, and the Slave Dynasty ended in 1290.

House of Khiljí, 1290–1320.—In that year, Jalál-ud-dín, a ruler of Khiljí, succeeded to the Delhi throne, and founded a line which lasted for thirty years. The Khiljí dynasty extended the Muhammadan power into Southern India. Alá-ud-dín, the nephew of Jalál-ud-dín, when governor of Karra near Allahábád, pierced through the Vindhya ranges with his cavalry, and plundered the Buddhist temple-city of Bhílsa, 300 miles off. After trying his powers against the rebellious Hindu princes of Bundelkhand and Málwá, Alá-ud-dín formed the idea of a grand raid into the Deccan. With a band of only 8000 horse, he rode into the heart of Southern India. On the way he gave out that he was flying from his uncle Jalál-ud-dín's court, to seek service with the Hindu King of Rájámahendri. The generous Rájput princes abstained from attacking a refugee in his flight; and Alá-ud-dín surprised the great city of Deogiri, the modern Daulatábád, at that time the capital of the Hindu kingdom of Maháráshtra. Having suddenly galloped into its streets, he announced himself as only the advance guard of the whole imperial army, levied an immense booty, and carried it back 700 miles to the seat of his governorship on the banks of the Ganges. He then lured the Sultán Jalál-ud-dín, his uncle, to Karra, in order to divide the spoil, and murdered the old man in the act of clasping his hand (1295 A.D.).

Reign of Alá-ud-dín, 1295-1315. Alá-ud-dín scattered his spoils in gifts or charity like a devout Musalmán, and proclaimed himself Sultán. The twenty years of his reign established the Muhammadan sway in Southern India. He reconquered Gujarát from the Hindus in 1297; captured Rintimbur, after a difficult siege, from the Jaipur Rájputs in 1300; took the fort of Chitor, and partially subjected the Sesodia Rájputs (1303); and, having thus reduced the Hindus on the north of the Vindhyas, prepared for the conquest of Southern India or the Deccan. But before starting on this great expedition he had to meet five Mughal inroads from Central Asia. In 1295, he defeated a Mughal invasion under the walls of his capital, Delhi; in 1304-5, he encountered four others, sending all his prisoners to Delhi, where the Chiefs were trampled by elephants, and the common soldiery slaughtered in cold blood. He crushed with equal cruelty several rebellions which took place among his own family during the same period—first putting out the eyes of his insurgent nephews, and then beheading them (1299-1300).

His Conquest of Southern India.—His affairs in Northern India being thus settled, he undertook the conquest of the south. In 1303, he had sent his eunuch slave, Málik Káfur, with an army, through Bengal, to attack Warangal, the capital of the south-eastern Hindu kingdom of Telingána. In 1306, Káfur marched victoriously through Málwá and Khándesh into the Maráthá country, where he captured Deogiri, and persuaded the Hindu king Rám Deo to return with him to do homage at Delhi. Meanwhile the Sultán Alá-ud-dín was conquering the Rájputs in Márwár. His slave general, Káfur, made expeditions through Maháráshtra and the Karnátik, as far south as Adam's Bridge, at the extremity of India, where he built a mosque.

Extent of the Muhammadan Power in India, 1306.—The Muhammadan Sultán of India was no longer merely an

Afghán King of Delhi. Three great waves of invasion from Central Asia had created a large Muhammadan population in Northern India. First came the Túrkís, represented by the house of Ghazní; then the Afgháns (commonly so called), represented by the house of Ghor; next the Mughals, having failed to conquer the Punjáb, took service in great numbers with the Sultáns of Delhi. Under the Slave Kings the Mughal mercenaries had become so powerful as to require to be massacred (1286). About 1292, three thousand Mughals, having been converted from their old Tartar rites to Islám, received a suburb of Delhi, still called Mughalpur, for their residence. Other Mughals followed. After various plots by them, Alá-ud-dín slaughtered 15,000 of the settlers, and sold their families as slaves (1311 A.D.). The unlimited supply of soldiers which he could thus draw upon from the Túrkí, Afghán, and Mughal settlers in Northern India and from countries beyond, enabled him to send armies farther south than any of his predecessors. But in his later years the Hindus revolted in Gujarát; the Rájputs reconquered Chitor; and many of the Muhammadan garrisons were driven out of the Deccan. On the capture of Chitor in 1303, the Rájput garrison had preferred death to submission. The peasantry still chant an early Hindí ballad, telling how the queen and thirteen thousand women threw themselves on a funeral pile, while the men rushed upon the swords of the besiegers. A remnant cut their way to the Arávalli hills; and the Rájput independence, although in abeyance during Alá-ud-dín's reign, was never crushed, Having imprisoned his sons, and given himself up to paroxysms of rage and intemperance, Alá-ud-dín died in 1315, helped to the grave, it is said, by poison given by his favourite general, Káfur.

A Renegade Hindu Emperor, 1316–1320.—During the four remaining years of the house of Khiljí, the actual power passed to Khusrú Khán, a low-caste renegade Hindu, who imitated the military successes and vices of his patron, the General Káfur, and in the end murdered him. Khusrú became all in all to the new Emperor, the debauchee Mubárik; then slew him, and seized the throne. While outwardly professing Islám, Khusrú desecrated the Kurán by using it as a seat, and degraded the pulpits of the mosques into pedestals for Hindu idols. In 1320 he was slain by his revolted soldiery, and the Khiljí dynasty disappeared.

House of Tughlak, 1320–1414.—The leader of the rebellion was Ghiyás-ud-dín Tughlak, who had started life as a Túrkí slave, and risen to the frontier governorship of the Punjab. He founded the Tughlak dynasty, which lingered on for ninety-six years, although submerged for a time by the invasion of Timúr (Tamerlane) in 1398. Ghiyás-ud-dín (1320–25 A.D.) removed the capital from Delhi to a spot about four miles farther east, and called it Tughlakábád.

Muhammad Tughlak, 1325-1351.—His son and successor, Muhammad Tughlak, was an accomplished scholar, a skilful general, and a man of severe abstinence. But his ferocity of temper, perhaps inherited from the tribes of the steppes of Central Asia, rendered him merciless as a judge, and careless of human suffering. The least opposition drove him into outbursts of insane fury. He wasted the treasures accumulated by Alá-ud-dín in buying off the Mughal hordes, who again and again swept through Afghánistán into the Punjab. On the other hand, in fits of ambition, he raised an army for the invasion of Persia, and is said to have sent out an expedition of 100,000 men against China. The force against Persia broke up for want of pay, and plundered his own dominions; the army against China perished almost to a man in the Himálayan passes. He planned great conquests into Southern India, and dragged the whole inhabitants of Delhi to Deogiri, to which he gave the name of Daulatábád, 800 miles off in the far south. Twice he allowed the miserable suppliants to return to Delhi; twice he compelled them on pain of death to quit it. One of these forced migrations took place amid the horrors of a famine; the citizens perished by thousands, and in the end the king had to give up the attempt. Having drained his treasury, he issued a forced currency of copper coins, by which he tried to make the king's brass equal to other men's silver. During the same century, the Mughal conqueror of China, Kublai Khán, had extended the use of paper notes, early devised by the Chinese; and Kai Khátú had introduced a bad imitation of them into Persia.

Tughlak's forced currency quickly brought its own ruin. Foreign merchants refused the worthless brass tokens, trade came to a stand, and the king had to take payment of his taxes in his own depreciated coinage.

Revolt of the Provinces, 1338–1351.—Meanwhile the Provinces began to throw off the Delhi yoke. Muhammad Tughlak had succeeded in 1324 to the greatest empire which had, up to that time, acknowledged a Muhammadan Sultán in India. But his bigoted zeal for Islám forbade him to confide in Hindu princes or Hindu officers; he dared not trust his own kinsmen; and he thus found himself compelled to fill every high post with foreign Muhammadan adventurers, who had no interest in the stability of his rule. The annals of the period present a long series of outbreaks, one part of the empire throwing off its allegiance as soon as another had been brought back to subjection. His own nephew rebelled in Málwá, and, being caught, was flayed alive (1338). The Punjab governor revolted (1339), was crushed, and put to death. The Musalmán viceroys of Lower Bengal and of the Coromandel coast set up for themselves (about 1340), and could not be subdued. The Hindu kingdoms of Karnáta and Telingána recovered their independence (1344), and expelled the Musalmán garrisons. The Muhammadan governors in the Deccan also revolted; while the troops in Gujarát rose in mutiny. Muhammad Tughlak rushed with an army to the south to take vengeance on the traitors, but hardly had he put down their rising than he was called away by insurrections in Gujarát, Málwá, and Sind. He died in 1351, while chasing rebels in the lower valley of the Indus.

Muhammad Tughlak's Revenue Exactions.—Muhammad Tughlak was the first Musalmán ruler of India who can be said to have had a regular revenue-system. He increased the land tax between the Ganges and the Jumna—in some Districts tenfold, in others twentyfold. The husbandmen fled before his tax-gatherers, leaving their villages to lapse into jungle, and formed themselves into robber clans. He cruelly punished all who trespassed on his game preserves; and he invented a kind of man-hunt without precedent in the annals of human wickedness. He surrounded a large tract with his army, 'and then gave orders that the circle should close towards the centre, and that all within it (mostly inoffensive peasants) should be slaughtered like wild beasts.' This sort of hunt was more than once repeated; and on another occasion there was a general massacre of the inhabitants of the great city of Kanauj. Such horrors led in due time to famine; and the miseries of the country exceeded all powers of description.

Fíruz Sháh Tughlak, 1351-1388.—His successor, Fíruz Tughlak, ruled mercifully, but had to recognize the independence of the Muhammadan kingdoms of Bengal and in the Deccan, and suffered much from bodily infirmities and court intrigues. He undertook many public works, such as dams across rivers for irrigation, tanks, caravan-saráis, mosques, colleges, hospitals, and bridges. But his greatest achievement was the old Jumna Canal. This Canal drew its waters from the Jumna near a point where it leaves the mountains, and connected that river with the Ghaggar and the Sutlej by irrigation channels. Part of it has been reconstructed by the British Government, and spreads a margin of fertility on either side at this day. But the dynasty of Tughlak soon sank amid Muhammadan mutinies and Hindu revolts; and under Mahmúd, its last real king, India fell an easy prey to the great Mughal invasion of 1398.

Timúr (Tamerlane's) Invasion, 1398.—In that year, Timúr (Tamerlane) swept through the Afghán passes at the head of the united hordes of Tartary. He defeated the Tughlak King Mahmúd under the walls of Delhi, and entered the capital. During five days a massacre raged; 'some streets were rendered impassable by heaps of dead'; while Timúr calmly looked on and held a feast in honour of his victory. On the last day of 1398, he resumed his march; first offering a 'sincere and humble tribute of grateful praise' to God, in Fíruz Sháh's marble mosque on the banks of the Jumna. Timúr then crossed the Ganges, and proceeded to Hardwár, after a great massacre at Meerut. After skirting the foot of the Himálayas, he retired westwards into Central Asia (1399). Timúr left no traces of his power in India, save desolate cities. On his departure, Mahmúd Tughlak crept back from his retreat in Gujarát, and nominally ruled till 1412.

The Sayyids and the Lodis.—The Tughlak line finally ended in 1414. The Sayyid dynasty ruled from 1414 till 1450; and the Afghán house of Lodi from 1450 to 1526. But some of these Sultáns reigned over only a few miles round Delhi; and during the whole period the Hindu princes and the local Muhammadan kings were practically independent throughout the greater part of India. The house of Lodi was crushed beneath the Mughal invasion of Bábar in 1526.

Hindu Kingdoms of the South.—Bábar founded the Mughal Empire of India, whose last representative died a British State prisoner at Rangoon in 1862. Before entering on the story of that empire, I turn to the kingdoms, Hindu and Muhammadan, on the south of the Vindhya range. The three ancient kingdoms, Chera, Chola, and Pándya, occupied the Dravidian country of Southern India, peopled by Támil-speaking races. Pándya, the largest of them, had its capital at Madura, and traces its foundation to the fourth century B.C. The Chola kingdom had its headquarters at Combaconum and Tanjore. Talkad, in Mysore, now buried by the sands of the Káveri, was the capital of the Chera kingdom from 288 to 900 A.D. The 116th king of the Madura or Pándya dynasty was overthrown by the Muhammadan general Málik Káfur in 1304. But the Musalmáns failed to establish their power in the extreme south, and a series of Hindu dynasties ruled from Madura over the old Pándya kingdom until the eighteenth century. No European kingdom can boast a continuous succession such as that of Pándya or Madura, traced back by the piety of genealogists for more than two thousand years. The Chera or Mysore and Travancore kingdom enumerates fifty kings, and the Chola or Tanjore sixty-six, besides minor offshoot dynasties.

Kingdom of Vijayanagar. — But authentic history in Southern India begins with the Hindu kingdom of Vijayanagar or Narsingha, from 1118 to 1565 A.D. The capital can still be traced within the Madras District of Bellary, on the right bank of the Tungabhadra river—vast ruins of temples, fortifications, tanks, and bridges, haunted by hyænas and snakes. For at least three centuries, Vijayanagar ruled over the southern part of the Indian peninsula. Its Hindu Rájás waged war and made peace on equal terms with the Muhammadan Sultáns of the Deccan.

Muhammadan States in the Deccan.—The Muhammadan kings of Southern India sprang out of the conquest of Alá-ud-dín (1303–1306). After a period of confused fighting, the Bahmaní kingdom of the Deccan emerged as the representative of Muhammadan rule in Southern India. Zafar Khán, an Afghán general during the reign of Muhammad Tughlak (1325–1351), defeated the Delhi troops, and set up as Musalmán sovereign of the Deccan. Having in early youth been the slave of a Bráhman, who had treated him kindly, and foretold his future greatness, he took the title of Bahmaní, and transmitted it to his successors.

The Bahmaní Dynasty.—The rise of the Bahmaní dynasty is usually assigned to the year 1347, and it lasted for 178 years, until 1525. Its capitals were successively at Gulbargah, Warangal, and Bídar, all in the modern Haidarábád territories; and it loosely corresponded with the Nizám's dominions of the present day. At the height of their power, the Muhammadan Bahmaní kings claimed sway over half the Deccan, from the Tungabhadra river in the south to Orissa in the north, and from Masulipatam on the east to Goa on the west. Their direct government was, however, much more confined. They derived support, in their early struggle against the Delhi throne, from the Hindu southern kingdoms of Vijayanagar and Warangal. But during the greater part of its career, the Bahmaní dynasty represented the cause of Islám against Hinduism on the south of the Vindhyas. Its alliances and its wars alike led to a mingling of the Musalmán and Hindu populations. For example, the King of Málwá invaded the Bahmaní dominions with a mixed force of 12,000 Muhammadan Afgháns and Hindu Rájputs. The Hindu Rájá of Vijayanagar recruited his armies from Afghán Musalmáns, whom he paid by assignments of land, and for whom he built a mosque. The Bahmaní Muhammadan troops, on the other hand, were frequently led by converted Hindus. The Bahmaní armies were themselves made up of two hostile sects of Musalmáns. One sect consisted of Shiás, chiefly Persians, Túrks, or Tartars from Central Asia; the other, of native-born Musalmáns of Southern India, together with Abyssinian mercenaries, professing the Sunní faith. The rivalry between these Musalmán sects frequently imperilled the Bahmaní throne. The dynasty reached its highest power under Alá-ud-dín II about 1437, and was broken up by its discordant elements between 1489 and 1525.

Five Muhammadan States of the Deccan, 1489–1688.—Out of its fragments, the five independent Muhammadan kingdoms in the Deccan were formed. These were—(1) The Adil Sháhí dynasty, with its capital at Bijápur, founded in 1489 by a son of Amurath II, Sultán of the Ottoman Túrks; annexed by the Mughal Emperor Aurangzeb in 1686–1688. (2) The Kutab Sháhí dynasty, with its capital at Golconda, founded in 1512 by a Túrkomán adventurer; also annexed by Aurangzeb in 1687–1688. (3) The Nizám Sháhí dynasty, with its capital at Ahmadnagar, founded in 1490 by a Bráhman renegade from the Vijayanagar Court; subverted by the Mughal Emperor Sháh Jahán in 1636. (4) The Imad Sháhí dynasty of Berar, with its capital at Ellichpur, founded in 1484 also by a Hindu from Vijayanagar; annexed to the Ahmadnagar kingdom (No. 3) in 1572. (5) The Baríd Sháhí dynasty, with its capital at Bídar, founded 1492–1498 by a Túrkí or Georgian slave. The Bídar territories were small and ill-defined; and were independent till after 1609. Bídar fort was taken by Aurangzeb in 1657.

Fall of Hindu Kingdom of Vijayanagar.—It is beyond my scope to trace the history of these local Muhammadan dynasties of Southern India. They preserved their independence until the firm establishment of the Mughal Empire in the north, under Akbar and his successors. For a time they had to struggle against the great Hindu kingdom of Vijayanagar. In 1565 they combined against that power, and, aided by a rebellion within Vijayanagar itself, they overthrew it at Tálikot in 1565. The battle of Tálikot marks the final downfall of Vijayanagar as a great Hindu kingdom. But its local Hindu Chiefs or Náyaks kept hold of their respective fiefs, and the Muhammadan kings of the south were only able to annex a part of its dominions. From the Náyaks are descended the well-known

Pálegárs (Polygars) of the Madras Presidency, and the Mahárájá of Mysore. One of the blood-royal of Vijayanagar fled to Chandragiri, and founded a line which exercised a prerogative of its former sovereignty, by granting the site of Madras to the English in 1639. Another scion, claiming the same high descent, lingers to the present day near the ruins of Vijayanagar, and is known as the Rájá of Anagundí, a feudatory of the Nizám of Haidarábád. The independence of the local Hindu Rájás in Southern India throughout the Muhammadan period is illustrated by the Manjarábád family, a line of petty Chiefs, which maintained its authority from 1397 to 1799.

Independence of the Provinces.—Lower Bengal threw off the authority of Delhi in 1340. Its Muhammadan governor, Fakír-ud-dín, set up as sovereign, with his capital at Gaur, and stamped coin in his own name. A succession of twenty kings ruled Bengal until 1538, when it was temporarily annexed to the Mughal Empire of Delhi by Humáyún. Bengal was finally incorporated into that empire by Akbar in 1576. The great Province of Gujarát in Western India had in like manner grown into an independent Muhammadan kingdom, which lasted for two centuries, from 1371 till conquered by Akbar in 1573. Málwá, which had also risen to be an independent State under its Muhammadan governors, was annexed by the King of Gujarát in 1531. Even Jaunpur, including the territory of Benares, in the centre of the Gangetic valley, maintained its independence as a Musalmán State for nearly a hundred years, from 1393 to 1478, during the disturbed rule of the Sayyids and the first Lodi at Delhi.

Weakness of the early Delhi Empire.—The position of the early Muhammadan rulers of Delhi was a very difficult one. Successive Musalmán hordes of Túrks, Afgháns, and Tartars swept down the passes, and wrested India from the preceding invaders of their own Muhammadan faith. The Delhi Empire was therefore beset by three perpetual dangers. First, new Muhammadan invasions from Central Asia; second, rebellious Muhammadan generals or Governors within India; third, the Hindu races whom the early Delhi kings neither conciliated nor crushed. It was reserved for Akbar the Great to remedy the inherent weakness of the position; and by incorporating the Hindus into his government, to put a curb alike on Muhammadan invaders from without, and on too powerful Muhammadan subjects within.

MATERIALS FOR REFERENCE.

The Honourable Mountstuart Elphinstone's *History of India* (Cowell's Edition) is still the standard popular work for the whole Muhammadan period; Sir Henry Elliot's eight volumes, entitled *The History of India as told by its own Historians*, i.e the Arab and Persian travellers and chroniclers (Dowson's edition), are the main original sources; also Edward Thomas' *Chronicles of the Pathán Kings of Delhi* (especially from 1193 to 1554); Blochmann's *Aín-i-Akbarí* (Calcutta, 1873) and Gladwin's older translation (1800); Stewart's *History of Bengal from the first Muhammadan Invasion to* 1757 (Calcutta, 1847); and Briggs' *Firishta* (subject to correction from Sir Henry Elliot's eight volumes). The District Gazetteers or Statistical Surveys of Northern India contain a mine of still unexhausted historical materials, which have, so far as permitted by the space allowed, been condensed in Hunter's *Imperial Gazetteer of India* (Second Edition) and his *Indian Empire*.

CHAPTER X.

The Mughal Dynasty, 1526–1761.

Bábar, 1482–1530.—When, therefore, Bábar the Mughal invaded India in 1526, he found it divided among a number of local Muhammadan kings and Hindu princes. An Afghán Sultán of the house of Lodi, with his capital at Agra, ruled over what little was left of the historical kingdom of Delhi. Bábar, literally 'the Lion,' born in 1482, was the sixth in descent from Timúr the Tartar. At the early age of twelve, he succeeded his father in the petty kingdom of Ferghána on the Jaxartes (1494); and, after romantic adventures, conquered Samarkand, the capital of Tamerlane's line, in 1497. Overpowered by a rebellion, and driven out of the valley of the Oxus, Bábar seized the kingdom of Kábul in 1504. During twenty-two years he grew in strength on the Afghán side of the Indian passes, till in 1526 he burst through them into the Punjab, and defeated the Delhi sovereign, Ibráhím Lodi at Pánípat. This was the first of three great battles which, within modern times, have decided the fate of India on that same plain of Pánípat, viz. in 1526, 1556, and 1761. Having entered Delhi, Bábar received the allegiance of the Muhammadans, but was speedily attacked by the Rájputs of Chitor. Those clans had brought all Ajmere, Mewár, and Málwá under their rule, and now threatened to found a Hindu empire. In 1527, Bábar defeated them at Fatehpur Síkri, near Agra, after a battle memorable for its perils, and for Bábar's vow in his extremity never again to touch wine. He rapidly extended his power as far as Múltán in the Southern Punjab, and Behar in the eastern valley of the Ganges. Bábar died at Agra in 1530, leaving an empire which stretched from the river Amu in Central Asia to the borders of the Gangetic delta in Lower Bengal.

Humáyún, Emperor, 1530–1556.—His son, Humáyún, succeeded him in India, but had to make over Kábul and the Western Punjab to his brother and rival, Kámrán. Humáyún was thus left to govern the new conquest of India, and at the same time was deprived of Afghánistán and the Punjab frontier from which his father had drawn his armies. The descendants of the early Afghán invaders, long settled in India, hated the new Muhammadan or Mughal hordes of Bábar even more than they hated the Hindus. After ten years of fighting, Humáyún was driven out of India by these Afgháns under Sher Sháh, the Governor of Bengal. While Humáyún was flying through the desert of Sind to Persia, his son Akbar was born in the petty fort of Umarkot (1542). Sher Sháh, the Afghán governor of Bengal, set up as emperor of Delhi, but was killed while storming the fortress of Kálinjar (1545). His son succeeded. But, under Sher Sháh's grandson, the Indian Provinces (including Málwá, the Punjab, and Bengal) revolted against the Afghán dynasty from Bengal. Humáyún returned to India, and Akbar, then only in his fourteenth year, defeated the Afghán army of Sher Sháh's dynasty after a desperate battle at Pánípat (1556). India now passed finally from the Afgháns to the Mughals. Sher Sháh's line disappears from Northern India and the Delhi throne, although it lingered on for a time in Lower Bengal. Humáyún, having recovered his Kábul dominions, reigned again for a few months at Delhi, but died in 1556.

The Reign of Akbar, 1556–1605.

Chronological Summary.

1542. Born at Umarkot in Sind.

1556. Regains the Delhi throne for his father, Humáyún, by the victory over the Afgháns at Pánípat (Bairám Khán in actual command). Succeeds his father a few months after, under the regency of Bairám Khán.

1560. Assumes the direct management of the kingdom. Revolt of Bairám Khán, who is defeated and pardoned.

1566. Invasion of the Punjab by Akbar's rival brother, Hákim, who is defeated.

1561–1568. Akbar subjugates the Rájput kingdoms to the Mughal Empire.

1572–1573. Campaign in Gujarát, and its re-annexation to the Delhi Empire.

1576. Akbar's conquest of Bengal; its final annexation to the Mughal Empire.

1581–1593. Insurrection in Gujarát. The Province finally subjugated in 1593 to the Mughal Empire.

THE REIGN OF AKBAR (*continued*).

1586. Conquest of Kashmír; its final revolt quelled in 1592.

1592. Conquest and annexation of Sind to the Mughal Empire.

1594. Subjugation of Kandahár, and consolidation of the Mughal Empire over all India north of the Vindhyas as far as Kábul and Kandahár.

1595. Unsuccessful expedition of Akbar's army into the Deccan against Ahmadnagar under his son, Prince Murád.

1599. Second expedition against Ahmadnagar by Akbar in person, who captures the town, but fails to establish Mughal rule.

1601. Annexation of Khándesh, and return of Akbar to Northern India.

1605. Akbar's death at Agra.

Akbar the Great, 1556-1605.—Akbar the Great, the real founder of the Mughal Empire as it existed for one and a half centuries, succeeded his father at the age of fourteen. Born in 1542, his reign lasted for almost fifty years, from 1556 to 1605, and was therefore contemporary with that of our own Queen Elizabeth (1558–1603). His father, Humáyún, left but a small kingdom in India, not so large as the present British Province of the Punjab: Akbar expanded that small kingdom into an Indian Empire. At the time of Humáyún's death, Akbar (a mere boy) was absent in the Punjab, under the guardianship of Bairám Khán, fighting the revolted Afgháns. Bairám, a Túrkomán by birth, had been the support of the exiled Humáyún, and held the real command of the army which restored him to his throne at Pánípat. He now became the regent for the youthful Akbar, under the honoured title of Khán Bába, equivalent to 'the King's Father.' Brave and skilful as a general, but harsh and overbearing, he raised many enemies; and Akbar, having endured four years of thraldom, took advantage of a hunting party to throw off his minister's yoke (1560). The fallen regent, after a struggle between his loyalty and his resentment, revolted, was defeated, and pardoned. Akbar granted him a liberal pension; and Bairám was in the act of starting on a pilgrimage to Mecca, when he fell beneath the knife of an Afghán assassin, whose father he had slain in battle.

Akbar's Work in India.—The reign of Akbar was a reign of pacification. On his accession in 1556 he found India split up into petty Hindu and Muhammadan kingdoms, and seething with discordant elements; on his death in 1605, he bequeathed it an almost united empire. The earlier invasions by Túrks,

Afgháns, and Mughals had left a powerful Muhammadan population in India under their own Kings. Akbar reduced these Musalmán States to Provinces of the Delhi Empire. Many of the Hindu kings and Rájput nations had also regained their independence: Akbar brought them into political dependence upon his authority. This double task he effected partly by force of arms, but in part also by alliances. He enlisted the Rájput princes by marriage and by a sympathetic policy in the support of his throne. He then employed them in high posts, and played off his Hindu generals and Hindu ministers alike against the Mughal party in Upper India, and against the Afghán faction in Lower Bengal.

Reduction of the Rájputs, 1561-1568.—Humáyún, as we have seen, left but a small kingdom, confined to the Punjab, with the Districts round Delhi and Agra. Akbar quickly extended it, at the expense of his nearest neighbours, namely, the Rájputs. Jaipur was reduced to a fief of the empire; and Akbar cemented his conquest by marrying the daughter of its Hindu prince. Jodhpur was in like manner overcome; and Akbar married his son, Salím, who afterwards reigned under the title of Jahángír, to the grand-daughter of the Rájá. The Rájputs of Chitor were overpowered after a long struggle, but would not mingle their high-caste Hindu blood even with that of a Muhammadan emperor. They found shelter among the mountains and deserts of the Indus, whence they afterwards emerged to recover most of their old dominions, and to found their capital of Udaipur, which they retain to this day. They still boast that alone, among the great Rájput clans, they never gave a daughter in marriage to a Mughal emperor.

Conciliation of the Hindus.—Akbar pursued his policy of conciliation towards all the Hindu States. He also took care to provide a career for the lesser Hindu nobility. He appointed his brother-in-law, the son of the Jaipur Rájá, Governor of the Punjab. Rájá Mán Singh, also a Hindu relative of the Emperor's family, did good war service for Akbar from Kábul to Orissa, and ruled as his Governor of Bengal from 1589 to 1604. Akbar's great finance minister, Rájá Todar Mall, was likewise a Hindu, and carried out the first regular land-settlement and survey of

India. Out of 415 *mansabdárs*, or commanders of horse, 51 were Hindus. Akbar abolished the *jaziah*, the hated tax on non-Musalmáns, and placed all his subjects upon a political equality. He had the Sanskrit sacred books and epic poems translated into Persian, and showed a keen interest in the religion of his Hindu subjects. He respected their laws, but he put down their inhumane rites. He forbade trial by ordeal, animal sacrifices, and child marriages before the age of puberty. He legalized the re-marriage of Hindu widows; but he failed to abolish widow-burning on the husband's funeral pile, although he took steps to ensure that the act should be voluntary.

Muhammadan States reduced.—Akbar thus incorporated his Hindu subjects into the effective force, both civil and military, of his empire. With their aid he reduced the independent Muhammadan kings of Northern India. He subjugated the petty Hindu potentates from the Punjab to Behar. After a struggle, he wrested Lower Bengal in 1576 from its Afghán princes of the house of Sher Sháh (see page 133). From the time of Akbar's conquest of Lower Bengal, it remained for nearly two centuries a province of the Mughal Empire, under governors from Delhi (1576–1765). In 1765, it passed by an imperial grant to the British. Orissa, on the Bay of Bengal, submitted to Akbar's armies, under his Hindu general, Todar Mall, in 1574. On the opposite coast of India, Gujarát was reconquered from its independent Muhammadan king (1572-73), although not finally subjugated until 1593. Málwá had been reduced in 1572. Kashmír was conquered in 1586, and its last revolt quelled in 1592. Sind was also annexed in 1592; and by the recovery of Kandahár in 1594, Akbar extended the Mughal Empire from the heart of Afghánistán across all India north of the Vindhyas, eastward to Orissa, and westward to Sind. He removed the seat of government from Delhi to Agra, and founded Fatehpur Síkri as the future capital of the empire. From this project he was afterwards dissuaded, by the superior position of Agra on the great waterway of the Jumna. In 1566, he built the Agra fort, whose red sandstone battlements majestically overhang the river to this day.

Akbar's Wars in Southern India.—Akbar's efforts to

establish the Mughal Empire in Southern India were less successful. Those efforts began in 1586, but during the first twelve years they were frustrated by the valour and statesmanship of Chánd Bíbí, the Musalmán queen of Ahmadnagar. This celebrated lady skilfully united the usually hostile Abyssinian and Persian settlers in Southern India, together with their armies, and strengthened herself by an alliance with Bijápur and other Muhammadan States of the south. In 1599, Akbar led his armies in person against the princess; but notwithstanding her assassination by her mutinous troops, Ahmadnagar was not reduced till the reign of Akbar's grandson, Sháh Jahán, in 1636. Akbar subjugated Khándesh, and with this somewhat precarious annexation his conquests in Southern India ceased. He returned to Northern India, perhaps feeling that the conquest of the south was beyond the strength of his young empire.

Akbar's Death.—His last years were embittered by the intrigues of his family, and by the misconduct of his beloved son, Prince Salím, afterwards the Emperor Jahángír. In 1605, he died, and was buried in the noble mausoleum at Sikandra, whose mingled architecture of Buddhist design and Saracenic tracery bears witness to the composite faith of the founder of the Mughal Empire. In 1873, the British Viceroy, Lord Northbrook, presented a cloth of honour to cover the plain marble slab beneath which Akbar lies.

Akbar's New Faith.—Akbar's conciliation of the Hindus, and his interest in their literature and religion, made him many enemies among the pious Musalmáns. His favourite wife was a Rájput princess; another of his wives is said to have been a Christian. On Fridays (the Sabbath of Islám), he loved to collect professors of many religions around him. He listened impartially to the arguments of the Bráhman and the Musalmán, the Zoroastrian, the Jew, the Jesuit, and the sceptic philosopher. The history of his life, the *Akbar-námah*, records such a conference, in which the Christian priest Redíf disputed with a body of Muhammadan *mullás* before an assembly of the doctors of all religions, and is allowed to have had the best of the argument. Starting from the broad ground of general toleration, Akbar was gradually led on by free discussion to question the truth of his inherited Muhammadan creed. The counsels of his friend Abul Fazl, coinciding with that sense of superhuman omnipotence which is bred of despotic imperial power, led Akbar at last to promulgate a new State religion, called 'The Divine Faith,' based upon natural theology, and comprising the best practices of all known forms of belief. Of this made-up creed Akbar himself was the prophet, or rather the head of the Church. Every morning he worshipped in public the sun, as the representative of the divine soul which animates the universe, while he was himself worshipped by the ignorant multitude. It is doubtful how far he encouraged this popular adoration of his person, but he certainly allowed his disciples to prostrate themselves before him in private. The stricter Muhammadans accused him, therefore, of accepting a homage permitted only to God.

Akbar's Organization of the Empire.—Akbar not only subdued all India to the north of the Vindhya mountains, he also organized it into an empire. He partitioned it into Provinces, over each of which he placed a governor, or viceroy, with full civil and military control. This control was divided into three departments—the military, the judicial, including the police, and the revenue. With a view to preventing mutinies of the troops, or assertions of independence by their leaders, he re-organized the army on a new basis. He substituted, as far as possible, money payments to the soldiers for the old system of grants of land (*jágírs*) to the generals. Where this change could not be carried out, he brought the holders of the old military fiefs under the control of the central authority at Delhi. He further checked the independence of his provincial generals, by a sort of feudal organization, in which the Hindu tributary princes took their place side by side with the Mughal nobles. The judicial administration was presided over by a lord justice (*mír-i-adl*) at the capital, aided by *kázís* or law-officers in the principal towns. The police in the cities were under a superintendent or *kotwál*, who was also a magistrate. In country districts, where police existed at all, they were left to the management of the landholders or revenue officers. But throughout rural India no regular police force can be said to have existed for the protection of person and property until after the establishment of British rule. The Hindu village-system had its hereditary watchman for each hamlet. These village watchmen were in many parts of the country taken from the predatory castes, and were as often leagued with the robbers as opposed to them. The landholders and revenue officers had each their own set of personal police, who plundered the peasantry in their names.

Akbar's Revenue System.—Akbar's revenue system was based on the ancient Hindu customs, and survives to this day. He first executed a survey or actual measurement of the fields. His officers then found out the produce of each acre of land, and settled the Government share, amounting to one-third of the gross produce. Finally, they fixed the rates at which this share of the crop might be commuted into a money payment. These processes, known as the land settlement, were at first repeated every year. But, to save the peasant from the extortions and vexations incident to an annual inquiry, Akbar's land settlement was afterwards made for ten years. His officers strictly enforced the payment of a third of the whole produce; and Akbar's land revenue from Northern India exceeded what the British levy at the present day. From his fifteen Provinces, including Kábul beyond the Afghán frontier, and Khándesh in Southern India, he demanded 14 millions sterling per annum; or, excluding Kábul, Khándesh, and Sind, 12⅛ millions. The British land tax from a much larger area of Northern India was only 12 millions in 1883. Allowing for the difference in area and in purchasing power of silver, Akbar's tax was about three times the amount which the British take. Two later returns show the land revenue of Akbar at 16½ and 17½ millions sterling. The Provinces had also to support a local militia (*búmí*), in contradistinction to the regular royal army, at a cost of at least 10 millions sterling. Excluding both Kábul and Khándesh, Akbar's demand from the soil of Northern India exceeded 22 millions sterling per annum, under the two items of land revenue and militia cess. There were also a number of miscellaneous taxes. Akbar's total revenue is estimated at 42 millions sterling.

Akbar's Ministers.—Akbar's Hindu minister, Rájá Todar Mall, conducted the revenue settlement, and his name is still a household word among the husbandmen of Bengal. Abul Fazl, the man of letters, and finance minister of Akbar, compiled a statistical survey of the empire, together with many vivid pictures of his master's court and daily life, in the *Aín-i-Akbarí*, which may be read with interest at the present day. Abul Fazl was killed in 1603, at the instigation of Prince Salím, the heir to the throne. The fate of Abul Fazl was the disgrace of Akbar's old age.

Jahángír, Emperor, 1605–1627.—Salím, the favourite son of Akbar, succeeded his father in 1605, and ruled until 1627, under the title of Jahángír, or Conqueror of the World. His reign of twenty-two years was spent in reducing the rebellions of his sons, in exalting the influence of his wife, and in festive self-indulgence. He carried on long wars in Southern India or the Deccan, but he added little to his father's territories. India south of the Vindhyas still continued apart from the northern Empire of Delhi. Málik Ambar, the Abyssinian minister of Ahmadnagar, maintained, in spite of reverses, the independence of that kingdom. At the end of Jahángír's reign, his own son, Prince Sháh Jahán, was a rebel and a refugee in the Deccan, in alliance with Málik Ambar against the imperial troops. The Rájputs also began to reassert their independence. In 1614, Prince Sháh Jahán, on behalf of his father the emperor, defeated the Udaipur Rájá. But the conquest was only partial and for a time. Meanwhile the Rájputs formed an important contingent of the imperial armies, and 5000 of their cavalry aided Sháh Jahán to put down a revolt in Kábul. The Afghán Province of Kandahár was wrested from Jahángír by the Persians in 1621. The land tax of the Mughal Empire remained at 17½ millions under Jahángír, but his total revenues are estimated at 50 millions sterling.

The Empress Núr Jahán.—The principal figure in Jahángír's reign is his empress, Núr Jahán, the 'Light of the World,' otherwise known as Núr Mahál, the 'Light of the Palace.' Born in great poverty, but of a noble Persian family, her beauty won the love of Jahángír while they were both in their first youth, during the reign of Akbar. The old emperor tried to put her out of his son's way, by marrying her to a brave soldier, who obtained high employment in Lower Bengal. Jahángír, on his accession to the throne, commanded her divorce. The husband refused, and was killed. The wife, being brought into the imperial palace, lived for some time in chaste seclusion as a widow, but in the end emerged as the Empress Núr Jahán, the Light of the World. She surrounded herself with her relatives, and at first influenced the self-indulgent emperor Jahángír for his good. But the jealousy of the imperial princes and of the Mughal generals against her party led to intrigue and rebellion. In 1626, her successful general, Mahábat Khán, found himself compelled, in self-defence, to turn against her. He seized the emperor, whom he kept, together with Núr Jahán, in captivity for six months. Jahángír died in the following year, 1627, in the midst of a rebellion against him by his son, Sháh Jahán, and his greatest general, Mahábat Khán.

Jahángír's Personal Character.—Jahángír's personal character is vividly portrayed by Sir Thomas Roe, the first British ambassador to India (1615). Agra continued to be the central seat of the government, but the imperial army on the march formed in itself a splendid capital. Jahángír thought that Akbar had too openly severed himself from the Muhammadan faith. The new emperor conformed more strictly to the outward observances of Islám, but lacked the inward religious feeling of his father. While he forbade the use of wine to his subjects, he spent his own nights in drunken revelry. He talked religion over his cups until he reached a certain stage of intoxication, when he 'fell to weeping, and to various passions, which kept them to midnight.' In public he maintained a strict appearance of virtue, and never allowed any person whose breath smelt of wine to enter his presence. On one occasion, a courtier who had shared his midnight revel, indiscreetly alluded to it next morning. The Sultán gravely examined him as to who could possibly have been the companions of such a debauch, and bastinadoed them so severely that one of them died.

When sober, Jahángír tried to work wisely for his empire. A

chain hung down from the citadel to the ground, and communicated with a cluster of golden bells in his own chamber, so that every suitor might apprise the emperor of his demand for justice, without the intervention of the courtiers. Many European adventurers repaired to his court, and Jahángír patronized alike their arts and their religion. In his earlier years he had accepted the new religion, or 'Divine Faith' of his father Akbar. It is said that on his accession he had even permitted the divine honours paid to Akbar to be continued to himself. Jahángír's first wife was a Hindu princess. Figures of Christ and the Virgin Mary adorned his rosary; and two of his nephews embraced Christianity with his approval.

Sháh Jahán, Emperor, 1628-1658.—On the news of his father's death, Sháh Jahán hurried north from the Deccan, and proclaimed himself emperor at Agra in January 1628. He put down for ever the court faction of the Empress Núr Jahán, by confining her to private life upon a liberal allowance; and by murdering his brother Shahriyár, with all the other members of the house of Akbar who might become rivals to the throne. But he was just to his people, blameless in his habits, a good financier, and as economical as a magnificent court, splendid public works, and distant military expeditions could permit. Under Sháh Jahán the Mughal Empire was finally shorn of its Afghán Province of Kandahár; but it extended its conquests in Southern India or the Deccan, and raised the magnificent buildings in Northern India which now form the most splendid memorials of the Mughal dynasty. After a temporary occupation of Balkh, and the actual reconquest of Kandahár by the Delhi troops in 1637, Sháh Jahán lost much of his Afghán territories, and the Province of Kandahár was severed from the Mughal Empire by the Persians in 1653. On the other hand, in the Deccan, the kingdom of Ahmadnagar (to which Ellichpur had been united in 1572) was at last annexed to the Mughal Empire in 1636; Bídar fort was taken in 1657; while the two other of the five kingdoms, namely Bijápur and Golconda, were forced to pay tribute, although not finally reduced until the succeeding reign of Aurangzeb. But the Maráthás now appear on the scene, and commenced, unsuccessfully at Ahmadnagar in 1637, that series of persistent Hindu attacks which were destined in the next century to break down the Mughal Empire. The imperial princes, Aurangzeb and his brothers, carried on the wars in Southern India and in Afghánistán for their father Sháh Jahán.

Sháh Jahán's Buildings.—Except during one or two military expeditions, Sháh Jahán lived a magnificent life in the north of India. At Agra he raised the exquisite mausoleum of the Táj Mahál, a dream in marble, 'designed by Titans and finished by jewellers.' His Pearl Mosque, the marble *Motí Masjíd*, within the Agra fort, is perhaps the purest and loveliest house of prayer in the world. Not content with enriching his grandfather Akbar's capital with these and other architectural glories, Sháh Jahán planned the re-transfer of the seat of government to Delhi, and adorned that city with buildings of unrivalled magnificence. Its Great Mosque, or *Jamá Masjíd*, was commenced in the fourth year of his reign, and completed in the tenth. The palace at Delhi, now the fort, covered a vast parallelogram, 1600 feet by 3200, with exquisite and sumptuous buildings in marble and fine stone. The entrance consists of a deeply recessed gateway leading into a vaulted hall, which springs up two storeys high, like the nave of a gigantic Gothic cathedral, 375 feet in length;—'the noblest entrance,' says Fergusson, the historian of architecture, 'to any existing palace.' The *Diwán-i-Khás*, or Court of Private Audience, overlooks the river,—a masterpiece of delicate inlaid work and poetic design. Sháh Jahán spent many years of his reign at Delhi, and prepared the city for its destiny as the most magnificent capital in the world under his successor Aurangzeb. But exquisite as are its public buildings, the manly vigour of Akbar's red-stone fort at Agra, with its bold sculptures and square Hindu construction, has given place to a certain effeminate beauty in the marble structures of Sháh Jahán.

Sháh Jahán's Revenues.—Under Sháh Jahán, the Mughal Empire attained its highest union of strength with magnificence. His son and successor, Aurangzeb, added to its extent, but at the same time sowed the seeds of its decay. Akbar's land revenue of $17\frac{1}{2}$ millions had been raised, chiefly by new conquests, to 22 millions sterling under Sháh Jahán. But this sum included Kashmír, and five Provinces in Afghánistán, some of which were lost during his reign. The land revenue of the Mughal Empire within India was $20\frac{3}{4}$ millions. The magnificence of Sháh Jahán's court was the wonder of European travellers. His Peacock Throne, with its tail blazing in the shifting natural colours of rubies, sapphires, and emeralds, was valued by the jeweller Tavernier at $6\frac{1}{2}$ millions sterling.

Rebellion of Prince Aurangzeb, 1657.—Akbar's dynasty lay under the curse of rebellious sons. As Jahángír had risen against his most loving father, Akbar, and as Sháh Jahán had mutinied against Jahángír; so Sháh Jahán in his turn suffered from the intrigues and rebellions of his family. In 1657, the old king fell ill; and Aurangzeb, after a treacherous conflict with his brethren, deposed his father, and proclaimed himself emperor in 1658. The unhappy emperor was kept in confinement for seven years, and died a State prisoner in the fort of Agra in 1666.

The Reign of Aurangzeb, 1658–1707.

Chronological Summary.

1658. Deposition of Sháh Jahán, and usurpation of Aurangzeb.

1659. Aurangzeb defeats his brothers Shujá and Dárá. Dárá, being betrayed by a chief with whom he had sought refuge, is put to death.

1660. Continued struggle of Aurangzeb with his brother Shujá, who ultimately flies to Arakan, and there perishes miserably.

1661. Aurangzeb executes his youngest brother, Murád, in prison.

1662. Unsuccessful invasion of Assam by Aurangzeb's general, Mír Jumlá. Disturbances in the Deccan. War between Bijápur and the Maráthás under Sivají. After various changes of fortune, Sivají, the founder of the Maráthá power, retains a considerable territory.

1662–1665. Sivají the Maráthá in rebellion against the Mughal Empire. In 1664, he assumes the title of Rájá, and asserts his independence. In 1665, on a large army being sent against him, he makes submission, and proceeds to Delhi, where he is placed under restraint, but soon afterwards escapes.

1666. Death of the deposed emperor, Sháh Jahán. War in the Deccan, and defeat of the Imperial Army from Delhi by the King of Bijápur.

1667. Sivají makes peace with Aurangzeb, and obtains an extension of territory. Sivaji levies tribute from Bijápur and Golconda.

THE REIGN OF AURANGZEB (*continued*).

1670. Sivají the Maráthá ravages Khándesh and the Deccan, and there levies for the first time *chauth*, or a contribution of one-fourth of the revenue.

1672. Defeat of the Mughal or Imperial troops by Sivají.

1677. Aurangzeb revives the *jaziah*, or poll-tax on non-Muhammadans.

1679. Aurangzeb at war with the Rájputs. Rebellion of Prince Akbar, Aurangzeb's youngest son, who joins the Rájputs, but whose army deserts him. Prince Akbar is forced to fly to the Maráthás.

1672–1680. Progress of the Maráthás in the Deccan. Sivají crowns himself an independent sovereign at Ráigarh in 1674. His wars with Bijápur and the Mughal or Imperial troops. Sivají dies in 1680, and is succeeded by his son, Sambhají.

1683. Aurangzeb invades the Deccan in person, at the head of his Grand Army.

1686–1688. Aurangzeb conquers Bijápur and Golconda, and annexes them to the empire.

1689. Aurangzeb captures Sambhají, the head of the Maráthás, and barbarously puts him to death.

1692. Guerilla war with the Maráthás under their various leaders.

1698. Aurangzeb's general captures Ginjí from the Maráthás.

1699–1701. Capture of Sátára and Maráthá forts by Aurangzeb. Apparent ruin of the Maráthás.

1702–1705. Fresh successes of the Maráthás.

1706. Aurangzeb retreats to Ahmadnagar; and,

1707. Miserably dies there.

Aurangzeb, Emperor, 1658–1707.—Aurangzeb proclaimed himself emperor in 1658, in the room of his imprisoned father, under the title of Alamgír, the Conqueror of the Universe, and reigned until 1707. Under Aurangzeb the Mughal Empire reached its widest limits. But his long rule of forty-nine years merely presents on a more magnificent stage the usual tragic drama of a Mughal reign. In its personal character, it began with his rebellion against his father; consolidated itself by the murder of his brethren; and darkened to a close amid the mutinies, intrigues, and jealousies of his own sons. Its public aspects consisted of a magnificent court in Northern India; conquests of the independent Muhammadan kings in the south; and wars against the Hindu powers, which, alike in Rájputána and in Southern India or the Deccan, were gathering strength for the overthrow of the Mughal Empire.

Aurangzeb murders his Brothers.—The year after his accession, Aurangzeb defeated and put to death his eldest brother, the noble but impetuous Dárá (1659). After another twelve months' struggle, he drove out of India his second brother, the self-indulgent Shujá (1660), who perished miserably among the insolent savages of Arakan. His remaining brother, the brave young Murád, was executed in prison the following year (1661). Aurangzeb had from boyhood been a Muhammadan of the stern puritan type. Having now killed off his rival brethren, he set up as an orthodox sovereign of the strictest sect of Islám, while his invalid father, Sháh Jahán, lingered on in prison, mourning over his murdered sons, until his own death in 1666.

Aurangzeb's Campaigns in Southern India.—Aurangzeb continued, as emperor, that persistent policy of the subjugation of Southern India which he had brilliantly commenced as his father's lieutenant. Of the five Muhammadan kingdoms of the Deccan, Bídar and Ahmadnagar with Ellichpur had fallen to his arms, as the prince in command of the Imperial armies, before his accession to the throne. The two others, Bijápur and Golconda, struggled longer, but Aurangzeb was determined at any cost to annex them to the Mughal Empire. During the first half of his reign, or exactly twenty-five years, he waged war in the south by means of his generals (1658–83). A new Hindu power had, as we have seen, arisen in the Deccan—the Maráthás, whose history will be traced in more detail in a subsequent chapter. The task before Aurangzeb's armies was not only the old one of subduing the Muhammadan kingdoms of Bijápur and Golconda, but also the new one of crushing the quick growth of the Hindu or Maráthá confederacy.

Slow Conquest of Southern India.—During a quarter of a century, his utmost efforts failed. Bijápur and Golconda were not conquered. In 1670, the Maráthá leader, Sivají, levied *chauth*, or one-fourth of the revenues, as tribute from the Mughal Provinces in Southern India; and in 1674 he crowned himself an independent sovereign at Ráigarh. In 1680–1681, Aurangzeb's son, Prince Akbar, having rebelled against his father, joined the Maráthá army. Aurangzeb felt that he must either give up his magnificent palace in the north for a soldier's tent in the Deccan, or he must relinquish his most cherished scheme of conquering Southern India. He accordingly prepared an expedition, on an unrivalled scale of numbers and splendour, to be led by himself. In 1683, he arrived at the head of his Grand Army in the Deccan, and spent the next half of his reign, or twenty-four years, in the field in Southern India. Golconda and Bijápur fell after another severe struggle, and were finally annexed to the Mughal Empire in 1688.

The Maráthás, 1688-1707.—But the conquests of these last of the five Muhammadan kingdoms of the Deccan only left the arena bare for the operations of the Maráthás. Indeed, the attacks of the Maráthás on the two Muhammadan States had prepared the way for their annexation by Aurangzeb. The emperor waged war during the remaining twenty years of his life (1688–1707) against the rising Hindu power of the Maráthás. Their first great leader, Sivají, had proclaimed himself king in 1674, and died in 1680. Aurangzeb captured his son and successor, Sambhají, in 1689, and cruelly put him to death; seized the Maráthá capital, with many of their forts; and seemed in the first year of the new century to have almost stamped out their existence (1701). But, after a guerilla warfare, the Maráthás again sprang up into a powerful fighting nation. In 1705, they recovered their forts; while Aurangzeb had exhausted his health, his treasures, and his troops, in the long and fruitless struggle. His soldiery murmured for arrears; and the emperor, now old and peevish, told the malcontents that if they did not like his service they might quit it, while he disbanded some of his cavalry to ease his finances.

Aurangzeb hemmed in.—Meanwhile the Maráthás were pressing hungrily on the imperial camp. The Grand Army of Aurangzeb had grown during a quarter of a century into an unwieldy capital. Its movements were slow, and incapable of concealment. If Aurangzeb sent out a rapid small expedition against the Maráthás, who plundered and insulted the outskirts of his camp, they cut it to pieces. If he moved out against them in force, they vanished. His own soldiery feasted with the enemy, who prayed, with mock ejaculations, for the health of the emperor as their best friend.

Aurangzeb's Death.—In 1706, the Grand Army was so

disorganized, that Aurangzeb opened negotiations with the Maráthás. He even thought of submitting the Imperial or Mughal Provinces to their tribute or *chauth*. But the insolent exultation of the Maráthá chiefs led to the treaty being broken off; and Aurangzeb, in 1706, found shelter in Ahmadnagar, where he died in February of the following year (1707). Dark suspicion of his sons' loyalty, and just fears lest they should subject him to the cruel fate which he had inflicted on his father, left him solitary in his last days. On the approach of death, he gave utterance in broken sentences to his worldly counsels and adieus, mingled with terror and remorse, and closing in an agony of desperate resignation: 'Come what may, I have launched my vessel on the waves. Farewell! Farewell! Farewell!'

Mír Jumlá's Expedition to Assam, 1662.—The conquest of the Deccan or Southern India was the one inflexible purpose of Aurangzeb's life, and has therefore been dealt with here in a continuous narrative. In the north of India, great events had also transpired. His general Mír Jumlá led the imperial troops as far as Assam, the extreme eastern Province of India (1662). But amid the pestilential swamps of the rainy season his army melted away, its supplies were cut off, and its march was surrounded by swarms of natives, who knew the country and were accustomed to the climate. Mír Jumlá succeeded in extricating the main body of his troops, but died of exhaustion and a broken heart before he reached Dacca, in the Bengal Delta.

Aurangzeb's Bigoted Policy.—In the north-west of India, Aurangzeb was not more fortunate. During his time the Sikhs (a theistic and military sect of Hindus) were growing into a power, but it was not till the succeeding reigns that they commenced the series of operations which in the end wrested the Punjab from the Mughal Empire. Aurangzeb's bigotry arrayed against him all the Hindu princes and peoples of Northern India. He revived the *jaziah*, or insulting poll-tax on non-Musalmáns (1677); drove the Hindus out of the administration; and oppressed the widow and children of his father's faithful Hindu general, Jaswant Singh. A local sect of Hindus in Northern India was persecuted into rebellion in 1676; and in

1677, the Rájput States combined against him. The emperor waged a protracted war against them,—at one time devastating Rájputána, at another time saving himself and his army from extermination only by a stroke of genius and rare presence of mind. In 1680, his rebel son, Prince Akbar, went over to the Rájputs with his division of the Mughal or Imperial army. From that year the permanent alienation of the Rájputs from the Mughal Empire dates; and the Hindu chivalry, which had been a source of strength to Akbar the Great, became an element of ruin to Aurangzeb and his successors. The emperor pillaged and slaughtered throughout the Rájput States of Jaipur, Jodhpur, and Udaipur. The Rájputs retaliated by ravaging the Muhammadan Provinces of Málwá, defacing the mosques, insulting the *mullás*, or priests of Islám, and burning the Kurán. In 1681, the emperor patched up a peace in order to allow him to lead the Grand Army into the Deccan, from which he was destined never to return. But Akbar's policy of conciliating the Hindus, and welding them into one empire with his Muhammadan subjects, came to an end under Aurangzeb.

Aurangzeb's Revenues.—All Northern India except Assam, and the greater part of Southern India, paid revenue to Aurangzeb. His Indian Provinces covered nearly as large an area as the British Empire at the present day, although their dependence on the central government was less direct. From these Provinces his net land revenue demand is returned at 30 to 38 millions sterling—a sum which represented at least three times the purchasing power of the land revenue of British India at the present day. But it is doubtful whether the enormous demand of 38 millions was fully realized during any series of years, even at the height of Aurangzeb's power, before he left Delhi for his long southern wars. It was estimated at only 30 millions sterling in the last year of his reign, after his absence of a quarter of a century in the Deccan. Fiscal oppressions led to evasions and revolts; and one or other of the Provinces was always in open war against the emperor. The standard return of Aurangzeb's land revenue was *net*, £34,505,890; and this remained the nominal demand in the accounts of the central exchequer during the next half-century, notwithstanding that the empire had fallen to pieces. When the Afghán invader, Ahmad Sháh Duráni, entered Delhi in 1761, the treasury officers presented him with a statement showing the land revenue of the empire at £34,506,640. The highest land revenue of Aurangzeb, after his annexations in Southern India, and before his final reverses, was returned at 38½ millions sterling; of which nearly 38 millions were from Indian Provinces, and the remainder from Kashmír and Kábul. The total revenue of the Mughal Empire under Aurangzeb, from all sources, was estimated in 1695 at 80 millions sterling, and in 1697 at 77½ millions sterling. The gross taxation levied from British India, deducting the opium excise, which is paid by the Chinese consumer, averaged 38 millions sterling during the ten years ending 1883.

Character of Aurangzeb.—Aurangzeb tried to live the life of a model Muhammadan emperor. Magnificent in his public appearances, simple in his private habits, diligent in business, exact in his religious observances, an elegant letter-writer, and ever ready with choice passages alike from the poets and from the Kurán, his life would have been a blameless one, if he had had no father to depose, no brethren to murder, and no Hindu subjects to oppress. But his bigotry made an enemy of every one who did not share his own faith; and the slaughter of his kindred compelled him to entrust his whole government to strangers. The Hindus never forgave him; and the Sikhs, the Rájputs, and the Maráthás, immediately after his reign, began to close in upon the empire. His Muhammadan generals and viceroys, as a rule, served him well during his vigorous life; but at his death they usurped his children's inheritance.

Decline of the Mughal Empire.—The succeeding emperors were puppets in the hands of the too powerful soldiers or statesmen who raised them to the throne, controlled them while on it, and killed them when it suited their purposes to do so. The subsequent history of the empire is a mere record of ruin. The chief events in its decline and fall are summarized on page 154. For a time Mughal emperors still ruled India from Delhi. But of the six immediate successors of Aurangzeb, two were under the control of an unscrupulous general, Zul-fikár Khán, while the four others were the creatures of a couple of Sayyid adventurers, who well earned their title of the 'king-makers.'

Independence of the Deccan and of Oudh.—From the year 1720 the breaking up of the empire took a more open form. The Nizám-ul-Múlk, or Governor of the Deccan, severed the largest part of Southern India from the Delhi rule (1720-1748). The Governor of Oudh, originally a Persian merchant, who had risen to the post of *wazír*, or prime minister of the empire, practically established his own dynasty as the Nawáb Wazír of Oudh which had been committed to his care (1732-1743).

Hindu Risings: Sikhs and Maráthás.—The Hindu subjects of the empire were at the same time asserting their independence. The Sikh sect in the Punjab was driven by the oppression of the Delhi Emperors into revolt, and was mercilessly crushed (1710-1716). The indelible memory of the cruelties then inflicted by the Mughal troops nerved the Sikh nation with that hatred to Delhi which served the British cause so well in 1857. Their leader, Banda, was carried about in an iron cage, tricked out in the mockery of imperial robes, with scarlet turban and cloth of gold. His son's heart was torn out before his eyes, and thrown in his face. He himself was then pulled to pieces with red-hot pincers; and the Sikhs were exterminated like mad dogs (1716). The Hindu princes of Rájputána were more fortunate. Ajít Singh of Jodhpur asserted his independence, and Rájputána practically severed its connection with the Mughal Empire in 1715. The Maráthás having enforced their claim to black-mail (*chauth*) throughout Southern India, burst through the Vindhyas into the north, and obtained from the Delhi emperors the cession of Málwá (1743) and Orissa (1751), with an imperial grant of tribute from Bengal (1751).

Invasions from Central Asia, 1739-1761.—While the Muhammadan governors and Hindu subjects of the empire were thus becoming independent of the Delhi emperors, two new sets of external enemies appeared; one set from Central Asia, the other set from the sea. In 1739, Nádir Sháh, the Persian monarch, swooped down on India, with his destroying host, and, after a massacre in the streets of Delhi and a fifty-eight days' sack, returned through the north-western passes with a booty estimated at 32 millions sterling. The destroying host of the Persian king was succeeded by a series of invasions from Afghánistán. Six times the Afgháns burst through the passes under Ahmad Sháh Duránf, pillaging, slaughtering, and then scornfully retiring to their homes with the plunder of the Mughal empire. In 1738, Kábul, the last Afghán Province of the Mughals, was severed from Delhi; and, in 1752, Ahmad Sháh obtained the cession of the Punjab from the miserable emperor. The cruelties inflicted upon Delhi and Northern India during these six Afghán invasions form an appalling tale of bloodshed and wanton cruelty. The wretched capital opened her gates, and was fain to receive the Afgháns as guests. Yet on one occasion it suffered for six weeks every enormity which a barbarian army can inflict upon a prostrate foe. Meanwhile the Afghán cavalry were scouring the country, slaying, burning, and mutilating, in the meanest hamlet as in the greatest town. They took especial delight in sacking the holy places of the Hindus, and murdering the defenceless votaries at the shrines.

Misery of the Provinces.—A single example must suffice to show the miseries inflicted by the invaders of India from the North-west. A horde of 25,000 Afghán horsemen swooped down upon the sacred city of Muttra during a festival, while it was thronged with peaceful Hindu pilgrims engaged in their devotions. 'They burned the houses,' says the Tyrolese Jesuit Tieffenthaler, who was in India at that time, 'together with their inmates, slaughtering others with the sword and the lance; haling off into captivity maidens and youths, men and women. In the temples they slaughtered cows' (the sacred animal of the Hindus), 'and smeared the images and pavement with the blood.' The borderland between Afghánistán and India lay silent and waste; indeed, Districts far within the Indian frontier, which had once been densely inhabited, and which are now again thickly peopled, were swept bare of inhabitants. Thus Gujránwála, the seat of the ancient capital of the Punjab in Buddhist times, was utterly depopulated. Its present inhabitants are immigrants of comparatively recent date.

The District, which was stripped of its inhabitants in the last century, has now a new population of a million.

Fall of the Empire, 1761–1765.—The other set of invaders came from over the sea. In the wars between the French and English in Southern India, the last vestiges of the Delhi authority in the Karnátik disappeared (1748–61). Bengal, Behar, and Orissa were handed over to the English by an imperial grant in 1765. We obtained these three fertile Provinces as the nominee of the emperor; but the battle of Pánípat had already reduced the throne of Delhi to a shadow. That battle was fought in 1761, between the Afghán invader Ahmad Sháh and the Maráthá powers, on the memorable plain of Pánípat on which Bábar and Akbar had twice won the sovereignty of India. The Afgháns defeated the Maráthás; but although the Muhammadans could still win victories, they could no longer rule India. During the anarchy which followed, the British patiently built up a new power out of the wreck of the Mughal Empire. Puppet emperors continued to reign at Delhi over a numerous seraglio, under such lofty titles as Akbar II. or Alamgír II. But their power was confined to the palace, while Maráthás, Sikhs, and Englishmen were fighting for the sovereignty of India. The last of these pensioned Mughal kings of Delhi emerged for a moment as a rebel during the Mutiny of 1857, and died a State prisoner in Rangoon, the capital of British Burma, in 1862.

Causes of its Fall.—Akbar had rendered a great Empire possible in India by conciliating the native Hindu races. He thus raised up a powerful third party, consisting of the native military peoples of India, which enabled him alike to prevent new Muhammadan invasions from Central Asia, and to keep in subjection his own Muhammadan Governors of Provinces. Under Aurangzeb and his miserable successors this wise policy of conciliation was given up. Accordingly, new Muhammadan hordes soon swept down from Afghánistán; the Muhammadan Governors of Indian Provinces set up as independent potentates: and the warlike Hindu races, who had helped Akbar to create the Mughal Empire, became, under his foolish posterity, the chief agents of its ruin.

The British won India, not from the Mughals, but from the Hindus.—Before we appeared as conquerors, the Mughal Empire had broken up. Our final and most perilous wars were neither with the Delhi king, nor with his revolted Muhammadan viceroys, but with the two Hindu confederacies, the Maráthás and the Sikhs. Muhammadan princes fought against us in Bengal, in the Karnátik, and in Mysore; but the longest opposition to the British conquest of India came from the Hindus. Our last Maráthá war dates as late as 1818, and the Sikh Confederation was overcome only in 1849.

The following summary must suffice to show the principal events in the ruin of the Mughal Empire after the death of Aurangzeb, the last of the great Mughal emperors, in 1707.

THE DECLINE AND FALL OF THE MUGHAL EMPIRE, 1707–1862.

1707. Succession contest between Muázzim and Alam, two sons of Aurangzeb; victory of the former, and his accession with the title of Bahádur Sháh; but under the complete control of his military prime minister, Zul-fikár Khán. Revolt of Prince Kambaksh; his defeat and death.

1710. Expedition by the Mughal emperor against the Sikhs.

1712. Death of the emperor Bahádur Sháh, and accession of his eldest son, Jahándar Sháh, who only ruled as the creature of his prime minister, Zul-fikár Khán. Revolt of his nephew, Farukhsiyyar; and murder of the emperor, Jahándar Sháh, and his *wazír*.

1713. Accession of Farukhsiyyar as emperor under the control of the two Sayyid 'king-makers,' Husáin Alí and Abdullá.

1716. Invasion of the imperial territories by the Sikhs; their defeat, and cruel persecution.

1719. Deposition and murder of the emperor Farukhsiyyar by the two Sayyids. They nominate in succession three boy emperors, the first two of whom die within a few months; the third, Muhammad Sháh, commences his reign in September 1719.

1720. Overthrow of the two Sayyids, the 'king-makers.'

1720–1748. The Governor of the Deccan or Southern India, or Nizám-ul-Múlk, establishes his independence at Haidarábád.

1732–1743. The Governor of Oudh, who was also *wazír* or prime minister of the empire, becomes practically independent of Delhi.

1735–1751. General decline of the empire; revolts within it: invasion of Nádir Sháh from Persia (1739). First invasion of India by Ahmad Sháh Duráni (1747). The Maráthás finally secure the cession of Málwá (1743); and of Southern Orissa and tribute from Bengal (1751).

1748–1750. Accession of the emperor Ahmad Sháh, son of Muhammad Sháh; disturbances by the Rohillás in Oudh, and defeat of the imperial troops.

1751. The Rohillá insurrection crushed by the imperial troops, with the aid of the Maráthás.

1751–1752. Second invasion from Afghánistán by Ahmad Sháh Duráni, and cession of the Punjab to him.

1754. Deposition of the emperor, and accession of Alamgír II.

1756. Third invasion from Afghánistán by Ahmad Sháh Duráni, and sack of Delhi.

1759. Fourth invasion of Ahmad Sháh Duráni, and murder of the emperor Alamgír II. by his prime minister, Ghází-ud-dín. Maráthá conquests in Northern India, and their capture of Delhi.

1761–1805. Third battle of Pánípat, and defeat of the Maráthás by the Afgháns (1761). The nominal emperor on the death of Alamgír II. is Sháh Alam II., who resides till 1771, at Allahábád, a pensioner of the British. The Maráthás then practically become masters of the Delhi territories and of the person of the emperor. The emperor is blinded and imprisoned by rebels; rescued by the Maráthás, but virtually a prisoner in their hands till 1803, when the Maráthá power is overthrown by Lord Lake.

1806–1837. Akbar II. succeeds as emperor, under British protection, but only to the nominal dignity.

1837–1862. Muhammad Bahádur Sháh, the seventeenth Mughal emperor, and last of the race of Timúr. For his complicity in the Mutiny of 1857 he was banished to Rangoon, where he died in 1862.

Materials for Reference.

The original sources for the Mughal Period are Sir Henry Elliot's eight volumes, Blochmann's *Ain-i-Akbari*, with Gladwin's older translation, Briggs' *Firishta*, and other works cited at p. 131. The popular narrative is still Elphinstone's *History of India*. Among valuable monographs may be cited Edward Thomas's *Revenue Resources of the Mughal Empire*, General Cunningham's letter on *Some Copper Coins of Akbar* (*Journal Asiatic Society of Bengal*, 1885), Aurangzeb's *Letters* (Persian lithograph), and the biographical or autobiographical memoirs of Bábar and other of the Mughal emperors, Graf Noer's *Kaiser Akbar* (Leiden, 1880), Erskine's *History of India, &c., under Bábar and Humáyún*, and the narratives of Bernier, Tavernier, and other travellers during the Mughal period. Mr. Stanley Lane-Poole's *History of the Moghul Emperors of Hindustan, illustrated by their Coins* (1892), gives a correct historical outline of the period together with valuable original data. The volumes on *Akbar* and *Aurangzeb* in the Rulers of India Series furnish a graphic account of the rise, the meridian and the fall of the Mughal empire.

CHAPTER XI.

The Maráthás, 1650-1818.

Rise of the Maráthás.—About the year 1634, a Maráthá soldier of fortune, SHÁHJÍ BHONSLA by name, began to play a conspicuous part in Southern India. He fought on the side of the two independent Muhammadan States, Ahmadnagar and Bijápur, against the Mughals; and left a band of followers, together with a military fief, to his son Sivají, born in 1627. Sivají formed a national party out of the Hindu tribes of the Deccan—a native Hindu party which was opposed alike to the imperial armies from the north, and to the independent Muhammadan kingdoms of the south. There were thus, from 1650 onwards, three powers in the Deccan,—first, the ever-invading troops of the Delhi Empire; second, the forces of the two remaining independent Muhammadan States of Southern India, namely, Ahmadnagar and Bijápur; third, the military organization of the local Hindu tribes, which ultimately grew into the Maráthá Confederacy.

Their Growth as a 'Third Party' in the Deccan.—During the eighty years' war of Sháh Jahán and Aurangzeb, with a view to the conquest of the independent Muhammadan kingdoms in Southern India (1627–1707), this third or Hindu party fought sometimes for the Delhi emperors, sometimes for the independent Muhammadan kingdoms, and obtained a constantly increasing importance. The Mughal armies from the north, and the independent Muhammadan kingdoms of the south, gradually exterminated each other. Being foreigners, they had to recruit their exhausted forces from outside. The Hindu or Maráthá Confederacy drew its inexhaustible native levies from the wide tract known as Maháráshtra, stretching from the Berars in Central India to near the south of the Bombay Presidency. The Maráthás were therefore courted alike by the imperial generals from Delhi and by the independent Muhammadan kingdoms of the Deccan. Those kingdoms, with the help of the Maráthás, long proved a match for the imperial troops. But no sooner were the Delhi armies driven back, than the Maráthás proceeded to despoil the independent Musalmán kingdoms. On the other hand, the Delhi generals, when allied with the Maráthás, could overpower the Muhammadan States.

Sivají, 1627–1680.—Sivají, the great Maráthá leader, saw the strength of his position, and, by a life of treachery, assassination, and hard fighting, he won for the Maráthás the practical supremacy in Southern India. As a basis for his operations, he perched himself safe in almost impregnable hill forts among the Western Gháts. His troops consisted of Hindu spearmen, mounted on hardy ponies. They were the peasant proprietors of Southern India, and they could be dispersed or promptly called together according to the season of the agricultural year. Except at seed time and harvest, they were always at leisure for war. Sivají had therefore the command of an unlimited body of men, without the expense of a standing army. With these he swooped down upon his enemies, exacted tribute, or forced them to come to terms. He then paid off his soldiery by a part of the plunder, and retreated with the lion's share to his hill forts. In 1659, he lured the general of the independent Muhammadan kingdom of Bijápur into an ambush, stabbed him at a friendly conference, and exterminated his army. In 1662, Sivají pillaged as far as the extreme north of the Bombay Presidency, and sacked the imperial city of Surat. In 1664, he assumed the title of king (Rájá), with the royal prerogative of coining money in his own name. The year 1665 found Sivají helping the Mughal armies against the independent Musalmán State of Bijápur. In 1666, he was induced to visit Delhi. Being coldly received by the Emperor Aurangzeb, and placed under restraint, he escaped to the south and raised the standard of revolt. In 1674, Sivají enthroned himself with great pomp at Ráigarh, weighing himself in a balance against gold, and distributing his weight in gold among his Bráhmans. After sending forth his hosts as far as the Karnátik in 1676, he died in 1680.

Aurangzeb's Mistaken Policy, 1688–1707.—The Emperor Aurangzeb would have done wisely to have left the independent Musalmán Kings of the Deccan alone, until he had crushed the rising Maráthá power. Indeed, a great statesman would have buried the old quarrel between the Muhammadans of the north and south, and would have united the whole forces of Islám against the Hindu Confederacy, which was rapidly growing to be the strongest power in the Deccan. But the fixed resolve of Aurangzeb's life was to annex to Delhi the Muhammadan kingdoms of Southern India. By the time he had carried out this scheme, he had wasted his armies, and left the Mughal Empire ready to break into pieces at the first touch of the Maráthá spear.

The Line of Sivají.—Sambhají succeeded his father, Sivají, in 1680, and ruled till 1689. His reign was spent in wars against the Portuguese settlements on the south-western coast of India, and against the armies of the Mughal Empire. In 1689, Aurangzeb captured him, blinded his eyes with a red-hot iron, cut out the tongue which had blasphemed the Prophet, and struck off his head. His son, Sahu, then six years of age, was also captured and kept a prisoner till the death of Aurangzeb. In 1707 he was restored, on acknowledging allegiance to Delhi. But his long captivity among the Mughals left him only half a Maráthá. He wasted his life in his seraglio, and resigned the government of his territories to his Bráhman minister, Bálají Vishwanáth, with the title of Peshwá. This office of Peshwá or prime minister became hereditary, and the power of the Peshwá superseded that of the Maráthá kings. The royal family of Sivají only retained the little principalities of Sátára and Kolhápur. Sátára lapsed to the British, for want of a direct heir, in 1849. Kolhápur has survived through British clemency, and is now ruled, under British control, by the representative of Sivají's line.

The Peshwás.—Meanwhile the Peshwás were building up at Poona the great Maráthá Confederacy. In 1718, Bálají, the first Peshwá, marched an army to Delhi in support of the Sayyid 'king-makers.' In 1720, he extorted an imperial grant of the *chauth*, or 'one-fourth' of the revenues of the Deccan. The Maráthás were also confirmed in the sovereignty of their own Southern countries round Poona and Sátára. The second

Peshwá, Bájí Ráo (1721–40), converted the grant of the tribute of the Deccan, which had been given by the Delhi emperor in 1720, into a Maráthá sovereignty over the Deccan. The second Peshwá also wrested the Province of Málwá from the Mughal Empire (1736), together with the country on the north-west of the Vindhyas, from the Narbadá to the Chambal. In 1739, he captured Bassein from the Portuguese. Málwá was finally ceded by the Delhi Emperor to the Maráthás in 1743.

Third Peshwá, 1740–1761.—The third Peshwá, Bálají Bájí Ráo, succeeded in 1740, and carried the Maráthá terror into the heart of the Mughal Empire. The Deccan became merely a starting-point for a vast series of their expeditions to the north and the east. Within the Deccan itself the Peshwá augmented his sovereignty, at the expense of the Muhammadan Nizám of Haidarábád, after two wars. The great centres of the Maráthá power were now fixed at Poona in Bombay and Nágpur in the Central Provinces. In 1741–42, a general of the Nágpur branch of the Maráthá Confederacy known as the Bhonslas, swept down upon Lower Bengal; but, after plundering to the suburbs of the Muhammadan capital of Murshidábád, he was driven back through Orissa by the Viceroy Alí Vardí Khán. The 'Maráthá Ditch,' or semi-circular moat around part of Calcutta, records to this day the panic which then spread throughout Lower Bengal. Next year, 1743, the head of the Nágpur branch, Raghují Bhonsla, invaded Lower Bengal in person. From this date, notwithstanding quarrels between the Poona and Nágpur Maráthás over the spoil, the fertile Provinces of the Lower Ganges became a plundering ground of the Bhonslas. In 1751, they obtained a formal grant from the Viceroy Alí Vardí of the *chauth*, or 'quarter revenue' of Lower Bengal, together with the cession of Orissa. In Northern India, the Poona Maráthás raided as far as the Punjab, and drew down upon them the wrath of Ahmad Sháh Duráni, the Afghán, who had already wrested that Province from Delhi. At the battle of Pánípat in 1761, as we have seen, the Maráthás were overthrown by the combined Muhammadan forces of the Afgháns and of the northern Provinces which still nominally remained to the Mughal Empire.

The Five Maráthá Houses.—The fourth Peshwá, Madhu Ráo, succeeded to the Maráthá sovereignty in this moment of ruin (1761). The Hindu Confederacy seemed doomed to destruction, alike by internal dissensions and by the superior force of the Afghán arms. As early as 1742, the Poona and Nágpur branches had taken the field against each other, in their quarrels over the plunder of Bengal. Before 1761, two other branches, under Holkar and Sindhia, held independent sway in the old Mughal Province of Málwá and the neighbouring tracts, now divided between the States of Indore and Gwalior. At Pánípat, Holkar, the head of the Indore branch, deserted the line of battle the moment he saw the tide turn, and his treachery rendered the Maráthá rout complete. The Peshwá was now little more than the nominal head of the five great Maráthá houses. These five Maráthá houses or dynasties had separate territories and armies. Their five capitals were at Poona, the seat of the Peshwás; at Nágpur, the capital of the Bhonslas, in the Central Provinces; at Gwalior, the residence of Sindhia; at Indore, the capital of Holkar; and at Baroda, the seat of the rising power of the Gáekwárs. Madhu Ráo, the fourth Peshwá, just managed to hold his own against the Muhammadan princes of Haidarábád and Mysore, and against the Bhonsla branch of the Maráthás in Berar. His younger brother, Náráyan Ráo, succeeded him as fifth Peshwá in 1772, but was quickly assassinated. The Peshwás were the great Maráthá power in Southern India; the other four or northern Maráthá branches were Sindhia and Holkar, the Bhonslas of Nágpur, and the Gáekwárs of Baroda. We shall briefly relate the fortunes of these four northern branches.

Sindhia and Holkar.—The Peshwá's power at Poona began to grow weak, as that of his nominal masters, the royal descendants of Sivají, had faded out of sight. The Peshwás came of a high Bráhman lineage, while the actual fighting force of the Maráthás consisted of low-caste Hindus. It thus happened that each Maráthá general who rose to independent territorial sway was inferior in caste to, although possessed of more real power, than the Peshwá, the titular head of the confederacy. Of the two great northern houses, Holkar was descended from a shepherd, and Sindhia from a slipper-bearer. The Maráthás under Holkar and Sindhia lay quiet for a time after their crushing disaster at Pánípat in 1761. But within ten years of that fatal field they had established themselves throughout Málwá, and proceeded to invade the Rájput, Ját, and Rohillá Provinces, from the Punjab on the west to Oudh in the east (1761–1771). In 1765, the titular emperor, Sháh Alam, had sunk into a British pensioner, after his defeat by Sir Hector Munro at Baxár in 1764. In 1771, the emperor gave himself over to the Maráthás. Sindhia and Holkar nominally maintained him on his throne at Delhi, but held him a virtual prisoner till 1803–4, when they were overthrown by our second Maráthá war. The dynasties of both Sindhia and Holkar have preserved to the present day their rule over the most fertile portion of Málwá.

The Bhonslas of Nágpur, 1751–1853.—The third of the northern Maráthá houses, namely the Bhonslas of Berar and the Central Provinces, occupied themselves with raids to the east. Operating from their base at Nágpur, they had (as we have seen) extorted in 1751 the *chauth*, or 'quarter revenue' of Lower Bengal, together with the sovereignty of Orissa. The acquisition of Lower Bengal by the British (1756–1765) put a stop to their raids. In 1803, a division of our army drove the Bhonsla Maráthás out of Orissa. In 1817, their power was finally broken by our last Maráthá war. Their headquarter territories, now forming the Central Provinces, were administered under the guidance of British Residents from 1817 to 1853. On the death of the last Raghují Bhonsla without a direct male heir, in 1853, the Nágpur Maráthá territories (now known as the Central Provinces), lapsed to the British.

The Gáekwárs of Baroda.—The fourth of the northern Maráthá houses, namely, Baroda, extended its power throughout Gujarát, on the north-western coast of Bombay, and the adjacent peninsula of Káthiáwár. The scattered but wealthy dominions known as the territories of the Gáekwár were thus formed. Since our last Maráthá war, in 1817, Baroda has been ruled by the Gáekwárs, with the help of an English Resident. In 1874, the reigning Gáekwár was tried by a High Commission, composed of three European and three Native members, on the charge of attempting to poison the Resident, and deposed. But the British Government refrained from annexing the State, and raised a descendant of the founder of the family from obscure poverty to the State cushion.

First Maráthá War with the British, 1779–1781.—While the four northern houses of the Maráthás were pursuing their separate careers, the Peshwá's power was being broken to pieces by family intrigues. The sixth Peshwá, Madhu Ráo Náráyan, was born after his father's death; and during his short life of twenty-one years the power remained in the hands of his minister, Náná Farnavis. Raghubá, the uncle of the late Peshwá, disputed the birth of the posthumous child (Madhu Ráo), and claimed for himself the office of Peshwá. The infant's guardian, Náná Farnavis, having called in the French, the British at Bombay sided with Raghubá. These alliances brought on the first Maráthá war (1779–1781), ending with the treaty of Salbái (1782). That treaty ceded the islands of Salsette and Elephanta near Bombay, together with two others to the British, secured to Raghubá a handsome pension, and confirmed the child-Peshwá in his sovereignty. But the young Peshwá only reached manhood to commit suicide at the age of twenty-one.

Second Maráthá War, 1802–1804.—His cousin, Bájí Ráo II., succeeded him in 1795 as the seventh and last Peshwá. The northern Maráthá house of Holkar now took the lead among the Maráthás, and forced the Peshwá to seek protection from the English. By the treaty of Bassein in 1802, Bájí Ráo the Peshwá agreed to receive a British force to maintain him in his dominions. The northern Maráthá houses combined to break down this treaty. The second Maráthá war followed (1802–1804). General Wellesley (afterwards Duke of Wellington) crushed the forces of the Sindhia and Nágpur branches of the Maráthás on the fields of Assaye and Argáum in the south, while Lord Lake disposed of the Maráthá armies at Laswári and Delhi in the north. In 1804, Holkar was completely defeated at Díg. These campaigns led to large cessions of territory to the British, to the final overthrow of French influence in India, and to the restoration of the titular Delhi Emperor under the protection of the English.

Last Maráthá War, 1817-1818.—In 1817-1818, the Peshwá, Holkar, and the Bhonsla at Nágpur, took up arms, each on his own account, against the British, and were defeated in detail. That war broke the Maráthá power for ever. The Peshwá, Bájí Ráo, surrendered himself to the British, and his territories were annexed to our Bombay Presidency. The Peshwá remained a British pensioner at Bithúr, near Cawnpur in Northern India, on a magnificent allowance, till his death. His adopted son grew up into the infamous Náná Sáhib of the Mutiny of 1857, when the last relic of the Peshwás disappeared from the eyes of men.

Materials for Reference.

Among the original authorities easily available to the English reader for Maráthá history may be mentioned:—(1) James Grant Duff's *History of the Maráthás*, 3 vols. (Bombay reprint, 1863); (2) Edward Scott Waring's *History of the Maráthás* (quarto, 1810); (3) Major William Thorn's *Memoir of the War in India conducted by General Lord Lake* (quarto, 1818); (4) Sidney J. Owen's *Selections from the Despatches of the Marquess Wellesley* (1877); (5) *Selections from the Indian Despatches of the Duke of Wellington* (1880); (6) Henry T. Prinsep's *Narrative of Political and Military Transactions of British India under the Marquess of Hastings* (quarto, 1820). The very brief notice of the Maráthás which the scope of the present work allows, precludes an exhaustive use of these storehouses. Keene's volume on *Mádhava Ráo Sindhia* in the Rulers of India Series gives an interesting account of the chief Maráthá leader in the second half of the eighteenth century. Interesting illustrations of Maráthá history are to be found in Acworth's *Ballads of the Maráthás*. The leading incidents of Maráthá history are described under the heading of their respective localities in the *Imperial Gazetteer of India*.

CHAPTER XII.

Early European Settlements, 1500–1700.

Europe and India before 1500 A.D.—The Muhammadan invaders of India had entered from the north-west. The Christian conquerors of India came by the sea from the south. From the time of Alexander the Great (327 B.C.) to that of Vasco da Gama (1498 A.D.), Europe held little direct intercourse with the East. An occasional traveller brought back stories of powerful kingdoms and of untold wealth. Commerce never ceased entirely. It was carried across Western Asia; or through Egypt and the Red Sea, and finally fell to the Italian cities on the Mediterranean which traded with the Asiatic ports of the Levant. In 1492, Christopher Columbus sailed westwards under the Spanish flag to seek India beyond the Atlantic, bearing with him a letter to the great Khán of Tartary. He found America instead.

Vasco da Gama, 1498.—An expedition under Vasco da Gama started from Lisbon five years later, in the opposite or eastern direction. It doubled the Cape of Good Hope, and cast anchor off the city of Calicut on the south-western coast of India on the 20th May 1498, after a voyage of nearly eleven months. From the first, Da Gama encountered hostility from the Moors, or rather Arabs, who monopolized the sea-borne trade of the Malabar coast; but he seems to have found favour with the Zamorin, or Hindu Rájá of Calicut. After staying nearly six months on the Malabar coast, he returned to Europe, bearing with him the following letter from the Zamorin to the King of Portugal:—'Vasco da Gama, a nobleman of your household, has visited my kingdom, and has given me great pleasure. In my kingdom there is abundance of cinnamon, cloves, ginger, pepper, and precious stones. What I seek from thy country is gold, silver, coral, and scarlet.'

Early Portuguese Governors.—In 1502, the King of Portugal obtained from Pope Alexander VI. a bull constituting him 'Lord of the Navigation, Conquests, and Trade of Ethiopia, Arabia, Persia, and India.' In that year Vasco da Gama set sail a second time for India, with a fleet numbering twenty vessels. He formed an alliance with the Rájás of Cochin and Cannanore against the Zamorin of Calicut, and bombarded the latter in his capital. In 1503, the great Affonso de Albuquerque sailed to the East in command of one of three expeditions from Portugal. In 1505, a large fleet of twenty-two sail and fifteen hundred men was sent under Francisco de Almeida, the first Portuguese Viceroy of India. In 1509, Albuquerque succeeded him as Governor, and widely extended the area of Portuguese influence. Having failed in an attack upon Calicut, Albuquerque seized Goa in 1510, which has since remained the capital of Portuguese India. Then, sailing round Ceylon, he captured Malacca, the key to the navigation of the Indian Archipelago, and opened up trade with Siam and the Spice Islands. Lastly, Albuquerque sailed back westwards, and, after penetrating into the Persian Gulf and the Red Sea, returned to Goa, only to die, in 1515. In 1524, Vasco da Gama came out to the East for the third time, and died at Cochin in the same year.

Cruelties of the Portuguese in India.—For exactly a century, from 1500 to 1600, the Portuguese enjoyed a monopoly of Oriental trade. But the Portuguese had neither the political strength nor the personal character necessary to found an empire in India. Their national temper had been formed in their contest with the Moors at home. They were not traders, but knights-errant and crusaders, who looked on every pagan as an enemy of Portugal and of Christ. Only those who have read the contemporary narratives of their conquests, can realize the superstition and the cruelty with which their history in the Indies is stained. Albuquerque alone endeavoured to win the goodwill of the natives, and to win the friendship of the Hindu princes. In such veneration was his memory held, that the Hindus of Goa, and even the Muhammadans, were wont to repair to his tomb, and there to utter their complaints, as if in the presence of his spirit, and to call upon God to deliver them from the tyranny of his successors.

Downfall of the Portuguese in India.—In 1580, the Portuguese crown was united with that of Spain under Philip II. The interests of Portugal in Asia were henceforth subordinated to the European interests of Spain. In 1640, Portugal again became a separate kingdom. But in the meanwhile two hardier rivals, the Dutch and English, had appeared in the Eastern seas, and the Portuguese empire of the Indies was withering away as rapidly as it had sprung up.

The Portuguese Possessions in 1892.—The only possessions in India now remaining to the Portuguese are Goa, Damán, and Diu, all on the west coast, with an area of 1100 square miles, and a population of under 500,000 souls. There are also about 500 Portuguese in British India, besides a larger number of mixed descent. Over 30,000 of mingled blood are found in Bombay ('Portuguese' half-castes), and 20,000 in Bengal, chiefly in the neighbourhood of Dacca and Chittagong. The latter are known as Firinghis; and, excepting that they retain the Roman Catholic faith and European surnames, are scarcely to be distinguished, either by colour, language, or habits of life, from the natives among whom they live.

The Dutch in India.—The Dutch were the first European nation who broke through the Portuguese monopoly. During the 16th century, Bruges, Antwerp, and Amsterdam became the great emporia whence Indian produce, imported by the Portuguese, was distributed to Germany, and even to England. At first the Dutch, following in the track of the English, attempted to find their way to India by sailing round the north coasts of Europe and Asia. William Barents is honourably known as the leader of three of these Dutch arctic expeditions, in the last of which he perished. The first Dutchman to double the Cape of Good Hope was Cornelius Houtman, who reached Sumatra and Bantam in 1596. Forthwith private companies for trade with the East were formed in many parts of Holland or the United Provinces; but in 1602 they were all amalgamated by the States-General into 'The Dutch East India Company.' In 1619, the Dutch laid the foundation of the city of Batavia in Java, as the seat of the supreme government of their possessions in the East Indies. Their principal factory had previously been at Amboyna. At about the same time the Dutch discovered the coast of Australia, and in North America they founded the city of New Amsterdam or Manhattan, now New York.

Dutch Supremacy in the Eastern Seas.—During the 17th century, the Dutch maritime power was the first in the world. Their memorable massacre of the English at Amboyna, in 1623, forced the British Company to retire from the Eastern Archipelago to the continent of India, and thus led to the foundation of our Indian Empire. The long naval wars and bloody battles between the English and the Dutch in the Eastern seas, were not terminated until William of Orange united the two countries in 1689. In the Indian Archipelago the Dutch ruled for a time without a rival, and gradually expelled the Portuguese from almost all their territorial possessions. In 1635, they occupied Formosa; in 1640, they took Malacca—a blow from which the Portuguese never recovered; in 1647, they were trading at Sadras, on the South-eastern coast of India; in 1651, they founded a colony at the Cape of Good Hope, as a half-way station to the East; in 1652, they built their first Indian factory at Pálakollu, on the Madras coast; in 1658, they captured Jaffnapatam, the last stronghold of the Portuguese in Ceylon. In 1664, they wrested from the Portuguese all the earlier Portuguese settlements on the pepper-bearing coast of Malabar; and in 1669, they expelled the Portuguese from St. Thomé and from Macassar.

Short-sighted Policy of the Dutch.—The fall of the Dutch colonial empire resulted from its short-sighted commercial policy. It was deliberately based upon a strict monopoly of the trade in spices, and remained from first to last destitute of sound economical principles. Like the Phœnicians of old, the Dutch stopped short of no acts of cruelty towards their rivals in commerce; but, unlike the Phœnicians, they failed to introduce their civilization among the natives with whom they came in contact. The knell of Dutch supremacy in India was sounded by Clive, when in 1758 he attacked the Dutch at Chinsurah both by land and water, and forced them to an ignominious capitulation. During the great French wars from 1793 to 1815, England wrested from Holland her Eastern colonies; but Java was restored in 1816, and Sumatra exchanged for Malacca in 1824. At the present time, the Dutch flag flies nowhere on the mainland of India. Quaint houses with Dutch tiles and ornaments in the now British towns of Chinsurah, Negapatam, Jaffnapatam, and at several petty ports on the Coromandel and Malabar coasts, together with the formal canals or water-channels in some of these old settlements, remind the traveller of scenes in the Netherlands.

Early English Adventurers, 1496–1596.—The earliest English attempts to reach India were made by the North-west or Arctic Sea. In 1496, Henry VII. granted letters patent to John Cabot and his three sons (one of whom was the famous Sebastian) to fit out two ships for the exploration of this North-western route. They failed, but discovered the island of Newfoundland, and sailed along the coast of America from Labrador to Virginia. In 1553, the ill-fated Sir Hugh Willoughby attempted to force a passage north-east, through the Arctic Sea along the north of Europe and Asia, the successful accomplishment of which has been reserved for a Swedish officer in our own day. Sir Hugh perished; but his second in command, Chancellor, reached a harbour on the White Sea, now Archangel. Many subsequent attempts were made to find a North-west passage from 1576 to 1616. They have left on our modern maps the imperishable names of Frobisher, Davis, Hudson, and Baffin. Meanwhile, in 1577, Sir Francis Drake had sailed round the globe, and on his way home had touched at Ternate, one of the Moluccas, the king of which island agreed to supply the English nation with all the cloves it produced. The first modern Englishman known to have visited India was Thomas Stephens, rector of the Jesuits' College in Salsette, in 1579. In 1583, three English merchants—Ralph Fitch, James Newberry, and Leedes—went out to India overland as mercantile adventurers. The jealous Portuguese threw them into prison at

Ormuz, and again at Goa. At length Newberry settled down as a shopkeeper at Goa; Leedes entered the service of the Mughal Emperor; and Fitch, after lengthened wanderings in Ceylon, Bengal, Pegu, Siam, Malacca, and other parts of the East Indies, returned to England. The defeat of the 'Invincible Armada,' sent by the united kingdom of Spain and Portugal against the English in 1588, gave a fresh stimulus to our maritime enterprise; and the successful voyage of Cornelius Houtman in 1596 showed the way round the Cape of Good Hope into waters hitherto monopolized by the Portuguese.

English East India Companies.—The English East India Company had its origin in the commercial rivalry between London and Amsterdam. In 1599, the Dutch raised the price of pepper against the English from 3*s*. to 6*s*. and 8*s*. per pound. The merchants of London held a meeting on the 22nd September 1599, at Founders' Hall, with the Lord Mayor in the chair, and agreed to form an association for the purposes of trading directly with India. Queen Elizabeth also sent Sir John Mildenhall by way of Constantinople to the Mughal Emperor to apply for privileges for an English company. On the 31st December 1600, the English East India Company was incorporated by royal charter, under the title of 'The Governor and Company of Merchants of London trading to the East Indies.' The original Company had only 125 shareholders, and a capital of £70,000, which was raised to £400,000 in 1612, when voyages were first undertaken on the joint-stock account. Courten's Association, known as 'The Assada Merchants,' from a factory subsequently founded by it in Madagascar, was established in 1635, but, after a period of keen rivalry, it combined with the London Company in 1650. In 1655, the 'Company of Merchant Adventurers' obtained a charter from Cromwell to trade with India, but united with the original Company two years later. A more formidable rival subsequently appeared in the English Company, or 'General Society trading to the East Indies,' which was incorporated under powerful patronage in 1698, with a capital of two millions sterling. However, a compromise was effected through the arbitration of Lord Godolphin, and the 'London' and the 'English' Companies were finally amalgamated in 1709, under the style of 'The United Company of Merchants of England trading to the East Indies.'

The First Voyages of the London Company.—The Indian Archipelago was the destination of the first English ships that penetrated into Eastern seas. Captain Lancaster, in the pioneer voyage of the Company (1602), established commercial relations with the King of Achín, and founded a factory, or 'house of trade,' at Bantam. In the following years, cargoes of pepper and rich spices were brought back from Sumatra and the Moluccas, Banda, Amboyna, and Bantam. The jealous Portuguese were still supreme along the western coast of India, and resisted English intrusion by force of arms. In 1611, Sir Henry Middleton resolutely took on board a cargo of Indian goods at Cambay in the teeth of Portuguese opposition. In 1615 occurred the famous sea-fight of Swally, near the mouth of the Tápti river off the Bombay coast, in which Captain Best four times beat back an overwhelming force of Portuguese ships, and for ever inspired the minds of the natives with respect for English bravery. In the same year, Sir Thomas Roe, sent out by King James I. as ambassador to the court of the Great Mughal (the Emperor Jahángír), succeeded in obtaining favourable concessions for English trade.

The Massacre of Amboyna, 1623.—The Dutch in the Spice Islands proved more dangerous rivals to the English than the Portuguese in India had done. The massacre of Amboyna, which made so deep an impression on the English mind, marked the climax of the Dutch hatred to us in the Eastern seas. After long and bitter recriminations, the Dutch seized our Captain Towerson at Amboyna, with 9 Englishmen, 9 Japanese, and 1 Portuguese sailor, in February 1623. They tortured the prisoners at their trial, and found them guilty of a conspiracy to surprise the garrison. The victims were executed in the heat of passion, and their torture and judicial murder led to an outburst of indignation in England. Ultimately, commissioners were appointed to adjust the claims of the Dutch and English nations; and the Dutch had to pay a sum of £3615 as satisfaction to the heirs of the servants of the English Company who had suffered. But from that time the Dutch remained masters of Banda and the Spice Islands. They monopolized the whole trade of the Indian Archipelago, until the great naval wars which commenced in 1793.

Early English Settlements in Madras.—The result of the massacre of Amboyna was to drive the English from the Spice Islands to the mainland of India. Their first settlements were on the Coromandel coast. An English agency had been established at Masulipatam as early as 1611; and this was now (1632) raised to the rank of a factory under the authority of a *farmán*, known as 'the golden *farmán*,' from the Sultán of Golconda. A few years earlier (1626) an English factory had also been founded at Armagáon (now a ruined place in Nellore District), which mounted 12 guns, and employed 23 European agents. At last, in 1639, Mr. Francis Day, the Chief of Armagáon, bought from the Rájá of Chandragiri a more favourable site lower down the coast, called Madaraspatam or Chennapatam. Here he built Fort St. George, and became the founder of Madras. Madras was the first territorial possession of the Company in India. For some years it remained subordinate to the English factory at Bantam in Java, but in 1653 it was created an independent Presidency.

Early English Settlements in Bombay.—On the west coast of India, Surat was long the headquarters of English trade. The factory was established here in 1612–15, with agencies at Gogra, Ahmadábád, and Cambay, as the first-fruits of the naval victory over the Portuguese off Swally. At this time Surat was the principal port in the Mughal Empire, through which flowed all trade between Northern India and Europe. In 1661, the island of Bombay was ceded by Portugal to the British Crown, as part of the dowry of Catharine of Braganza, queen of Charles II.; but it was not delivered up by the Portuguese until 1665. In 1668, King Charles II. sold his rights over Bombay to the East India Company for an annual payment of £10. The city of Bombay was then a mere fishing village, dominated by an old Portuguese fort, and notorious even in the East for its unhealthiness. But it had the supreme advantage of being placed on an island, secure from the raids of

Maráthá horsemen. In 1663, the city of Surat, although not the English factory, had been pillaged by the Maráthá leader, Sivají. Accordingly, it was thought wiser to withdraw the seat of the Western Presidency from Surat to Bombay. This was ordered in 1685, and accomplished two years afterwards (1687).

Early English Settlements in Bengal.—The settlements in Bengal were later in time, and at first more precarious, than those in Madras or Bombay. Small agencies, offshoots from Surat, were opened at Ajmere, at Agra, and as far east as Patná, by 1620; but access was not gained to the Bengal seaboard until 1634. In that year a *farmán* was granted by the Mughal Emperor, allowing the Company to trade in Bengal. Their ships, however, were to resort only to Pipplí, in Orissa, a port now left far inland by the sea, and of which the very site has to be guessed. The factory at Húglí in Lower Bengal was established in 1640, and that at Balasor in Orissa in 1642. Three years later, in 1645, Mr. Gabriel Broughton, surgeon of the *Hopewell*, obtained from the Emperor Sháh Jahán exclusive privileges of trading for the Company in Bengal, as a reward for his professional services. In 1681, the English factories in Bengal were separated from Madras; and Mr. Hedges was appointed agent and governor of the Company's affairs in the Bay of Bengal, and of the subordinate factories at Kásimbázár, Patná, Balasor, Maldah, and Dacca. But the English had not yet acquired any territorial possessions in Bengal, as they had in Madras and Bombay. Their little settlements, planted in the midst of populous cities, were exposed to every outburst of hostility or caprice of the Native governors. In 1686, the Nawáb of Bengal, Shaistá Khán, issued orders confiscating all the English factories in Bengal. The merchants at Húglí, under their president, Job Charnock, retreated about 26 miles down the river Húglí to Sutánatí, then a village amid the swamps, now a northern quarter of Calcutta. Here they laid the foundations of the original Fort William; and in 1700 they purchased from Prince Azím, son of the Emperor Aurangzeb, the three villages of Sutánatí, Kalikata, and Govindpur, which were united to form the modern Calcutta.

The English Company embarks on Territorial Sway.—It was about this same time (1689) that the Company determined to build up its power in India by acquiring territorial possessions, so as to enable it to resist the oppression of the Mughals and Maráthás. With that view they passed the following resolution for the guidance of their servants in India:—'The increase of our revenue is the subject of our care, as much as our trade; 'tis that must maintain our force when twenty accidents may interrupt our trade; 'tis that must make us a nation in India.' With the same view, Sir John Child was appointed 'Governor-General and Admiral of India,' with full power to make peace or war, and to arrange for the safety of the Company's possessions.

Other 'East India Companies.'—The Portuguese at no time attempted to found a large mercantile company, but kept their Eastern trade as a royal monopoly. The first private company was the English, established in 1600. It was quickly followed by the Dutch, in 1602. The Dutch conquests, however, were made in the name of the State, and ranked as national colonies, not as private possessions. Next came the French, whose first East India Company was founded in 1604; the second, in 1611; the third, in 1615; the fourth (Richelieu's), in 1642; the fifth (Colbert's), in 1644. The sixth was formed by the union of the French East and West India, Senegal, and China Companies, under the name of 'The Company of the Indies,' in 1719. The exclusive privileges of this Company were, by the French King's decree, suspended in 1769; and the Company was abolished by the National Assembly in 1790. The first Danish East India Company was formed in 1612, and the second in 1670. The Danish settlements of Tranquebar and Serampur were both founded in 1616, and acquired by the English by purchase from Denmark in 1845. Other Danish settlements on the mainland of India were Porto Novo, with Eddova and Holcheri, on the Malabar coast. The Company started by the Scotch in 1695 may be regarded as having been still-born. The 'Royal Company of the Philippine Islands,' incorporated by the King of Spain in 1733, had little to do with the Indian continent. Of more importance was 'The Ostend

Company,' incorporated by the Austrian monarch Charles VI, in 1723, its factors being chiefly persons who had served the Dutch and English Companies. But the opposition of the European maritime powers forced the Court of Vienna in 1727 to suspend the Company's charter for seven years. The Ostend Company, after a precarious existence, prolonged by the desire of the Austrian Government to participate in the growing East India trade, became bankrupt in 1784. The last nations of Europe to engage in maritime trade with India were Sweden and Prussia. When the Ostend Company was suspended, a number of its servants were thrown out of employment. Mr. Henry Köning, of Stockholm, took advantage of the knowledge which these men had acquired of the East, and obtained a charter for the 'Swedish Company,' dated 13th June 1731. Its operations were, however, of little importance. King Frederick the Great of Prussia gave his patronage in 1750 and 1753 to two short-lived Prussian Companies trading to the East.

The Survival of the Fittest.—The Indian trade was thus a prize for which many of the European nations strove with each other during four hundred years; and dreams of an Indian Empire had allured some of the greatest European monarchs. The English East India Company outlived all its rivals. To the Portuguese and Spaniards, India seemed a second Peru where diadems might be torn from the brows of princes: another New World to plunder and to convert. To the Dutch, it formed a great market which afforded, however, little room for individual enterprise, as the profit from the India trade was a strictly guarded national monopoly. To the French, India was a theatre for lucrative intrigue, in which splendid reputations might be won; but reputations fatal in the end to their owners, and sterile of results to the nation. The methods of the English Company were less showy, but more sure. Its youth was passed under the stern self-restraints imposed by having to make a hazardous private enterprise pay. It laid in a store of knowledge of the country before it embarked on any scheme of conquest. At length, when the breaking up of the Mughal Empire compelled it to choose between being driven out of India or ruling over India, it firmly made up its mind. No sufferings, no disasters ever shook for a moment its resolution; nor did the British nation ever fail its East India Company in any crisis of peril.

MATERIALS FOR REFERENCE.

A chronological list of the most noteworthy of the mediæval travellers to India from the ninth to the sixteenth centuries is given in my *Indian Empire*, chapter xiv. Among authorities available to the English reader may be noted—(1) Sir George Birdwood's *Report on the Miscellaneous Old Records in the India Office*; (2) Peter Auber's *Analysis of the Constitution of the East India Company* and Bruce's *Annals of the Honourable East India Company*; (3) the Abbé Raynal's *History of the Settlements and Trade of the Europeans in the East and West Indies* (not always accurate); (4) Orme's *History of Military Transactions in Indostan* (a masterpiece of minute history); (5) Hamilton's *New Account of the East Indies*; (6) Colonel Malleson's admirable *History of the French in India*; (7) Mr. G. W. Forrest's valuable *Reports on the Government Records at Calcutta, Madras, and Bombay*; (8) Mr. Morse Stephens' *Albuquerque, and the Portuguese Settlements in India*, in the Rulers of India Series; (9) the articles on the various settlements in *The Imperial Gazetteer of India*; (10) the chapters in Mill's *History of British India*, which deal with this period, are fairly trustworthy. To this list must be added Sir W. W. Hunter's own *History of British India*, vols. 1 and 2 (1899, 1900).

CHAPTER XIII.

The Foundation of British Rule in India, 1746-1805.

THE object of this history is to give a concise survey of the Indian peoples. What English rule has done for those peoples may best be realized by comparing India under the Muhammadans, as shown in Chapters IX. and X., with India at the present day. Such a comparison lies beyond the scope of this work; and a brief narrative of events must here suffice.

CHRONOLOGY: CLIVE TO THE EARL OF MINTO.

BRITISH GOVERNORS AND GOVERNORS-GENERAL OF INDIA UNDER THE EAST INDIA COMPANY, 1758-1858.

GOVERNORS.

1758. Colonel (afterwards Lord) Clive.
1760. J. Z. Holwell (officiating).
1760. H. Vansittart.
1764. John Spencer (officiating).
1765. Lord Clive (second time).
1767. Harry Verelst.
1769. John Cartier.
1772. Warren Hastings.

GOVERNORS-GENERAL.

1774. Warren Hastings.
1785. Sir John Macpherson, Bart. (officiating).
1786. Earl (aft. Marquess) Cornwallis.
1793. Sir John Shore, Bart. (Lord Teignmouth).
1798. Sir Alured Clarke (officiating).
1798. Earl of Mornington (Marquess Wellesley).
1805. Marquess Cornwallis (second time).
1805. Sir George Barlow, Bart. (temporary).
1807. Lord (aft. Earl of) Minto.
1813. Earl of Moira (Marquess of Hastings).
1823. John Adam (officiating).
1823. Lord (aft. Earl) Amherst.
1828. Wm. Butterworth Bayley (officiating).
1828. Lord William Cavendish Bentinck.
1835. Sir Charles Metcalfe, afterwards Lord Metcalfe (temporary).
1836. Lord (aft. Earl of) Auckland.
1842. Lord (aft. Earl of) Ellenborough.
1844. Sir Henry (aft. Viscount) Hardinge.
1848. Earl (afterwards Marquess) of Dalhousie.
1856. Viscount (aft. Earl) Canning.

VICEROYS OF INDIA UNDER THE CROWN, 1858–1906.

1858. Earl Canning.
1862. Earl of Elgin.
1863. Sir Robert Napier, aft. Lord Napier of Magdala (officiating).
1863. Sir William Denison (officiating).
1864. Sir John Lawrence, Bart. (Lord Lawrence).
1869. Earl of Mayo.
1872. Sir John Strachey (officiating).
1872. Lord Napier of Merchistoun (officiating).
1872. Lord (aft. Earl of) Northbrook.
1876. Lord (aft. Earl of) Lytton.
1880. Marquess of Ripon.
1884. Earl of Dufferin (afterwards Marquess of Dufferin and Ava).
1888. Marquess of Lansdowne.
1894. Earl of Elgin.
1898. Lord Curzon of Kedleston.
1905. Earl of Minto.

The French and English in the South.—The political history of the British in India begins in the eighteenth century with the French wars in the Karnátik. It was at Arcot, in the Madras Presidency, that Clive's star first shone forth; and it was on the field of Wandiwash in the same Presidency that the French dream of an Indian Empire was for ever shattered. Fort St. George, or Madras, was, as we have seen, the first territorial possession of the English on the mainland of India, having been founded by Mr. Francis Day in 1639. The French settlement of Pondicherri, about 100 miles lower down the Coromandel coast, was established in 1674; and for many years the English and French traded side by side without rivalry or territorial ambition.

Southern India after 1707.—On the death of the Mughal emperor, Aurangzeb, in 1707, Southern India gradually became independent of Delhi. In the Deccan proper, the Nizám-ul Múlk founded a hereditary dynasty, with Haidarábád for its capital, which exercised a nominal authority over the entire south. The Karnátik, or the lowland tract between the central plateau and the Bay of Bengal, was ruled by a deputy of the Nizám, known as the Nawáb of Arcot, who in his turn asserted claims to hereditary sovereignty. Farther south, Trichinopoli was the capital of a Hindu Rájá; Tanjore formed another Hindu kingdom under a degenerate descendant of the Maráthá leader, Sivají. Inland, Mysore was gradually growing into a third Hindu State; while everywhere local chieftains, called *pálegárs* or *náyaks*, were in semi-independent possession of citadels or hill-forts. These represented the feudal chiefs or fief-holders of the ancient Hindu kingdom of Vijayanagar; and many of them had maintained a practical independence, subject to irregular payments of tribute, since the fall of that kingdom in 1565 (see *ante*, pp. 129, 130).

Our First War in the Karnátik, 1746–1748.—Such was the condition of affairs in Southern India when war broke out between the English and the French in Europe in 1743. Dupleix was at that time the French Governor of Pondicherri, and in 1744 Clive was a young civil servant or 'writer' at Madras. An English fleet appeared first on the Coromandel coast, but Dupleix by a judicious present induced the Nawáb of Arcot to interpose and forbid hostilities. In 1746, a French squadron arrived, under the command of La Bourdonnais. Madras surrendered to it almost without a blow; and the only settlement left to the English was Fort St. David, some miles south of Pondicherri, where Clive and a few other fugitives sought shelter. The Nawáb of Arcot, faithful to his impartial policy, marched with 10,000 men to drive the French out of Madras, but was defeated. In 1748, an English fleet arrived under Admiral Boscawen, and attempted the siege of Pondicherri, while a land force co-operated under Major Stringer Lawrence. The French repulsed all attacks; but the treaty of Aix-la-Chapelle, in the same year, restored Madras to the English.

Dupleix.—The first war with the French was merely an incident in the greater contest in Europe. The second war had its origin in Indian politics, while England and France were at peace. The easy success of the French arms had inspired Dupleix with the ambition of founding a French empire in India, under the shadow of the Muhammadan powers. Disputed successions among the reigning families both at Haidarábád and at Arcot gave him his opportunity. On both thrones Dupleix placed nominees of his own, and for a time he posed as the arbiter of the entire south. In boldness of conception, and in knowledge of Oriental diplomacy, Dupleix has probably had no equal. But he was no soldier, and he was destined to encounter in the field the 'heaven-born genius' of Clive. The English of Madras, under the instinct of self-preservation, had maintained the cause of another candidate to the throne of Arcot, in opposition to the nominee of Dupleix. Their candidate was Muhammad Alí, afterwards known in history as Wálá-jáh.

Clive.—The war which ensued between the French and English in Southern India has been exhaustively described by Orme. The one incident that stands out conspicuously is the capture and subsequent defence of Arcot by Clive in 1751. This heroic feat, even more than the battle of Plassey, spread the fame of English valour throughout India. Shortly afterwards, Clive returned to England in ill-health, but the war continued fitfully for many years. On the whole, the English influence predominated in the Karnátik or Madras coast, and their candidate, Muhammad Alí, maintained his position at Arcot. But, inland, the French were supreme in Southern India, and they were also able to seize the maritime tract called 'the Northern Circars.'

Battle of Wandiwash, 1760.—The final struggle did not take place until 1760. In that year, Colonel (afterwards Sir Eyre) Coote won the decisive victory of Wandiwash over the French general, Lally, and proceeded to invest Pondicherri, which was starved into capitulation in January 1761. A few months later, the hill fortress of Ginjí (Gingi) also surrendered. In the words of Orme, 'that day terminated the long hostilities between the two rival European powers in Coromandel, and left not a single ensign of the French nation avowed by the authority of its Government in any part of India.'

Native Rulers of Bengal, 1707-1756.—Meanwhile the narrative of British conquests shifts with Clive to Lower Bengal. At the time of Aurangzeb's death, in 1707, the Nawáb or Governor of Lower Bengal was Murshid Kulí Khán, known also in European history as Jáfar Khán. By birth a Bráhman, and brought up as a slave in Persia, he united the administrative ability of a Hindu to the fanaticism of a renegade. Hitherto the capital of Lower Bengal had been at Dacca, on the eastern frontier of the empire, whence the piratical attacks of the Portuguese and of the Arakanese or Maghs could be most easily checked. Murshid Kulí Khán transferred his residence to Murshidábád, in the immediate neighbourhood of Kásimbázár, which was then the river port of the Gangetic trade. The

English, the French, and the Dutch had each factories at Kásimbázár, as well as at Dacca, Patná, and Maldah. But Calcutta was the separate headquarters of the English, Chandarnagar of the French, and Chinsurah of the Dutch,—these three towns being situated not far from one another on the lower reaches of the Húglí, where the river was navigable for sea-going ships. Murshid Kulí Khán ruled over Lower Bengal prosperously for twenty-one years, and left his power to a son-in-law and a grandson. The hereditary succession was broken in 1740 by Alí Vardí Khán, a usurper, but the last of the great Nawábs of Bengal. In his days the Maráthá horsemen ravaged the country, and the inhabitants of Calcutta obtained permission in 1742 to erect an earthwork, known to the present day as the 'Maráthá Ditch.'

'Black Hole' of Calcutta.—Alí Vardí Khán died in 1756, and was succeeded by his grandson, Siráj-ud-daulá (Surajah Dowlah), a youth of only eighteen years, whose ungovernable temper led to a rupture with the English within two months after his accession. In pursuit of one of his own family who had escaped from his vengeance, he marched upon Calcutta with a large army. Many of the English fled down the river in their ships. The remainder surrendered after some resistance, and were thrust for the night into the 'Black Hole' or military jail of Fort William, a room about 18 feet square, with only two small windows barred with iron. It was our ordinary garrison prison in those times of cruel military discipline. But although the Nawáb does not seem to have been aware of the consequences, it meant death to a crowd of English men and women in the stifling heats of June. When the door of the prison was opened next morning, only 23 persons out of 146 remained alive.

Clive and Watson.—The news of this disaster fortunately found Clive back again at Madras, where also was a squadron of King's ships under Admiral Watson. Clive and Watson promptly sailed to the mouth of the Ganges with all the troops they could get together. Calcutta was recovered with little fighting; and the Nawáb consented to a peace, which restored to the English Company all their privileges, and gave them ample compensation for their losses.

Battle of Plassey, 1757.—It is possible that matters might have ended thus, if a fresh cause of hostilities had not suddenly arisen. War had just been declared between the English and French in Europe; and Clive, following the traditions of warfare in the Karnátik, captured the French settlement of Chandarnagar on the Húglí. Siráj-ud-daulá, enraged by this breach of neutrality within his dominions, sided with the French. But Clive, again acting upon the policy which he had learned from Dupleix in Southern India, provided himself with a rival candidate (Mír Jáfar) to the throne. Undaunted, he marched out to the grove of Plassey, about 70 miles north of Calcutta, at the head of 1000 Europeans and 2000 sepoys, with 8 pieces of artillery. The Bengal Viceroy's army numbered 35,000 foot and 15,000 horse, with 50 cannon. Clive is said to have fought in spite of his council of war. The truth is, he could scarcely avoid a battle. The Nawáb attacked with his whole artillery, at 6 a.m.; but Clive kept his men well under shelter, 'lodged in a large grove, surrounded with good mud-banks.' At noon the enemy drew off into their entrenched camp for dinner. Clive only hoped to make a 'successful attack at night.' Meanwhile, the enemy being probably undressed over their cooking-pots, he sprang upon one of their advanced posts, which had given him trouble, and stormed 'an angle of their camp.' Several of the Nawáb's chief officers fell. The Nawáb himself, dismayed by the unexpected confusion, fled on a camel; his troops dispersed in a panic; and Clive found he had won a great victory. Mír Jáfar's cavalry, which had hovered undecided during the battle, and had been repeatedly fired on by Clive, 'to make them keep their distance,' now joined our camp; and the road to Murshidábád, the Nawáb's capital, lay open.

Mír Jáfar, 1757.—The battle of Plassey was fought on June 23, 1757, an anniversary afterwards remembered when the Mutiny of 1857 was at its height. History has agreed to adopt this date as the beginning of the British Empire in the East. But the immediate results of the victory were comparatively small, and several years passed in hard fighting before even the Bengalis would admit the superiority of the British arms. For the moment, however, all opposition was at an end. Clive, again following in the steps of Dupleix, placed his nominee, Mír Jáfar, upon the viceregal throne at Murshidábád, as Nawáb of Bengal, and obtained for his appointment a *farmán* from the Mughal emperor of Delhi. Enormous sums were exacted from Mír Jáfar as the price of his elevation. The Company claimed ten million rupees as compensation for its losses. For the English, Hindu, and Armenian inhabitants of Calcutta were demanded, respectively, 5 million, 2 million, and 1 million rupees; for the naval squadron and the army, 2½ million rupees apiece. The members of the Council received the following amounts:—Mr. Drake, the Governor, and Colonel Clive, as second member of the Select Committee, 280,000 rupees each; and Mr. Becher, Mr. Watts, and Major Kilpatrick, 240,000 rupees each. Colonel Clive also received 200,000 rupees as Commander-in-Chief, and 1,600,000 rupees 'as a private donation.' Additional 'donations' were likewise made to the other Members of the Council, amounting in the case of Mr. Watts to 800,000 rupees. The whole claim of the British amounted to £2,697,750. The English still cherished extravagant ideas of Indian wealth. But no funds existed to satisfy their inordinate demands, and they had to be content with one-half the stipulated sums. Even of this reduced amount one-third had to be taken in jewels and plate, there being neither coin nor ingots left.

Grant of the Twenty-four Parganás, 1757.—At the same time the new Nawáb of Bengal made a grant to the Company of the *zamíndárí* or landholder's rights over an extensive tract of country round Calcutta, now known as the District of the Twenty-Four Parganás. The area of this tract was 882 square miles. In 1757, the Company obtained only the *zamíndárí* rights,—i. e. the right to collect the cultivator's rents, together with the revenue jurisdiction attached, subject to the obligation of paying over the assessed land-tax to the Nawáb, as the representative of the Delhi Emperor. But, in 1759, the land-tax also was granted by the emperor, the nominal suzerain of the Nawáb, in favour of Clive, who thus became the landlord of his own masters, the Company. This military fief, or Clive's *jágír*, as it was called, subsequently became a matter of inquiry in England. Lord Clive's claims to the property as feudal suzerain over the Company were contested by it in 1764. But finally in 1765, when he returned to Bengal, a new deed was issued, confirming the unconditional *jágír* to Lord Clive for ten years, with reversion afterwards to the Company in perpetuity. This deed, having received the Delhi emperor's sanction on the 12th August, 1765, gave absolute validity to the original *jágír* grant in favour of Lord Clive. It transferred eventually to the Company the Twenty-four Parganás as a perpetual property, based upon a *jágír* grant. The annual sum of Rs. 222,958, the amount at which the land-rent was assessed when first made over to the Company in 1757, was paid to Lord Clive from 1765 until his death in 1774, when the whole proprietary right reverted to the Company.

Clive, First Governor of Bengal, 1758.—In 1758, Clive was appointed by the Court of Directors the first Governor of all the Company's settlements in Bengal. Two powers threatened hostilities. On the north-west, the Sháhzáda or imperial prince, afterwards the Emperor Sháh Alam, with a mixed army of Afgháns and Maráthás, and supported by the Nawáb Wazír of Oudh, was advancing his own claims to the Province of Bengal. In the south, the influence of the French under Lally and Bussy was overshadowing the British at Madras. The name of Clive exercised a decisive effect in both directions. Our Nawáb of Bengal, Mír Jáfar, was anxious to buy off the Sháhzáda, who had already invested Patná. But Clive marched in person to the rescue, with an army of only 450 Europeans and 2500 sepoys, and the Mughal army dispersed without striking a blow. In the same year, Clive despatched a force southwards under Colonel Forde, which recaptured Masulipatam on the Madras coast from the French, and permanently established British influence in the Northern Circars, and at the Nizám's court of Haidarábád in Southern India. Clive next attacked the Dutch, the only other European nation who might yet prove a rival to the English. He defeated them both by land and water; and their settlement at Chinsurah existed thenceforth only on sufferance.

Mismanagement, 1760–1764.—From 1760 to 1765, Clive was in England. He had left no system of government in Bengal, but merely the tradition that unlimited sums of money might be extracted from the natives by the terror of the English name. In 1761, it was found expedient and profitable to dethrone Mír Jáfar, our Nawáb of Murshidábád, and to substitute his son-in-law, Mír Kásim, in his place. On this occasion, besides private donations, the English received a grant of the three Districts of Bardwán, Midnapur, and Chittagong, estimated to yield a net revenue of half a million sterling a year.

Revolt of Mír Kásim, 1763.—But the freshly appointed Nawáb of Bengal, Mír Kásim, soon began to show a will of his own, and to cherish dreams of independence. He retired from Murshidábád to Monghyr, a strong position on the Ganges which commanded the line of communication with the north-west. There he proceeded to organize an army, drilled and equipped after European models, and to carry on intrigues with the Nawáb Wazír of Oudh. He was resolved to try his strength with the English, and he found a good pretext. The Company's servants claimed the privilege of carrying on their private trade throughout Bengal, free from the Nawáb's inland imposts. The assertion of this claim caused affrays between the customs officers of the Nawáb and the native traders, who, whether truly or not, represented that they were acting on behalf of the servants of the Company. The Nawáb alleged that his civil authority was everywhere set at nought. The majority of the Council at Calcutta would not listen to his complaints. The Governor, Mr. Vansittart, and Warren Hastings, then a junior member of Council, attempted to effect some compromise. But the controversy had become too hot. The Nawáb's officers fired upon an English boat, and a general rising against the English took place. Two thousand of our sepoys were cut to pieces at Patná; about 200 Englishmen, who there and in other various parts of Bengal fell into the hands of the Muhammadans, were massacred.

Re-conquest of Bengal, 1764.—But as soon as regular warfare commenced, Mír Kásim met with no more successes. His trained regiments were defeated in two pitched battles by Major Adams, at Gheriá and at Udhunálá; and he himself took refuge with the Nawáb Wazír of Oudh, who refused to deliver him up to us. This led to a prolongation of the war. Sháh Alam, who had now succeeded his father as emperor, and Shujá-ud-daulá, the Nawáb Wazír of Oudh, united their forces, and threatened Patná, which the English had recovered. A more formidable danger appeared in the English camp, in the form of the first sepoy mutiny. It was quelled by Major (afterwards Sir Hector) Munro, who ordered twenty-four of the ringleaders to be blown from guns, an old Mughal punishment. In 1764, Major Munro won the decisive battle of Baxár, which laid Oudh at the feet of the conquerors, and brought the Mughal Emperor, Sháh Alam, as a suppliant to the English camp. The old deposed Nawáb of Bengal, Mír Jáfar, was brought forth from his retirement, and was again appointed Nawáb in place of Mír Kásim, who had risen against us. The English Council in Calcutta had thus twice found the profitable opportunity which they loved, of creating a new Nawáb of Bengal, and of receiving the donations and large sums of money distributed to them by each of the Nawábs on his accession.

Clive's Second Governorship, 1765–1767.—But, in 1765, Clive (now Baron Clive of Plassey in the peerage of Ireland) arrived at Calcutta, as Governor of Bengal for the second time. Two landmarks stand out in his policy. First, he sought the substance, although not the name, of territorial power, under the fiction of a grant from the Mughal Emperor. Second, he desired to purify the Company's service, by prohibiting illicit gains, and guaranteeing a reasonable salary from honest sources. In neither respect were his plans carried out by his immediate successors. But our efforts at good government in India date from this second governorship of Clive in 1765, as our military supremacy had dated from his victory at Plassey in 1757.

Grant of the Díwání of Bengal, 1765.—Clive advanced rapidly up from Calcutta to Allahábád, and there settled in person the fate of nearly the northern half of India. Oudh was given back to the Nawáb Wazír, on condition of his paying half a million sterling towards the expenses of the war. The Provinces of Allahábád and Kora, lying between the Ganges and the Jumna, were handed over to the Emperor Sháh Alam, who in his turn granted to the English Company the *díwání* or fiscal administration of [Lower] Bengal, Behar, and Orissa, and also the territorial jurisdiction of the Northern Circars. A puppet Nawáb was still maintained at Murshidábád, who received an annual allowance from us of £600,000. Half that amount, or about £300,000, we paid to the emperor as tribute from Bengal, Behar, and Orissa. Thus was constituted the dual system of government, by which the English received all the revenues of Bengal, Behar, and Orissa, and undertook to maintain the army; while the criminal jurisdiction was vested in the Nawáb. In Indian phraseology, the Company was *díwán*, and the Nawáb was *nizám*. The actual collection of the revenues still remained for seven years in the hands of native officials (1765–1772).

Clive's Reorganization of the Bengal Service, 1766.—Clive's other great task was the reorganization of the Company's service. All the officers, civil and military alike, were tainted with the common corruption. Their legal salaries were paltry, and quite insufficient for a livelihood. But they had been permitted to augment them, sometimes a hundredfold, by means of private trade and by gifts from the Native powers. Despite the united resistance of the civil servants, and an actual mutiny of two hundred military officers, Clive carried through his reforms. Private trade and the receipt of presents were prohibited for the future, while a fair increase of pay was provided out of the monopoly of salt.

Dual System of Administration, 1767–1772.—Lord Clive quitted India for the third and last time in 1767. Between that date and the governorship of Warren Hastings in 1772, little of importance occurred in Bengal, beyond the terrible famine of 1770, which is officially reported to have swept away one-third of the inhabitants. The dual system of government established in 1765 by Clive had proved a failure. The English were the real rulers, but the administration of the districts was still carried on by native officials. There was thus a divided responsibility, and when any disaster occurred it was impossible to find out who was really to blame. Even the distant Court of Directors in England discerned that a complete change had become necessary in the government of Bengal. Warren Hastings, a tried servant of the company, distinguished alike for intelligence, for probity, and for knowledge of Oriental manners, was nominated Governor by the Court of Directors, with express instructions to carry out a predetermined series of reforms. In their own words, the Court had resolved to 'stand forth as *díwán*, and to take upon themselves, by the agency of their own servants, the entire care and administration of the revenues.' In the execution of this plan, Hastings removed the exchequer from Murshidábád to Calcutta, and appointed European officers, under the now familiar title of Collectors, to superintend the collections and preside in the revenue courts.

Warren Hastings, 1772–1785.—Clive had laid the territorial foundations of the British Empire in Bengal. Hastings may be said to have created a British administration for that empire. The wars forced on him by Native powers in India, the clamours of his masters in England for money, and the virulence of Sir Philip Francis with a faction of his colleagues at the Council table in Calcutta, retarded the completion of his schemes. But the manuscript records disclose the patient statesmanship and indomitable industry which he brought to bear upon them. From 1765 to 1772, Clive's dual system of government, by corrupt Native underlings and rapacious English chiefs, had prevailed. Thirteen years were now spent by Warren Hastings in experimental efforts at rural administration by means of English officials (1772–1785). The completion of the edifice was left to his successor. But Hastings was the administrative organizer, as Clive had been the territorial founder, of our Indian Empire.

Hastings' Work in India.—Hastings rested his claims as an Indian ruler on his administrative work. He reorganized the Indian service, reformed every branch of the revenue collections, created courts of justice and laid the basis of a police. But history remembers his name, not for his improvements in the internal administration, but for his bold foreign policy in dealing with the Native States. From 1772 to 1774, he was Governor of Bengal; from the latter date to 1785, he was the first Governor-General of India, presiding over a Council nominated, like himself, under a statute of Parliament known as the Regulating Act (1773). In his domestic policy he was greatly hampered by the opposition of his colleague in council, Sir Philip Francis, whom he ultimately wounded in a duel. But in his external relations with Oudh, with the Maráthás and with

Haidar Alí, Hastings was generally, although not always, able to compel assent to his views.

Hastings' Policy to Native Rulers.—His relations with the Native powers, like his domestic policy, formed a well-considered scheme. Hastings had to find money for the Court of Directors in England, whose thirst for the wealth of India was not less keen, although more decorous, than that of their servants in Bengal. He had also to protect the Company's territory from the Native powers, which, if he had not destroyed them, would have annihilated him. Beyond the Bengal frontier a group of Muhammadan viceroys or governors of the old Mughal Empire had established independent States, the most important of which was Oudh. Beyond this group of Muhammadan States, the Maráthás were practically the masters of Northern India, and held the nominal Emperor of Delhi as a puppet under their control. The wise policy of Warren Hastings was to ally himself with the independent Muhammadan States, that is to say principally with Oudh, just beyond his own frontier. If he could make these Muhammadan States strong, he hoped that they would prevent the Maráthás from pouring down into Bengal. But these Muhammadan States were themselves so weak that this policy only obtained a partial success. In the end Warren Hastings found himself compelled to advance the British territories further up the Ganges, and practically to bring the Muhammadan States under his own control.

Hastings makes Bengal pay.—Warren Hastings had in the first place to make Bengal pay. This he could not do under Clive's dual system of administration. When he abolished that double system, he cut down the Nawáb of Bengal's allowance to one-half, and so saved about £160,000 a year. As a matter of fact, the titular Nawáb, being then a minor, had ceased to render even any nominal service for his enormous income. Clive had himself reduced the original £600,000 to £450,000 on the accession of a new Nawáb in 1766; and the grant was again cut down to £350,000 on a fresh succession in 1769. The allowance had practically been of a fluctuating and personal character. Its further reduction in 1772 in the case of the new child-Nawáb had, moreover, been expressly ordered by the Court of Directors six months before Hastings took office as Governor of Bengal.

Hastings stops the Tribute to Delhi, 1773.—Hastings' next financial stroke was to stop payment of the tribute of £300,000 to the Delhi emperor, which Clive had agreed to, in return for the grant of Bengal to the Company. But the emperor had now been seized by the Maráthás. Hastings held that His Majesty was no longer independent, and that to pay money to the emperor would practically be paying it to the Maráthás, who were our most formidable enemies, and whom he clearly saw that we should have to crush, unless we were willing to be crushed by them. Hastings therefore withheld the tribute of £300,000 from the puppet emperor, or rather from his Maráthá custodians.

Hastings sells Allahábád and Kora, 1773-1774.—On the partition of the Gangetic valley in 1765, Clive had also allotted the Provinces of Allahábád and Kora to the emperor Sháh Alam. The emperor, now in the hands of the Maráthás, made them over to his new masters. Warren Hastings held that by so doing His Majesty had forfeited his title to these Provinces. Hastings accordingly resold them to the Wazír of Oudh. By this measure he freed the Company from a military charge of nearly half a million sterling, and obtained a price of over half a million for the Company. The terms of sale included the loan of British troops to subdue the Rohillá Afgháns, who had seized and for some time kept hold of a tract on the north-western frontier of Oudh. The Rohillás were Muhammadans and foreigners; they had cruelly lorded it over the Hindu peasantry; and they were now intriguing with the Maráthás, our most dangerous foes. The Wazír of Oudh, supported by the British troops lent to him by Hastings, completely defeated the Rohillás. He compelled most of their fighting men to seek new homes on the other side of the Ganges river, in a neighbouring and equally fertile district, but one in which they could no longer open the northern frontier of Oudh to the Maráthás. By the foregoing series of measures, Hastings ceased to furnish the Maráthá custodians of the Delhi emperor with the Bengal tribute; he also strengthened our ally the Wazír of Oudh, and closed his frontier against Maráthá invasions; he bettered the Company's finances in Bengal by a million sterling a year in both its revenue and expenditure: say two millions *per annum.*

Fines on Chait Singh and on the Oudh Begam.—Hastings further improved the financial position of the Company by contributions from Chait Singh and from the Begam of Oudh. Chait Singh, the Rájá of Benares, had grown rich under British protection. He resisted the just demand of Warren Hastings to subsidize a military force, and entered into correspondence with the enemies of the British Government. This led to his arrest. He escaped, headed a rebellion, and was crushed. His estates were forfeited, but transferred to his nephew, subject to an increased tribute. The Begam, or Queen-Mother, of Oudh was charged with abetting Chait Singh, the Benares Rájá, in his rebellion. A heavy fine was laid upon her, which she resisted to the utmost. But after severe pressure on herself and the eunuchs of her household, over a million sterling was obtained.

Hastings' Trial in England, 1788–1795.—On his return to England, Warren Hastings was impeached by the House of Commons for these and other alleged acts of oppression. He was solemnly tried by the House of Lords, and the proceedings dragged themselves out for seven years (1788–1795). They form one of the most celebrated State trials in English history, and ended in a verdict of not guilty on all the charges. Meanwhile the cost of the defence had ruined Warren Hastings, and left him dependent upon the generosity of the Court of Directors,—a generosity which never failed.

First Maráthá War, 1779–1781.—The Bombay Government looked with envy on the territorial conquests of Madras and Bengal. It accordingly resolved to establish its supremacy at the Maráthá court of Poona. This ambition found scope, in 1775, by the treaty of Surat, by which Raghubá, one of the claimants to the headship of the Maráthás as Peshwá, agreed to cede Salsette and Bassein to the English, in consideration of being himself restored to Poona. The military operations that followed are known as the first Maráthá war (see p. 162). Warren Hastings, who in his capacity of Governor-General claimed a right of control over the decisions of the Bombay Government, strongly disapproved of the treaty of Surat. But when war actually broke out, he threw the whole force of the Bengal army into the scale. One of his favourite officers, Colonel Goddard, marched across the peninsula of India from sea to sea, and conquered the rich Province of Gujarát almost without a blow. Another, Captain Popham, stormed the rock-fortress of Gwalior, which was regarded as the key of Hindustán. These brilliant successes of the Bengal troops atoned for the disgrace of the convention of Wargaum in 1779, when the Maráthás had overpowered and dictated terms to our Bombay force; but the war was protracted until 1781. It was closed in 1782 by the treaty of Salbái, which practically restored the *status quo*. Raghubá, the English nominee for the Peshwáship, was set aside on a pension; Gujarát was restored to the Maráthás; and only Salsette, with Elephanta and two other small islands, was retained by the English.

War with Mysore, 1780–1784.—Meanwhile, Warren Hastings had to deal with a more dangerous enemy than even the Maráthá Confederacy. The reckless conduct of the Madras Government had roused the hostility of Haidar Alí of Mysore and also of the Nizám of the Deccan, the two strongest Musalmán powers in India. These attempted to draw the Maráthás into an alliance against the English. The diplomacy of Hastings won back the Nizám and the Maráthá Rájá of Nágpur; but the army of Haidar Alí fell like a thunderbolt upon the British possessions in the Karnátik. A strong detachment under Colonel Baillie was cut to pieces at Perambákam, and Haidar Alí's Mysore cavalry ravaged the country up to the walls of Madras. For the second time the Bengal army, stimulated by the energy of Hastings, saved the honour of the English name. He despatched Sir Eyre Coote, the victor of Wandiwash, to relieve Madras by sea, with all the men and money available, while Colonel Pearse marched south overland to overawe the Rájá of Berar and the Nizám. The war was hotly contested, for the aged Sir Eyre Coote had lost his energy, and the Mysore army was not only well-disciplined and equipped, but skilfully handled by Haidar and his son Tipú. Haidar died in

1782, and peace was finally concluded with Tipú in 1784, on the basis of a mutual restitution of all conquests. Warren Hastings retired from the Governor-Generalship in 1785.

Marquess Cornwallis, 1786-1793.—In 1786 arrived Lord Cornwallis, the first English nobleman who undertook the office of Governor-General of India. Between these two great names an interregnum of twenty months took place under Sir John Macpherson, a civil servant of the Company (Feb. 1785 to Sept. 1786). Lord Cornwallis twice held the high post of Governor-General. His first rule lasted from 1786 to 1793, and is celebrated for two events,—the introduction of the Permanent Settlement into Bengal, and the second Mysore war. If the foundations of the system of civil administration were laid by Hastings, the superstructure was raised by Corn wallis. He made over the higher criminal jurisdiction to European officers, and established the Nizámat Sadr Adálat, or Supreme Court of Criminal Judicature, at Calcutta; in the rural districts, he separated the functions of Revenue Collector and Civil Judge. The system thus organized in Bengal was afterwards extended to Madras and Bombay, when those Presidencies also grew into great territorial divisions of India.

The Revenue Settlement of Bengal.—But the achievement most familiarly associated with the name of Cornwallis is the Permanent Settlement of the land revenue of Bengal. Up to this time the revenue had been collected pretty much according to the old Mughal system. The *zamíndár's*, or Government farmers, whose office always tended to become hereditary, were recognized as having a right to collect the revenue from the actual cultivators. But no principle of assessment existed, and the amount actually realized varied greatly from year to year. Hastings tried to obtain experience, from a succession of five years' settlements, so as to furnish a standard rate for the future. Sir Philip Francis, the great rival of Hastings, advocated, on the other hand, a limitation of the State demand in perpetuity. The same view recommended itself to the authorities at home, partly because it would place their finances on a more stable basis, partly because it seemed to identify the *zamíndár* with the landlord of the English system of property. Accordingly,

Cornwallis took out with him in 1787 instructions to introduce a Permanent Settlement of the land-tax of Bengal.

The Permanent Settlement, 1793.—The process of assessment began in 1789, and terminated in 1791. No attempt was made to measure the fields or calculate the out-turn, as had been done by Akbar, and as is now done whenever settlements are made in the British Provinces. The amount to be paid in the future was fixed by reference to what had been paid in the past. At first the settlement was decennial, or 'for ten years,' but in 1793 it was declared permanent. The total assessment amounted to Sikka Rs. 26,800,989, or about three millions sterling for Bengal. Lord Cornwallis carried the scheme into execution; but the praise or blame, so far as details are concerned, belongs to Sir John Shore, afterwards Lord Teignmouth, a civil servant, whose knowledge of the country was unsurpassed in his time. Shore would have proceeded more cautiously than Cornwallis' preconceived idea of a proprietary body, and the Court of Directors' haste after fixity, permitted.

Second Mysore War, 1790–1792.—The second Mysore war of 1790–1792 is noteworthy on two accounts. Lord Cornwallis, the Governor-General, led the British army in person, with a pomp and a magnificence of supply which recalled the campaigns of Aurangzeb. The two great southern powers, the Nizám of the Deccan and the Maráthá Confederacy, co-operated as allies of the British. In the end, Tipú Sultán submitted when Lord Cornwallis had commenced to beleaguer his capital. He agreed to yield one-half of his dominions to be divided among the allies, and to pay three millions sterling towards the cost of the war. These conditions he fulfilled, but ever afterwards he burned to be revenged upon his English conquerors. Lord Cornwallis retired in 1793, and was succeeded by Sir John Shore, afterwards Lord Teignmouth.

Marquess Wellesley, 1798–1805.—The period of Sir John Shore's rule as Governor-General, from 1793 to 1798, was uneventful. In 1798, Lord Mornington, better known as the Marquess Wellesley, arrived in India, already inspired with imperial projects which were destined to change the map of the country. Lord Mornington was the friend and favourite of Pitt, from whom he is thought to have derived his far-reaching political vision, and his antipathy to the French name. From the first he laid down as his guiding principle, that the English must be the one paramount power in the Indian peninsula, and that Native princes could only retain the insignia of sovereignty by surrendering their political independence. The history of India since his time has been but the gradual development of this policy, which received its finishing touch when Queen Victoria was proclaimed Empress of India on the 1st of January 1877.

French Influence in India, 1798–1800.—To frustrate the possibility of a French invasion of India, led by Napoleon in person, was the immediate governing idea of Wellesley's foreign policy. France at this time, and for many years later, filled the place afterwards occupied by Russia in the minds of Indian statesmen. Nor was the danger so remote as might now be thought. French regiments guarded and overawed the Nizám of Haidarábád. The soldiers of Sindhia, the military head of the Maráthá Confederacy, was disciplined and led by French adventurers. Tipú Sultán of Mysore carried on a secret correspondence with the French Directory, allowed a tree of liberty to be planted in his dominions, and enrolled himself in a republican club as 'Citizen Tipú.' The islands of Mauritius and Bourbon afforded a convenient half-way rendezvous for French intrigue and for the assembling of a hostile expedition. Above all, Napoleon Buonaparte was then in Egypt, dreaming of the Indian conquests of Alexander the Great, and no man knew in what direction he might turn his hitherto unconquered legions.

India before Lord Wellesley, 1798.—Wellesley conceived the scheme of crushing for ever the French hopes in Asia, by placing himself at the head of a great Indian confederacy. In Lower Bengal, the sword of Clive and the policy of Warren Hastings had made the English paramount. Before the end of the century, our power was consolidated from the seaboard to Benares, high up the Gangetic valley. Beyond our frontier, the Nawáb Wazír of Oudh had agreed to pay a subsidy for the aid of British troops. This sum in 1797 amounted to £760,000 a year; and the Nawáb, being always in arrears, entered into negotiations for a cession of territory in lieu of a cash payment. In 1801, the treaty of Lucknow made over to the British the Doáb, or fertile tract between the Ganges and the Jumna, together with Rohilkhand. In Southern India, our possessions were chiefly confined, before Lord Wellesley, to the coast Districts of Madras and Bombay. Wellesley resolved to make the British supreme as far as Delhi in Northern India, and to compel the great powers of the south to enter into subordinate relations to the Company's government. The intrigues of the Native princes gave him his opportunity for carrying out this plan without a breach of faith. The time had arrived when the English must either become supreme in India, or be driven out of it. The Mughal Empire was completely broken up; and the sway had to pass either to the local Muhammadan governors of that empire, or to the Hindu Confederacy represented by the Maráthás, or to the British. Lord Wellesley determined that it should pass to the British.

Lord Wellesley's Policy.—His work in Northern India was at first easy. The treaty of Lucknow in 1801 made us territorial rulers as far as the heart of the present North-Western Provinces, and established our political influence in Oudh. Beyond those limits, the northern branches of the Maráthás practically held sway, with the puppet emperor in their hands. Lord Wellesley left them untouched for a few years, until the second Maráthá war (1802–1804) gave him an opportunity for dealing effectively with their nation as a whole. In Southern India, he saw that the Nizám at Haidarábád stood in need of his protection, and he converted him into a useful follower throughout the succeeding struggle. The other Muhammadan power of the south, Tipú Sultán of Mysore, could not be so easily handled. Lord Wellesley resolved to crush him, and had ample provocation for so doing. The third power of Southern India—namely, the Maráthá Confederacy—was so loosely organized, that Lord Wellesley seems at first to have hoped to live on terms with it. When several years of fitful alliance had convinced him that he had to choose between the supremacy of the Maráthás or of the British in Southern India, he did not hesitate to decide.

Treaty with the Nizám, 1798.—Lord Wellesley first

addressed himself to the weakest of the three southern powers, the Nizám of Haidarábád. Here he won a diplomatic success, which turned a possible rival into a subservient ally. The French battalions at Haidarábád were disbanded, and the Nizám bound himself by treaty not to take any European into his service without the consent of the English Government,—a clause since inserted in every engagement entered into with Native powers.

Third Mysore War, 1799.—Wellesley next turned the whole weight of his resources against Tipú, whom Cornwallis had defeated, but not subdued. Tipú's intrigues with the French were laid bare, and he was given an opportunity of adhering to the new subsidiary system. On his refusal, war was declared, and Wellesley came down in viceregal state to Madras to organize the expedition in person, and to watch over the course of events. One English army marched into Mysore from Madras, accompanied by a contingent from the Nizám. Another advanced from the western coast. Tipú, after a feeble resistance in the field, retired into Seringapatam, his capital, and, when it was stormed, died fighting bravely in the breach (1799). Since the battle of Plassey, no event so greatly impressed the Natives as the capture of Seringapatam, which won for General Harris an eventual peerage, and for Wellesley an Irish marquessate. In dealing with the territories of Tipú, Wellesley acted with moderation. The central portion, forming the old State of Mysore, was restored to an infant representative of the Hindu Rájás, whom Haidar Alí had dethroned; the rest of Tipú's dominion was partitioned between the Nizám, the Maráthás, and the English. At about the same time, the Karnátik, or the part of South-Eastern India ruled by the Nawáb of Arcot, and also the principality of Tanjore, were placed under direct British administration, thus constituting the Madras Presidency almost as it has existed to the present day. The sons of the slain Tipú were treated by Lord Wellesley with paternal tenderness. They received a magnificent allowance, with a semi-royal establishment, first at Vellore, and afterwards in Calcutta. The last of them, Prince Ghulám Muhammad, who survived to 1877, was long a well-known citizen of Calcutta, and an active Justice of the Peace.

The Maráthás in 1800.—The Maráthás had been the nominal allies of the English in both their wars with Tipú. But they had not rendered active assistance, nor were they secured to the English side as the Nizám had been. The Maráthá powers at this time were five in number. The recognized head of the confederacy was the Peshwá of Poona, who ruled the hill country of the Western Gháts, the cradle of the Maráthá race. The fertile Province of Gujarát was annually harried by the horsemen of the Gáekwár of Baroda. In Central India, two military leaders, Sindhia of Gwalior and Holkar of Indore, alternately held the pre-eminence. Towards the east, the Bhonsla Rájá of Nágpur reigned from Berar to the coast of Orissa. Wellesley laboured to bring these several Maráthá powers within the net of his subsidiary system. In 1802, the necessities of the Peshwá, who had been defeated by Holkar, and driven as a fugitive into British territory, induced him to sign the treaty of Bassein. By that he pledged himself to the British to hold communications with no other power, European or Native, and granted to us Districts for the maintenance of a subsidiary force. This greatly extended the English territorial influence in the Bombay Presidency. But it led to the second Maráthá war, as neither Sindhia nor the Rájá of Nágpur would tolerate the Peshwá's betrayal of the Maráthá independence.

Second Maráthá War, 1802-1804.—The campaigns which followed are perhaps the most glorious in the history of the British arms in India. The general plan, and the adequate provision of resources, were due to the Marquess Wellesley, as also the indomitable spirit which refused to admit of defeat. The armies were led by Sir Arthur Wellesley (afterwards Duke of Wellington) and General (afterwards Lord) Lake. Wellesley operated in the Deccan, where, in a few short months, he won the decisive victories of Assaye and Argáum, and captured Ahmadnagar. Lake's campaign in Hindustán was equally brilliant, although it has received less notice from historians. He won pitched battles at Alígarh and Laswári, and took the cities of Delhi and Agra. He scattered the French troops of Sindhia, and at the same time stood forward as the champion of the Mughal Emperor in his hereditary capital. Before the end of 1803, both Sindhia and the Bhonsla Rájá of Nágpur sued for peace. Sindhia ceded all claims to the territory north of the Jumna, and left the blind old Emperor Sháh Alam once more under British protection. The Bhonsla forfeited Orissa to the English, who had already occupied it with a flying column in 1803, and Berar to the Nizám, who gained fresh territory by every act of complaisance to the British Government. The freebooter Jaswant Ráo Holkar alone remained in the field, supporting his troops by raids through Málwá and Rájputána. The concluding years of Wellesley's rule were occupied with a series of operations against Holkar, which brought little credit on the British name. The disastrous retreat of Colonel Monson through Central India (1804) recalled memories of the convention of Wargaum, and of the destruction of Colonel Baillie's force by Haidar Alí. The repulse of Lake in person at the siege of Bhartpur (Bhurtpore) is memorable as an instance of a British army in India having to turn back with its object unaccomplished (1805). Bhartpur was not finally taken till 1827.

India after Lord Wellesley, 1805.—Lord Wellesley during his six years of office carried out almost every part of his territorial scheme. In Northern India, Lord Lake's campaigns brought the North-Western Provinces (the ancient *Madhya-desa*) under British rule, together with the custody of the puppet emperor. The new Districts were amalgamated with those previously acquired from the Nawáb Wazír of Oudh into the 'Ceded and Conquered Provinces.' This arrangement of Northern India remained till the Sikh wars of 1845 and 1849 gave us the Punjab. In South-Eastern India, we have seen that Lord Wellesley's conquests constituted the Madras Presidency almost as it exists at the present date. In South-Western India, the Peshwá was reduced to a vassal of the Company. But the territories now under the Governor of Bombay were not finally built up into their existing form until the last Maráthá war in 1818.

Materials for Reference.

James Mill's *History of British India* would be the standard work on this and the subsequent periods dealt with in the present *Brief History*, but for the unfortunate prejudices and misrepresentations which disfigure that able writer's work. H. H. Wilson's edition of Mill to some extent corrects those misrepresentations; but an accurate history of British India from the original sources has yet to be written. Among trustworthy works available to the English reader may again be noted Orme's *History of the Military Transactions of the British Nation in Indostan*, Cambridge's *War on the Coast of Coromandel*, Wilk's *Historical Sketches of the South of India*, Dirom's *Narrative of the Campaign in India, which terminated the War with Tippoo Sultan in* 1792, and Malleson's *History of the French in India*, together with his *Final Struggles of the French in India*, and his *Decisive Battles of India*. Also Anderson's *English in Western India*, which well deserves to be reprinted; Keene's *Moghul Empire from the Death of Aurangzeb to the Overthrow of the Maráthá Power*; Owen's *India on the Eve of the British Conquest*. Sir Charles Aitchison's *Treaties and Engagements relating to India* form the foundation of any accurate political history of the period. Sir John Strachey's *Hastings and the Rohilla War*, with Sir James Stephen's work on the trial of Nuncomar and Mr. Busteed's *Old Calcutta* are valuable monographs. Among the very numerous biographies of the statesmen and soldiers who laid the foundations of the British Rule, may be mentioned as most easily available to the English reader, the half-crown volumes on *Lord Clive*, *Dupleix*, *Warren Hastings*, the *Marquess Cornwallis*, and the *Marquess Wellesley*, in the 'Rulers of India' Series (Clarendon Press).

CHAPTER XIV

The Consolidation of British India.

Marquess Cornwallis again, 1805.—The financial strain caused by these great operations of Lord Wellesley had meanwhile exhausted the patience of the Court of Directors at home. In 1805, Lord Cornwallis was sent out as Governor-General a second time, with instructions to bring about peace at any price, while Holkar was still unsubdued, and with Sindhia threatening a fresh war. But Cornwallis was now an old man, and broken in health. Travelling up to the north-west during the rainy season, he sank and died at Gházípur, before he had been ten weeks in the country.

Sir George Barlow, 1805.—His immediate successor was Sir George Barlow, a civil servant of the Company, who as a *locum tenens* had no alternative but to carry out the commands of his employers. Under these orders he curtailed the area of British territory, and, in violation of engagements, abandoned the Rájput Chiefs to the cruel mercies of Holkar and Sindhia. During his administration, also, occurred the mutiny of the Madras sepoys at Vellore (1806), which, although promptly suppressed, sent a shock of insecurity through the empire. The feebly economical policy of this interregnum proved most disastrous. But fortunately the rule soon passed into firmer hands.

Earl of Minto, 1807–1813.—Lord Minto, Governor General from 1807 to 1813, consolidated the conquests which Wellesley had acquired. His only military exploits were the occupation of the island of Mauritius, and the conquest of Java by an expedition which he accompanied in person. The condition of Central India continued to be disturbed, but Lord Minto succeeded in preventing any violent outbreaks without himself having recourse to the sword. The Company had ordered him to follow a policy of non-intervention, and he managed to obey this instruction without injuring the prestige of the British name.

Under his auspices, the Indian Government opened relations with a new set of foreign powers, by sending embassies to the Punjab, to Afghánistán, and to Persia. The ambassadors had been trained in the school of Wellesley, and formed perhaps the most illustrious trio of 'politicals' whom the Indian services have produced. Metcalfe went as envoy to the Sikh Court of Ranjít Singh at Lahore; Elphinstone met the Sháh of Afghánistán at Peshawar; and Malcolm was despatched to Persia. It cannot be said that these missions were fruitful of permanent results; but they introduced the English to a new set of diplomatic relations, and widened the sphere of their influence. In 1813 the East India Company's Charter was renewed for twenty years, but its monopoly as a trading Company with India was abolished.

Lord Moira, 1814-1823.—The successor of Lord Minto was the Earl of Moira, better known by his later title as the Marquess of Hastings. The Marquess of Hastings completed Lord Wellesley's conquests in Central India, and left the Bombay Presidency almost as it stands at present. His long rule of nine years, from 1814 to 1823, was marked by two wars of the first magnitude, namely the campaigns against the Gúrkhas of Nepál, and the last Maráthá struggle.

Nepál War, 1814-1815.—The Gúrkhas, the present ruling race in Nepál, are Hindu immigrants, who claim a Rájput origin. The indigenous inhabitants, called Newars, belong to the Indo-Tibetan stock, and profess Buddhism. The sovereignty of the Gúrkhas over Nepál dates only from 1767, in which year they overran the valley of Khátmándu, and gradually extended their power over the hills and valleys of Nepál. Organized upon a feudal basis, they soon became a terror to their neighbours, marching east into Sikkim, west into Kumáun, and south into the Gangetic plains. In the last quarter their victims were British subjects, and it became necessary to check their advance. Sir George Barlow and Lord Minto had remonstrated in vain, and nothing was left to Lord Moira but to take up arms. The campaign of 1814 was at first unsuccessful. After overcoming the natural difficulties of a malarious climate and precipitous hills, our troops were on several occasions fairly worsted by the impetuous bravery of the little Gúrkhas, whose heavy knives or *kukris* dealt terrible execution. But, in the cold weather of 1814, General Ochterlony, who advanced by way of the Sutlej, stormed one by one the hill forts which still stud the Himálayan States, now under the Punjab Government, and compelled the Nepál *darbár* to sue for peace. In the year 1816, the same general made his brilliant march from Patná into the lofty valley of Khátmándu, and finally dictated the terms which had before been rejected, within a few miles of the capital. By the treaty of Segauli, which defines the English relations with Nepál to the present day, the Gúrkhas withdrew on the south-east from Sikkim; and on the south-west, from their advanced posts in the outer ranges of the Himálayas, which have supplied to the English the health-giving stations of Náini Tál, Mussooree, and Simla.

The Pindárís, 1804–1817.—Meanwhile the condition of Central India was every year becoming more unsatisfactory. The great Maráthá Chiefs had learned to live as princes rather than as predatory leaders. But their old example of lawlessness was being followed by a new set of freebooters, known as the Pindárís. As opposed to the Maráthás, who were at least a Hindu nationality bound by traditions of confederate government, the Pindárís were merely plundering bands, corresponding to the free companies of mediæval Europe. Of no common race, and without any common religion, they welcomed to their ranks the outlaws and broken tribes of all India—Afgháns, Maráthás, or Játs. They represented the *débris* of the Mughal Empire, the broken men who had not been incorporated by the Muhammadan or the Hindu powers which sprang out of its ruins. For a time, indeed, it seemed as if the inheritance of the Mughal might pass to these armies of banditti. In Bengal, similar hordes had formed themselves out of the disbanded Muhammadan troops and the Hindu predatory castes. But they had been dispersed under the vigorous rule of Warren Hastings. In Central India, the evil lasted longer, attained a greater scale, and was only stamped out by a regular war.

Pindárí War, 1817.—The Pindárí headquarters were in Málwá, but their depredations were not confined to Central

India. In bands, sometimes of a few hundreds, sometimes of many thousands, they rode out on their forays as far as the opposite coasts of Madras and of Bombay. The most powerful of the Pindárí captains, Amír Khán, had an organized army of many regiments, and several batteries of cannon. Two other leaders, known as Chítu and Karím, at one time paid a ransom to Sindhia of £100,000. To suppress the Pindárí hordes, who were supported by the sympathy, more or less open, of all the Maráthá Chiefs, Lord Hastings (1817) collected the strongest British army which had been seen in India, numbering 120,000 men. One-half operated from the north, the other half from the south. Sindhia was overawed, and remained quiet. Amír Khán disbanded his army, on condition of being guaranteed the possession of what is now the Principality of Tonk. The remaining bodies of Pindárís were attacked in their homes, surrounded, and cut to pieces. Karím threw himself upon the mercy of the conquerors. Chítu fled to the jungles, and was killed by a tiger.

Last Maráthá War, 1817–1818.—In the same year (1817), and almost in the same month (November), as that in which the Pindárís were crushed, the three great Maráthá powers at Poona, Nágpur, and Indore rose separately against the British. The Peshwá Bájí Ráo had long been chafing under the terms imposed by the treaty of Bassein (1802). A new treaty of Poona, in June 1817, now freed the Gáekwár from his control, ceded fresh districts to the British for the pay of the subsidiary force, and submitted all future disputes to the decision of our Government. The Hon. Mountstuart Elphinstone, then our Resident at his court, foresaw a storm, and withdrew to Kirki, whither he had ordered up a European regiment. The Residency was burnt down by the Maráthás, and the Peshwá attacked Kirki with his whole army. The attack was bravely repulsed, and the Peshwá immediately fled from his capital. Almost the same plot was enacted at Nágpur, where the honour of the British name was saved by the sepoys, who defended the hill of Sítábaldi against enormous odds. The Maráthá army of Holkar was defeated in the following month at the pitched battle of Mehidpur.

Results of last Maráthá War.—All open resistance was

now at an end. Nothing remained but to follow up the fugitives, and to impose conditions for a general pacification. In both these duties Sir John Malcolm played a prominent part. The dominions of the Peshwá were annexed to the Bombay Presidency, and the nucleus of the present Central Provinces was formed out of the territory rescued from the Pindárís. The Peshwá himself surrendered, and was permitted to reside at Bithúr, near Cawnpur, on a pension of £80,000 a year. His adopted son was the infamous Náná Sáhib of the Mutiny of 1857. To fill the Peshwá's place as the traditional head of the Maráthá Confederacy, the lineal descendant of Sivají was brought forth from obscurity, and placed upon the throne of Sátára. An infant was recognized as the heir of Holkar; and a second infant was proclaimed Rájá of Nágpur under British guardianship. At the same time, the States of Rájputána accepted the position of feudatories to the paramount British power. The map of India, as thus drawn by Lord Hastings, remained substantially unchanged until the time of Lord Dalhousie. But the proudest boast of Lord Hastings and Sir John Malcolm was, not that they had advanced the British frontier, but that they had conferred the blessings of peace and good government upon millions who had groaned under the extortions of the Maráthás and Pindárís.

Earl Amherst, 1823–1828.—The Marquess of Hastings was succeeded by Lord Amherst, after the interval of a few months, during which Mr. Adam, a civil servant, acted as Governor-General. The Maráthá war in the peninsula of India was hardly completed, when our armies had to face new enemies beyond the sea. Lord Amherst's administration lasted for five years, from 1823 to 1828. It is known in history by two prominent events—the first Burmese war, and the capture of Bhartpur.

Burma in Ancient Times.—For years our eastern frontier of Bengal had been disturbed by Burmese raids. The peninsula was known to the Greeks in ancient times as the 'Golden Chersonese.' Burmese traditions pretend that a pious Indian Prince from Benares founded a kingdom on the coast of Arakan, centuries before the birth of Christ. They also assert that the southern parts of Burma were peopled by settlers from the coast of Coromandel on the Madras side of the Bay of Bengal. However this may be, it is certain that the Buddhist religion, which is professed by the Burmese at the present day, came from India at a very early date. Indeed, the State establishment of Buddhism in Burma is said to have taken place in 164 A.D. While a stream of civilisation reached Burma from India on the north-west, the wild Shan tribes and other races of Tibeto-Chinese origin poured into the Irawadi valley from the north-east. Waves of invaders thus passed over Burma during many centuries, some coming from Siam on the south-east, others from the wild mountains of the Chinese frontier on the north-east. These gradually established themselves into three separate kingdoms, namely, Arakan on the Burmese coast; Ava in the upper valleys of the Irawadi; and Pegu in the delta of that river. They became the ruling races of Burma, races of Tibeto-Chinese descent, who professed or adopted the Buddhist religion which had originally come from India. The three Burmese kingdoms fought against each other with all the cruelties and massacres which characterize the Tibeto-Chinese tribes; but the learning and civilization of Buddhism survived every shock and flourished around its ancient pagodas. European travellers in the sixteenth century visited Pegu and Tenasserim, which they describe as flourishing marts of maritime trade. During the period of Portuguese predominance in the East, Arakan became the asylum for desperate European adventurers. With their help, the Arakanese extended their power inland, occupied Chittagong, and (under the name of the Maghs) became the terror of the Gangetic delta. About 1750, a new dynasty arose in Burma, founded by Alaungpaya or Alompra, with its capital at Ava. His descendants ruled over Independent Burma until 1885.

First Burmese War, 1824-1826.—The successors of Alompra, after having subjugated all Burma, and overrun Assam, which was then an independent kingdom, began a series of encroachments upon the British Districts of Bengal. As they rejected all peaceful proposals with scorn, Lord Amherst was at last compelled to declare war in 1824. One expedition with gunboats proceeded up the Brahmaputra into Assam.

Another marched by land through Chittagong into Arakan, for the Bengal sepoys refused to go by sea. A third, and the strongest, sailed from Madras direct to the mouth of the Irawadi. The war was protracted over two years. After a loss to us of about 20,000 lives, chiefly from the pestilential climate, and an expenditure of £14,000,000, the King of Ava signed, in 1826, the treaty of Yandabu. By this he abandoned all claim to Assam, and ceded to us the Provinces of Arakan and Tenasserim, already in the military occupation of the British. He retained the whole valley of the Irawadi, down to the sea at Rangoon.

Bhartpur taken, 1827.—A disputed succession led to the British intervention in Bhartpur, the great Ját State of Central India. The capture of the city by Lord Combermere, in January 1827, wiped out the repulse which Lord Lake had received in January 1805. Artillery could make little impression upon the massive walls of mud. But at last a breach was effected by mining, and Bhartpur was taken by storm, thus removing the popular notion throughout India, that it was impregnable—a notion which had threatened to become a political danger.

Lord William Bentinck, 1828–1835.—The next Governor-General was Lord William Bentinck, who had been Governor of Madras twenty years earlier, at the time of the mutiny of Vellore (1806). His seven years' rule is not signalized by any of those victories or extensions of territory by which chroniclers measure the growth of an empire. But it forms an epoch in administrative reform, and in the slow process by which a subject population is won over to venerate as well as to obey its foreign rulers. The modern history of the British in India, as benevolent administrators, ruling the country with a single eye to the good of the natives, may almost be said to begin with Lord William Bentinck. According to the inscription upon his statue at Calcutta, from the pen of Macaulay: 'He abolished cruel rites; he effaced humiliating distinctions; he gave liberty to the expression of public opinion; his constant study was to elevate the intellectual and moral character of the nations committed to his charge.'

Bentinck's Financial Reforms.—Lord William Bentinck's first care on arrival in India was to restore equilibrium to the finances, which were tottering under the burden imposed upon them by the Burmese war. This he effected by three series of measures—first, by reductions in permanent expenditure, amounting to 1½ millions sterling a year; second, by augmenting the revenue from land which had unfairly escaped assessment; third, by duties on the opium of Málwá. He also widened the gates by which educated Natives could enter the service of the Company. Some of these reforms were distasteful to the covenanted service and to the officers of the army. But Lord William was staunchly supported by the Court of Directors and by the Ministry at home.

Abolition of Satí, and Suppression of Thagí.—His two most memorable acts are the abolition of *satí* (suttee), or widow-burning, and the suppression of the *thags* (thugs). At this distance of time, it is difficult to realize the degree to which these two barbarous practices had corrupted the social system of the Hindus. European research has proved that the text in the Vedas adduced to authorize the immolation of Hindu widows was a wilful mistranslation. But the practice had been enshrined in Hindu opinion by the authority of centuries, and had acquired the sanctity of a religious rite. The Emperor Akbar tried to prohibit it, but failed to put it down. The early English rulers did not dare to violate the religious traditions of the people. In the year 1817, no fewer than 700 widows are said to have been burned alive in the Bengal Presidency alone. To this day, the holy spots of Hindu pilgrimage are thickly dotted with little white pillars, each commemorating a *satí*. In spite of strenuous opposition, both from Europeans and Natives, Lord William Bentinck carried a regulation in Council, on the 4th December 1829, by which all who abetted *satí* were declared guilty of 'culpable homicide.' The honour of suppressing *thagí* must be shared between Lord William Bentinck and Captain Sleeman. *Thags* were hereditary assassins, who made strangling their profession. They travelled in gangs, disguised as merchants or pilgrims, and were banded together by an oath based on the rites of the bloody goddess Kálí. Between 1826 and 1835, as many as 1562 *thags* were apprehended in different parts of British India; and, by the evidence of approvers, this moral plague-spot was gradually stamped out.

Renewal of Charter, 1833.—Two other historical events are connected with the administration of Lord William Bentinck. In 1833, the charter of the East India Company was again renewed for twenty years, but on condition that the Company should abandon its trade entirely, alike with India and China, and permit Europeans to freely settle in India. At the same time, a fourth or Law Member was added to the Governor-General's Council, who need not necessarily be a servant of the Company; and a Commission was appointed to revise and codify the law. Macaulay was the first legal member of Council, and the first President of the Law Commission.

Mysore protected and Coorg annexed.—In 1830, it was found necessary to take Mysore under British administration. This arrangement continued until March 1881, when Mysore was restored to Native government. In 1834, the frantic misrule of the Rájá of Coorg brought on a short and sharp war. The Rájá was permitted to retire to Benares; and the brave and proud inhabitants of his mountainous little territory decided to place themselves under the sway of the Company. This was the only annexation effected by Lord William Bentinck, and it was done 'in consideration of the unanimous wish of the people.' He retired in 1835.

Lord Metcalfe, 1835-1836.—Sir Charles (afterwards Lord) Metcalfe succeeded Lord William Bentinck, being senior member of Council. His short term of office is memorable for the measure which his predecessor had initiated, but which he carried into execution, for giving entire liberty to the press. Public opinion in India, as well as the express wish of the Court of Directors at home pointed to Metcalfe as the fittest person to carry out the policy of Bentinck, not provisionally, but as Governor-General for a full term.

Lord Auckland, 1836-1842.—Party exigencies, however, led to the appointment of Lord Auckland. From this date commences a new era of war and conquest, which may be said to have lasted for twenty years. All looked peaceful, until Lord

Auckland, prompted by his evil genius, attempted to place Sháh Shujá upon the throne of Kábul—an attempt conducted with gross mismanagement, and ending in the annihilation of the British garrison placed in that city.

Afghánistán under the Duránís, 1747–1826.—Almost for the first time since the days of the Sultáns of Ghazní and Ghor, Afghánistán had obtained a national king, in 1747, in Ahmad Sháh Durání. This resolute soldier found his opportunity in the confusion which followed the death of the Persian conqueror, Nádir Sháh. Before his own decease in 1773, Ahmad Sháh had conquered a wide empire, from Herat to Peshάwar, and from Kashmír to Sind. His intervention on the field of Pánípat (1761) turned back the tide of Maráthá conquest, and replaced a Muhammadan emperor on the throne of Delhi. But Ahmad Sháh never cared to settle down in India, and kept state alternately at his two Afghán capitals of Kábul and Kandahár. The Durání kings were prolific in children, who fought to the death with one another on each succession. At last, in 1826, Dost Muhammad, head of the powerful Bárakzái family, succeeded in establishing himself as ruler of Kábul, with the title of Amír, while two fugitive brothers of the Durání line were living under British protection at Ludhiána, on the Punjab frontier.

Our Early Dealings with Kábul.—The attention of the English Government had been directed to Afghán affairs ever since the time of Lord Wellesley, who feared that Zemán Sháh, then holding his court at Lahore (1800), might follow in the path of Ahmad Sháh, and overrun Hindustán. The growth of the powerful Sikh kingdom of Ranjít Singh, however, gradually dispelled such alarms for the future. Subsequently, in 1809, while a French invasion of India was still a possibility to be guarded against, Mountstuart Elphinstone was sent by Lord Minto on a mission to Sháh Shujá, brother of Zemán Sháh, to form a defensive alliance. Before the year expired, Sháh Shujá had been driven into exile, and a third brother, Mahmúd Sháh, was on the throne.

Restoration of Sháh Shujá by the British, 1839.—In 1837, when the curtain rises upon the drama of English interference in Afghánistán, the usurper Dost Muhammad Bárakzái was firmly established at Kábul. His great ambition was to recover Pesháwar from the Sikhs. When, therefore, Captain Alexander Burnes arrived on a mission from Lord Auckland, with the ostensible object of opening trade, the Dost was willing to promise everything, if only he could get Pesháwar. But Lord Auckland had another and more important object in view. At this time the Russians were advancing rapidly in Central Asia; and a Persian army, not without Russian support, was besieging Herát, the traditional bulwark of Afghánistán on the east. A Russian envoy was at Kábul at the same time as Burnes. The latter was unable to satisfy the demands of Dost Muhammad in the matter of Pesháwar, and returned to India unsuccessful. Lord Auckland forthwith resolved upon the hazardous plan of placing a more subservient ruler upon the throne of Kábul. Sháh Shujá, one of the two royal Afghán exiles at Ludhiána, was selected for the purpose. At this time both the Punjab and Sind were independent kingdoms; and both lay between British India and Afghánistán. Sind was the less powerful of the two, and accordingly a British army escorting Sháh Shujá made its way through Sind into Southern Afghánistán by way of the Bolán Pass. Kandahár surrendered, Ghazní was taken by storm, Dost Muhammad fled across the Hindu Kush, and Sháh Shujá was triumphantly led into the Bala Hissár at Kábul in August 1839. After one more brave struggle, Dost Muhammad surrendered, and was sent to Calcutta as a State prisoner. The Governor-General, Baron Auckland, was created Earl of Auckland in 1839.

British Retreat from Afghánistán, 1841–1842.—But although we could enthrone Sháh Shujá, we could not win for him the hearts of the Afgháns. To that nation he seemed a degenerate exile thrust back upon them by foreign arms. During two years Afghánistán remained in the military occupation of the British. The catastrophe occurred in November 1841, when our Political Agent, Sir Alexander Burnes, was assassinated in the city of Kábul. The troops in the cantonments were under the command of General Elphinstone (not to be confounded with the able civilian and historian, the Hon.

Mountstuart Elphinstone, formerly Governor of Bombay). Sir William Macnaghten was the Political Officer. General Elphinstone, an old man, proved unequal to the responsibilities of the position. Macnaghten was treacherously murdered at an interview with the Afghán chief Akbar Khán, son of Dost Muhammad. After lingering in its cantonments for two months, the British army set off in the depth of winter, under a fallacious guarantee from the Afghán leaders, to find its way back to India through the passes. When it started, it numbered 4000 fighting men, with 12,000 camp-followers. A single survivor, Dr. Brydon, reached the friendly walls of Jalálábád, where General Sale was gallantly holding out. The rest perished in the snowy defiles of Khurd-Kábul and Jagdalak, from the knives and matchlocks of the Afgháns, or from the effects of cold. A few prisoners, chiefly women, children, and officers, were considerately treated by the orders of Akbar Khán.

Lord Ellenborough, 1842-1844: The Army of Retribution, 1842.—The first Afghán enterprise, begun in a spirit of aggression, and conducted amid dissensions and mismanagement, had ended in the disgrace of the British arms. The real loss, which amounted only to a single garrison, was magnified by the horrors of the winter march, and by the completeness of the annihilation. Within a month after the news reached Calcutta, Lord Auckland had been superseded by Lord Ellenborough, whose first impulse was to be satisfied with drawing off in safety the garrisons from Kandahár and Jalálábád. But bolder counsels were forced upon him. General Pollock, who was marching straight through the Punjab to relieve General Sale, was allowed to penetrate to Kábul. General Nott, although ordered to withdraw from Kandahár, resolved to go round by way of Kábul. Lord Ellenborough gave his commands in well-chosen words, which would leave his generals responsible for any disaster. General Nott accepted that responsibility, and, instead of retreating south-east to the Indus, boldly marched north to Kábul. After hard fighting, the two British armies, under Pollock and Nott, met at their common destination in Kábul, in September 1842. The great *bázár* of Kábul was blown up with gunpowder, to fix a stigma upon the city; the

British prisoners were recovered; and our armies marched back to India, leaving Dost Muhammad to take undisputed possession of his throne. The drama closed with a bombastic proclamation from Lord Ellenborough, who had caused the gates from the tomb of Mahmúd of Ghazní to be carried back as a memorial of 'Somnáth revenged.' The gates were a modern forgery; and their theatrical procession through the Punjab formed a vainglorious sequel to Lord Ellenborough's timidity while the fate of our armies hung in the balance.

Conquest of Sind, 1843.—Lord Ellenborough, who loved military pomp, had his tastes gratified by two more wars. In 1843, the Muhammadan rulers of Sind, known as the Mírs or Amírs, whose chief fault was that they would not surrender their independence, were crushed by Sir Charles Napier. The victory of Miáni, in which 3000 British troops defeated 12,000 Balúchís, is one of the brilliant feats of arms in Anglo-Indian history. But valid reasons can scarcely be found for the annexation of the country. In the same year a disputed succession at Gwalior, fomented by feminine intrigue, resulted in an outbreak of the overgrown army which the Sindhia family kept up. Peace was restored by the battles of Mahárájpur and Panniár, at the former of which Lord Ellenborough was present in person.

Lord Hardinge, 1844-1848.—In 1844, Lord Ellenborough was recalled by the Court of Directors, who differed from him on points of administration, and distrusted his erratic genius. He was succeeded by a veteran soldier, Sir Henry (afterwards Lord) Hardinge, who had served through the Peninsular war, and lost a hand at Ligny. It was felt on all sides that a trial of strength between the British and the one remaining Hindu power in India, the great Sikh nation, was near.

The Sikhs.—The Sikhs were not a nationality like the Maráthás, but originally a religious sect, bound together by the additional tie of military discipline. They trace their origin to Nának Sháh, a pious Hindu reformer, born near Lahore in 1469, before the ascendency of either Mughals or Portuguese in India. Nának, like other zealous preachers of his time, preached the abolition of caste, the unity of the Godhead, and the duty of leading a pure life. From Nának, ten *gurus* or apostles are traced down to Govind Singh in 1708, with whom the succession stopped. Cruelly persecuted by the ruling Muhammadans, almost exterminated under the miserable successors of Aurangzeb, the Sikh martyrs clung to their faith with unflinching zeal. At last the downfall of the Mughal Empire transformed the sect into a territorial power. It was the only political organization remaining in the Punjab. The Sikhs in the north, and the Maráthás in Southern and Central India, grew into the two great Hindu powers who partitioned the Mughal Empire.

Ranjít Singh, 1780–1839.—Even before the rise of Ranjít Singh, offshoots from the Sikh *misls* or confederacies, each led by its elected *sardár* or chief, had carved out for themselves feudal principalities along the banks of the Sutlej, some of which endure to the present day. Ranjít Singh, the founder of the Sikh kingdom of the Punjab, was born in 1780. In his twentieth year he obtained the appointment of Governor of Lahore from the Afghán king, and formed the project of building up his personal rule on the religious fanaticism of his countrymen. He organized the Sikhs, or 'the liberated,' into an army under European officers, which for steadiness and religious fervour has had no parallel since the 'Ironsides' of Cromwell. From Lahore, as his capital, he extended his conquests south to Múltán, west to Pesháwar, and north to Kashmír. On the east side alone, he was hemmed in by the Sutlej, up to which river the authority of the British Government had advanced in 1804. Till his death in 1839, Ranjít Singh was ever loyal to the engagements which he entered into with Metcalfe in 1809. But he left no son capable of wielding his sceptre. Lahore was torn by dissensions between rival generals, ministers, and queens. The only strong power in the Punjab was the army of the *khálsá*, or Central Council of the Sikhs, which, since our disaster in Afghánistán, burned to measure its strength with the British sepoys. Ranjít Singh's skilful European Generals, Avitabile and Court, were foolishly ousted from their commands in the Sikh army, and the supreme military power was vested in a series of *pancháyats*, or elective committees of five.

First Sikh War, 1845.—In 1845, the Sikh army, numbering 60,000 men, with 150 guns, crossed the Sutlej and invaded British territory. Sir Hugh Gough, the Commander-in-Chief, accompanied by the Governor-General, hurried up to the frontier. Within a few weeks, four pitched battles were fought, at Múdkí, Firozsháh, Aliwál, and Sobráon. The British loss on each occasion was heavy; but by the last victory the Sikhs were fairly driven back across the Sutlej, and Lahore surrendered to the British. By the terms of peace which we granted, Dhulíp Singh, a supposed infant son of Ranjít and a dancing-girl, was recognized as Rájá; the Jálandhar Doáb, or tract between the Sutlej and the Beas, was annexed; the Sikh army was limited to a specified number; Major Henry Lawrence was appointed to be Resident at Lahore; and a British force sent to garrison the Punjab for a period of eight years. Sir H. Hardinge received a peerage, and returned to England in 1848.

Earl (afterwards Marquess) of Dalhousie, 1848-1856.—Lord Dalhousie succeeded. The eight years' rule of this greatest of Indian proconsuls left more conspicuous results than that of any Governor-General since Lord Wellesley, perhaps even since Clive. A high-minded statesman, of a most sensitive conscience, and earnestly desiring peace, Lord Dalhousie found himself forced against his will to fight two wars, and to embark on a policy of annexation. His campaigns in the Punjab and in Burma ended in large acquisitions of territory; while Nágpur, Oudh, and several minor States also came under British rule, through failure of direct heirs. But Dalhousie's deepest interest lay in the improvement of the moral and material condition of the country. The system of administration carried out in the conquered Punjab, by the two Lawrences and their assistants, is probably the most successful piece of governing ever accomplished by Englishmen. British Burma has prospered under our rule not less than the Punjab. In both cases, Lord Dalhousie himself laid the foundations of our administrative success, and deserves a large share of the credit. No branch of the administration escaped his reforming hand. He founded the Public Works Department, with a view to creating the network of roads and canals which now cover India. He opened the Ganges Canal, still the largest work of the kind in the country; he turned the sod of the first Indian railway. He promoted steam communication with England *viâ* the Red Sea; he introduced cheap postage and the electric telegraph. It is Lord Dalhousie's misfortune that these benefits are too often forgotten in the recollections of the Mutiny, which followed his policy of annexation, after the firm hand which had remodelled British India was withdrawn.

Second Sikh War, 1848–1849.—Lord Dalhousie had not been six months in India before the second Sikh or Punjab war broke out. Two British officers were treacherously assassinated at Múltán. Unfortunately, Henry Lawrence, our Resident at Lahore, was at home on sick leave. The British army was not ready to act in the hot weather; and, despite the single-handed exertions of Lieutenant (afterwards Sir Herbert) Edwardes, this outbreak of fanaticism led to a general rising in the Punjab. The *khálsá* army of the Sikhs again came together, and once more fought on even terms with the British. On the fatal field of Chilianwála, which English patriotism prefers to call a drawn battle, the British lost 2400 officers and men, four guns, and the colours of three regiments (13th January 1849). Before reinforcements could come out from England, with Sir Charles Napier as Commander-in-Chief, Lord Gough had restored his reputation by the crowning victory of Gujrát, which absolutely destroyed the Sikh army. Múltán had previously fallen, and the allied Muhammadan cavalry from Afghánistán, who had forgotten their religious antipathy to the Sikhs, and joined with them in a common hatred of the British name, were chased back with ignominy to their native hills. The Punjab, annexed by proclamation on the 29th March 1849, became a British Province—a virgin field for the administrative talents of Dalhousie and the two Lawrences. Mahárájá Dhulíp Singh received an allowance of £58,000 a year, on which he lived for many years as an English country gentleman in Norfolk. In 1849 the Earl of Dalhousie was advanced to a Marquessate.

Pacification of the Punjab.—The first step in the pacification of the Punjab was a general disarmament, which resulted in the delivery of no fewer than 120,000 weapons of various kinds. Then followed a settlement of the land tax, village by village, at an assessment much below the rates to which it had been raised by Sikh exactions; and the introduction of a loose but equitable code of civil and criminal procedure. Roads and canals were laid out by Colonel Robert Napier (afterwards Lord Napier of Magdala). The security of British peace, and the personal influence of British officers, inaugurated a new era of prosperity, which was felt to the farthest corners of the Province. It thus happened that, when the Mutiny broke out in 1857, the Punjab remained not only quiet, but loyal.

Second Burmese War, 1852.—The second Burmese war, in 1852, arose out of the ill-treatment of some European merchants at Rangoon, and the insults offered to the captain of a British frigate who had been sent to remonstrate. The whole valley of the Irawadi, from Rangoon up to Prome, was occupied in a few months. As the King of Ava refused to treat, the conquered tracts of Lower Burma were annexed by proclamation, on the 20th December 1852, under the name of Pegu, to the Provinces of Arakan and Tenasserim, which we had acquired in 1826, after the first Burmese war.

Prosperity of British Burma.—Since annexation, the inhabitants of Rangoon had multiplied fourteenfold by 1891. The trade of the port, which four years after its annexation (1857–58) amounted to £2,131,055, had increased in 1881–82 to £11,723,781. The towns and the rural tracts have alike prospered. Before 1826, Amherst District was the scene of perpetual warfare between the Kings of Siam and Pegu, and was stripped of inhabitants. In February 1827, a Talaing Chief with 10,000 followers settled in the neighbourhood of Maulmain; and, after a few years, a further influx of 20,000 immigrants took place. In 1855, the population of Amherst District amounted to 83,146 souls; in 1860, to 130,953; and in 1881, to 301,086. Or, to take the case of a seaport. In 1826, when we annexed the Province of Arakan, Akyab was a poor fishing village; its trade multiplied nearly four hundredfold in fifty years. The population of Burma (including some other districts), which was incompletely enumerated in 1891, has increased from 7½ millions in that year, to 10½ millions in 1901.

Lord Dalhousie and the Native States.—Lord Dalhousie's dealings with the Feudatory States of India revealed the whole nature of the man. That rulers only exist for the good of the ruled, was his supreme axiom of government, of which he gave a conspicuous example in his own daily life. That British administration was better for the people than Native rule, seemed to him to follow from this axiom. The truth is that the system of British protectorates, as developed by Lord Wellesley and his successors, had proved by no means a complete success. It practically secured to the Native Chiefs their principalities and revenues, however they might abuse their position and oppress their subjects. A remedy for this state of things has since been worked out in the India of the Queen by enforcing a higher standard of personal responsibility on the Feudatory princes of India. But in Lord Dalhousie's time the old unreformed system was bearing its last and worst fruits. Dalhousie was thus led to regard Native Chiefs as mischievous anomalies, to be abolished by every fair means. Good faith must be kept with princes on the throne, and with their legitimate heirs. But no false sentiment should preserve dynasties which had forfeited our sympathies by generations of misrule, or prolong those that had no natural successor. The 'doctrine of lapse' was the practical application of these principles, complicated by the Indian practice of adoption. It has never been doubted that, according to Hindu private law, an adopted son entirely fills the place of a natural son, whether to perform the religious obsequies of his father or to inherit his property. In all respects he continues the rights of the deceased. But it was argued, both as a matter of historical fact and on grounds of political expediency, that the succession to a throne stood upon a different footing. The paramount power could not recognize such a right, which might be used as a fraud to hand over the happiness of millions to a base-born impostor. Here came in Lord Dalhousie's maxim of 'the good of the governed.' In his mind, the benefits to be conferred through British administration weighed heavier than a superstitious and often fraudulent fiction of inheritance.

Lord Dalhousie's Doctrine.—When a Native Chief left direct male heirs of his body, Lord Dalhousie recognized their right to succeed alike to the private fortune and the public government of their father. But when there was only an adopted son, Lord Dalhousie, while scrupulously respecting the claims of the heirs to the private fortune of the late chief, denied the right of the adopted son to succeed to the public government of the State. He held the government of a Native State to be a public trust; he also held that, in the absence of direct male issue with a lawful claim to succeed, the succession must be decided by the British Government, not in the interests of the family of the late chief, but in the interests of the people. Those interests he believed to be most effectually protected by bringing them under direct British rule.

Lapsed Native States.—The first State to escheat to the British Government, in accordance with these principles, was Sátára, which had been reconstituted by Lord Hastings on the downfall of the Peshwá in 1818. The Rájá of Sátára, the last direct representative of Sivají, died without a son in 1848, and his deathbed adoption of a son was set aside (1849). In the same year, the Rájput State of Karauli was saved by the Court of Directors, who drew a fine distinction between a dependent principality and a protected ally. In 1853, Jhánsi suffered the same fate as Sátára. But the most conspicuous application of the doctrine of lapse was the case of Nágpur. The last of the Maráthá Bhonslas, a dynasty older than the British Government in India, died without a son, natural or adopted, in 1853. His territories were annexed, and became the Central Provinces. That year also saw British administration extended to the Berars, or the Assigned Districts, which the Nizám of Haidarábád was induced to hand over to us as a territorial guarantee for the subsidies which he perpetually left in arrear. The relics of three other dynasties also passed away in 1853, although without any attendant accretion to British territory. In the extreme south, the titular Nawáb of the Karnátik and the titular Rájá of Tanjore both died without heirs. Their rank and their pensions died with them, but compassionate allowances were continued to their families. In the north of India, Bájí Ráo, the ex-Peshwá, who had been dethroned in 1818, lived on till 1853 in the enjoyment of his annual pension of £80,000. His adopted son,

Náná Sáhib, inherited his accumulated savings, but could obtain no further recognition.

Annexation of Oudh, 1856.—Lord Dalhousie annexed the Kingdom of Oudh on different grounds. Ever since the Nawáb Wazír, Shujá-ud-daulá, received back his forfeited territories of Oudh from Lord Clive in 1765, the existence of his dynasty had depended on the protection of British bayonets. Guarded alike from foreign invasion and from domestic rebellion, the line of Oudh Nawábs had sunk into private debauchees and public oppressors. Their one virtue was steady loyalty to the British Government. The fertile districts between the Ganges and the Gogra, which now support a denser agricultural population than almost any rural area of the size on this globe, had been groaning for generations under an anarchy for which each British Governor-General felt himself in part responsible. Warning after warning had been given to the Nawábs (who had assumed the title of Sháh or King since 1819) that they must put their house in order. What the benevolent Bentinck and the soldierly Hardinge had only threatened, was now performed by Lord Dalhousie, who united an equal honesty of purpose with sterner decision of character. He laid the whole case before the Court of Directors. After long and painful hesitation, the Court of Directors resolved on annexation. Lord Dalhousie, then on the eve of retiring, felt that it would be unfair to bequeath this perilous task to his successor in the first moments of his rule. The tardy decision of the Court of Directors left him, however, only a few weeks to carry out the work. But he solemnly believed that work to be his duty to the people of Oudh. 'With this feeling on my mind,' he wrote privately, 'and in humble reliance on the blessing of the Almighty (for millions of His creatures will draw freedom and happiness from the change), I approach the execution of this duty gravely and not without solicitude, but calmly and altogether without doubt.'

Grounds of Annexation.—Accordingly, at the commencement of 1856, the last year of his rule, Dalhousie gave orders to General (afterwards Sir James) Outram, then Resident at the Court of Lucknow, to assume the administration of Oudh, on the ground that 'the British Government would be guilty in the sight of God and man if it were any longer to aid in sustaining by its countenance an administration fraught with suffering to millions.' The proclamation was issued on the 13th February 1856. The King of Oudh, Wájid Alí, bowed to irresistible force, although he refused to recognize the justice of his deposition. After a mission to England by way of protest and appeal, he settled down in the pleasant suburb of Garden Reach, near Calcutta, in the enjoyment of a pension of £120,000 a year. Oudh was thus annexed without a blow. But this measure, on which Lord Dalhousie looked back with the proudest sense of rectitude, was perhaps the act of his rule that most alarmed Native public opinion.

Lord Dalhousie's Work in India.—The Marquess of Dalhousie resigned office in March 1856, being then only forty-four years of age; but he carried home with him the seeds of a lingering illness, which resulted in his death in 1860. Excepting Cornwallis, he was the first, though by no means the last, of English statesmen who have fallen victims to their devotion to India's needs. Lord Dalhousie completed the fabric of British rule in India. The Indian Empire, as mapped out by Lord Wellesley and Lord Hastings during the first quarter of the century, had received the addition of Sind in 1843. The Marquess of Dalhousie finally filled in the wide spaces covered by Oudh, the Central Provinces, and smaller States within India, together with the great outlying territories of the Punjab on the north-western frontier, and the richest part of British Burma beyond the sea.

Lord Canning, 1856-1862.—The great Governor-General was succeeded by his friend Lord Canning, who, at the farewell banquet in England given to him by the Court of Directors, uttered these prophetic words: 'I wish for a peaceful term of office. But I cannot forget that in the sky of India, serene as it is, a small cloud may arise, no larger than a man's hand, but which, growing larger and larger, may at last threaten to burst and overwhelm us with ruin.' In the following year, the sepoys of the Bengal army mutinied, and all the valley of the Ganges from Patná to Delhi was enveloped in the flame.

Materials for Reference.

In addition to the more general histories of India cited *ante*, p. 199, the following are a few of the leading and easily available works bearing more specially on the half-century (1805 to 1856) dealt with in this chapter. Malcolm's *Political History of India from* 1784 *to* 1823 (London, ed. 1826); *Life and Letters of Lord Minto in India*; H. T. Prinsep's *Political and Military Transactions in India*, 1813 *to* 1823; Major Ross of Bladensburg's *Marquess of Hastings*, in the 'Rulers of India' Series; Malcolm's *Memoir of Central India* (ed. 1832); Cotton's *Mountstuart Elphinstone and the Making of South-Western India*, in the 'Rulers of India' Series; Phayre's *History of Burma* (1883), and the *British Burma Gazetteer* (2 vols., Rangoon, 1879-80). Boulger's *Lord Williàm Bentinck*, in the 'Rulers of India' Series, condenses the materials available for 1828 to 1835. Kaye's *History of the War in Afghánistán* is still the standard work on that sad period; Miss Eden's *Journal in India in* 1837 *and* 1838 portrays the social aspects of Lord Auckland's rule; Lord Colchester's *Indian Administration of Lord Ellenborough* unconsciously but definitely reveals from Lord Ellenborough's own letters the vainglorious meanness of that Governor-General. The volumes on *Lord Hardinge*, by his son, and on the *Marquess of Dalhousie*, in the 'Rulers of India' Series, with the lives of Sir Henry Lawrence, Sir Herbert Edwardes, and Lord Lawrence, indicate the materials for the succeeding period from 1844 to 1856.

CHAPTER XV.

The Sepoy Mutiny of 1857.

Causes of the Sepoy Mutiny.—The various motives assigned for the Mutiny appear inadequate to the European mind. The truth seems to be that Native opinion throughout India was in a ferment, predisposing men to believe the wildest stories, and to rush into action in a paroxysm of terror. Panic acts on an Oriental population like drink upon a European mob. The annexation policy of Lord Dalhousie, although dictated by the most enlightened considerations, was distasteful to the Native mind. The spread of education, the appearance at the same moment of the steam-engine and the telegraph wire, seemed to reveal a deep plan for substituting an English for an Indian civilization. The Bengal sepoys especially thought that they could see further than the rest of their countrymen. Most of them were Hindus of high caste; many of them were recruited from Oudh. They regarded our reforms on Western lines as attacks on their own nationality, and they knew at first hand what annexation meant. They believed it was by their prowess that the Punjab had been conquered, and that all India was held. The numerous dethroned princes, or their heirs and widows, were the first to learn and take advantage of this spirit of disaffection and panic. They had heard of the Crimean war, and were told that Russia was the perpetual enemy of England. Our munificent pensions had supplied the funds with which they could buy the aid of skilful intriguers.

Other alleged causes of the Mutiny.—On the other hand, the Company had not sufficiently opened up the higher posts in its service to natives of education, talent, or proved fidelity. It had taken important steps in this direction in respect to the lower grades of appointments. But the prizes of Indian official life, many of which are now thrown open to natives of India by the Crown, were then the monopoly of a handful of Englishmen. Shortly before the Mutiny, Sir Henry Lawrence pointed out that even the army supplied no career to a native officer, which could satisfy the reasonable ambition of an able man. He insisted on the serious dangers arising from this state of things; but his warnings were unheeded till too late. In the crisis of the Mutiny they were remembered. He was nominated provisional Governor-General in event of any accident happening to Lord Canning; and the Queen's proclamation, on the transfer of the Government from the Company to the Crown at the end of the great struggle, affirmed the principle which he had so powerfully urged. 'And it is our further will,' are Her Majesty's gracious words, 'that, so far as may be, our subjects, of whatever race or creed, be freely and impartially admitted to offices in our service, the duties of which they may be qualified by their education, ability, and integrity duly to discharge.' Under the Company this liberal policy was unknown. The Sepoy Mutiny of 1857, therefore, found many of the Indian princes, especially the dethroned dynasties, hostile to the Company; while a multitude of its own native officers were either actively disloyal or indifferent to its fate.

The 'Greased Cartridges.'—In this critical state of affairs, a rumour ran through the Native army that the cartridges served out to the Bengal regiments had been greased with the fat of pigs—animals which are unclean alike to Hindu and Muhammadan. No assurances could quiet the minds of the Sepoys. Indeed the evidence shows that a disastrous blunder had in truth been made in this matter—a blunder which, although quickly remedied, was remedied too late. Fires occurred nightly in the Native lines; officers were insulted by their men; confidence was gone, and only the form of discipline remained.

The Army drained of its Talent.—In addition, the outbreak of the storm found the Native regiments denuded of many of their best officers. The administration of the great empire to which Dalhousie had put the corner-stone, required a larger staff than the civil service could supply. The practice of selecting able military men for civil posts, which had long existed, received a sudden and vast development. Oudh, the Punjab, the Central Provinces, British Burma, were administered to a large extent by picked officers from the Company's regiments. Good and skilful commanders remained; but the Native army had nevertheless been drained of many of its brightest intellects and firmest wills at the very crisis of its fate. At the same time the British troops in India had, in spite of Lord Dalhousie's remonstrances, been reduced far below the strength which the great Governor-General declared to be essential to the safety of our rule. His earnest representations on this subject, and as to the urgent necessity for a reform alike of the Native and the British armies of India, were lying disregarded in London when the panic about the 'greased cartridges' spread through the Native regiments, and the storm burst upon Bengal.

Outbreak of the Mutiny, May 1857.—On the afternoon of Sunday, 10th May 1857, the sepoys at Meerut (Mírath) broke into open mutiny. They forced open the jail, and rushed in a wild torrent through the cantonments, cutting down any European whom they met. They then streamed off to the neighbouring city of Delhi, to stir up the Native garrison and the criminal population of that great city, and to place themselves under the authority of the discrowned Mughal emperor. Meerut was then the largest military station in Northern India, with a strong European garrison of foot, horse, and guns, sufficient to overwhelm the mutineers long before they could have reached Delhi. But as the Sepoys acted in irrational panic, so the British officers, in but too many cases, behaved with equally irrational indecision. The news of the outbreak was telegraphed to Delhi, and nothing more was done at Meerut that night. At the moment when one strong will might have saved India, no soldier in authority at Meerut seemed able to think or act. The next morning the Muhammadans of Delhi rose, and all that the Europeans there could do was to blow up the magazine.

Spread of the Mutiny, June 1857.—A rallying centre and a traditional name were thus given to the revolt, which forthwith spread like wild-fire through the North-Western Provinces and Oudh down into Lower Bengal. The same narrative must suffice for all the outbreaks, although each episode has its own story of sadness and devotion. The sepoys rose on their officers, usually without warning, sometimes after protestations of fidelity—protestations in some cases perhaps true at the moment. The Europeans, or persons of Christian faith, were often massacred; occasionally, also, the women and children. The jail was broken open, the treasury plundered, and the mutineers marched off to some centre of revolt, to join in what had now become a national war. Only in the Punjab were the sepoys anticipated by stern measures of repression and disarmament, carried out by Sir John Lawrence and his lieutenants, among whom Edwardes and Nicholson stand conspicuous. The Sikh population never wavered. Crowds of willing Muhammadan recruits joined us from the Afghán hills. And thus the Punjab, instead of being itself a source of danger, was able to furnish a portion of its own garrison for the siege of Delhi. In Lower Bengal most of the sepoys mutinied, and then dispersed in different directions. The Native armies of Madras and Bombay remained, on the whole, true to their colours. In Central India, the contingents of some of the great Chiefs sooner or later threw in their lot with the rebels, but the Muhammadan State of Haidarábád was kept loyal by the authority of its able minister, Sir Sálar Jang.

Cawnpur.—The main interest of the Sepoy War gathers round the three cities of Cawnpur, Lucknow and Delhi. The cantonments at Cawnpur contained one of the great Native garrisons of India. At Bithúr, not far off, was the palace of Dundhu Panth, the heir of the last Peshwá, whose more familiar name of Náná Sáhib will ever be handed down to infamy. At first the Náná was profuse in his professions of loyalty; but when the sepoys mutinied at Cawnpur on the 6th June, he put himself at their head, and was proclaimed Peshwá of the Maráthás. The Europeans at Cawnpur, numbering more women and children than fighting men, shut themselves up in an ill-chosen hasty entrenchment, where they heroically bore a siege for nineteen days under the sun of a tropical June. Every one had courage and endurance to suffer or to die; but the directing mind was again absent. On the 27th June, trusting to a safe-conduct from the Náná—a safe-conduct supposed to hold good as far as Allahábád—they surrendered; and to the number of 450 embarked in boats on the Ganges. A murderous fire was opened upon them from the river bank. Only a single boat escaped; and four men, who swam across to the protection of a friendly Rájá, survived to tell the tale. The rest of the men were massacred on the spot. The women and children, numbering 125, were reserved for the same fate on the 15th July, when the avenging army of Havelock was at hand.

Lucknow.—Sir Henry Lawrence, the Chief Commissioner of Oudh, had foreseen the storm. He fortified and provisioned the Residency at Lucknow; and thither he retired, with all the European inhabitants and a weak British regiment, on 2nd July. Two days later, he was mortally wounded by a shell. But the clear head was here in authority. Sir Henry Lawrence had deliberately chosen his position; and the little garrison held out, under unparalleled hardships and against enormous odds, until relieved by Havelock and Outram on 25th September. But the relieving force was itself invested by fresh swarms of rebels; and it was not till November that Sir Colin Campbell (afterwards Lord Clyde) cut his way into Lucknow, and effected the final deliverance of the garrison (16th November 1857). Our troops then withdrew to more urgent work, and did not permanently reoccupy Lucknow till March 1858.

Siege of Delhi.—The siege of Delhi began on 8th June, a month after the original outbreak at Meerut. Siege in the proper sense of the word it was not; for our army, encamped on the historic 'ridge' of Delhi, never exceeded 8000 men, while the rebels within the walls were more than 30,000 strong. In the middle of August, Nicholson arrived with a reinforcement from the Punjab; his own inspiring presence was perhaps even more valuable than the reinforcement he brought. On 14th September the assault was delivered; and, after six days' desperate fighting in the streets, Delhi was again won. Nicholson fell heroically at the head of the storming party. Hodson, the daring but unscrupulous leader of a corps of irregular horse, hunted down next day the old Mughal Emperor, Bahádur Sháh, and his sons. The emperor was afterwards sent a State prisoner to Rangoon, where he lived till 1862. As the mob pressed in on the guard around the emperor's sons, near Delhi, Hodson thought it necessary to shoot down the princes (who had been captured unconditionally) with his own hand.

Oudh reduced by Lord Clyde.—After the fall of Delhi and the final relief of Lucknow, the war loses its dramatic interest, although fighting still went on in various parts of the country for about eighteen months. The population of Oudh and Rohilkhand, stimulated by the presence of the Begam of Oudh, the Nawáb of Bareilly, and Náná Sáhib himself, had joined the mutinous sepoys *en masse.* In this quarter of India alone, it was the revolt of a people rather than the mutiny of an army that had to be quelled. Sir Colin Campbell (afterwards Lord Clyde) conducted the campaign in Oudh, which lasted through two cold seasons. Valuable assistance was lent by Sir Jang Bahádur of Nepál, at the head of his gallant Gúrkhas. Town after town was occupied, fort after fort was stormed, until the last gun had been recaptured, and the last fugitive had been chased across the frontier by January 1859.

Central India reduced by Sir Hugh Rose.—In the meanwhile, Sir Hugh Rose (afterwards Lord Strathnairn), with another army from Bombay, was conducting an equally brilliant campaign in Central India. His most formidable antagonists were the disinherited Rání or Princess of Jhánsi, and Tántia Topí, whose military talent had previously inspired Náná Sáhib with all the capacity for resistance that he ever displayed. The princess fell fighting bravely at the head of her troops in June 1858. Tántia Topí, after doubling backwards and forwards through Central India, was at last betrayed and run down in April 1859.

Summary of the Company's Charters, 1600 to 1784.—The Mutiny sealed the fate of the East India Company, after a life of more than two and a half centuries. The original Company received its charter of incorporation from Elizabeth in 1600. Its political powers, and the constitution of the Indian Government, were derived from the Regulating Act of 1773, passed by the ministry of Lord North. By that statute the Governor of Bengal was raised to the rank of Governor-General; and, in conjunction with his Council of four members, he was entrusted with the duty of controlling the Governments of Madras and Bombay, so far as regarded questions of peace and war: a Supreme Court of Judicature was appointed at Calcutta, to which the judges were nominated by the Crown; and a power of making rules and regulations was conferred upon the Governor-General and his Council. Next came the India Bill of Pitt (1784), which founded the Board of Control in England; strengthened the supremacy of Bengal over the other Presidencies; and first authorized the historic phrase, 'Governor-General-in-Council.'

Renewals of the Company's Charter, 1813–1853.—The renewed charter of 1813 abolished the Company's monopoly of Indian trade, and compelled it to direct its energies to the good government of the people. The Act of 1833, at the next renewal of the Company's charter for another twenty years, did away with its remaining trade to China. It also introduced successive reforms into the constitution of the Indian Government. It added to the Council a new (legal) member, who need not be chosen from among the Company's servants, and who was at first entitled to be present only at meetings for making laws and regulations; it accorded the authority of Acts of Parliament to the laws and regulations so made, subject to the disallowance of the Court of Directors; it appointed a Law Commission; and it finally gave to the Governor-General-in-Council a control over the other Presidencies, in all points relating to the civil or military administration. The charter of the Company was renewed for the last time in 1853, not for a definite period of years, but only for so long as Parliament should see fit. On this occasion the number of Directors was reduced, and their patronage as regards appointments to the civil service was taken away, to make room for the principle of open competition.

India transferred to the Crown, 1858.—The Act for the Better Government of India (1858), which finally transferred the administration from the Company to the Crown, was not passed without an eloquent protest from the Directors, nor without bitter party discussions in Parliament. It enacted that India shall be governed by, and in the name of, the Queen of

England through one of her Principal Secretaries of State, assisted by a Council of fifteen members. The Governor-General received the new title of Viceroy. The European troops of the Company, numbering about 24,000 officers and men, were amalgamated with the royal service, and the Indian navy was abolished. By the Indian Councils Act (1861), the Governor-General's Council, and also the Councils at Madras and Bombay, were augmented by the addition of non-official members, either Natives or Europeans, for legislative purposes only; and, by another Act passed in the same year, High Courts of Judicature were constituted out of the old Supreme Courts at the Presidency towns.

Materials for Reference.

The literature of the Indian Mutiny is too copious, too recent, and still in too active a state of production to permit of its being safely summarized. The standard work is Kaye and Malleson's *History of the Sepoy War and the Indian Mutiny* (6 vols.). The original authorities are to be fonnd in the official pnblications of the period; particularly the reports and evidence laid before Parliament; in the published personal journals and the Indian newspapers of the period, and in the numerous memoirs and biographies of the actors in the great drama. Among the last class may be mentioned especially Bosworth Smith's *Life of Lord Lawrence*; with the volumes by Sir Henry Cunningham on *Lord Canning*, by Sir Charles Aitchison on *Lord Lawrence*, and by Major-General Sir Owen Tudor Burne on *Lord Clyde and Lord Strathnairn*, in the 'Rulers of India' Series. Many questions connected with the period are still in dispute. The brief narrative which I have given in this chapter is based upon the carefully verified evidence of those who had the best opportunities of observing the facts and discerning the causes with their own eyes, and particularly of Sir John (afterwards Lord) Lawrence.

CHAPTER XVI.

India under the British Crown.

The Queen's Proclamation, 1st November 1858.—It fell to the lot of Lord Canning both to suppress the Mutiny and to introduce the peaceful revolution which followed. He preserved his equanimity unruffled in the darkest hours of peril; and the strict impartiality of his conduct incurred alternate praise and blame from partisans of both sides. The epithet then scornfully applied to him, of 'Clemency' Canning, is now remembered only to his honour. On 1st November 1858, at a grand *darbár* held at Allahábád, he sent forth the royal proclamation, which announced that the Queen had assumed the government of India. This document, which is, in the truest and noblest sense, the Magna Charta of the Indian people, declared in eloquent words the principles of justice and religious toleration as the guiding policy of the Queen's rule. It also granted an amnesty to all except those who had directly taken part in the murder of British subjects. Peace was proclaimed throughout India on the 8th July 1859. In the following cold weather, Lord Canning made a viceregal progress through the Northern Provinces, to receive the homage of loyal Princes and Chiefs, and to guarantee to them the right of adoption.

Mr. Wilson's Financial Reforms.—The suppression of the Mutiny increased the debt of India by about 40 millions sterling; and the military changes which ensued augmented the annual expenditure by about 10 millions. To grapple with this deficit, a distinguished political economist and parliamentary financier, the Right Honourable James Wilson, was sent out from England as financial member of Council. He reorganized the customs system, imposed an income tax and a licence duty, and created a State paper currency. He died in the midst of his splendid task; but his name still lives as that of the first and greatest finance minister of India. The Bengal Tenancy Act, a memorable measure which secured the land-rights of the peasantry of Bengal, was passed under Lord Canning's auspices in 1859; the Penal Code, originally drawn up by Macaulay in 1837, became law in 1860; with Codes of Civil and Criminal Procedure in 1861.

Lord Elgin, 1862–1863.—Lord Canning left India in March 1862, and died before he had been a month in England. His successor, Lord Elgin, only lived till November 1863. He expired at the Himálayan station of Dharmsála, and there he lies buried.

Lord Lawrence, 1864–1869.—He was succeeded by Sir John Lawrence, the saviour of the Punjab. The chief incidents of his rule were the Bhután war, followed by the annexation of the Dwárs (*Dooars*), a submontane strip on the North-Eastern frontier of Bengal, in 1864, and the terrible Orissa famine of 1866. In a later famine in Bundelkhand and Upper Hindustán in 1868–1869, Lord Lawrence laid down the principle, for the first time in Indian history, that the officers of the Government would be held personally responsible for taking every possible means to avert death by starvation. An inquiry was conducted into the status of the peasantry of Oudh, and an Act was passed with a view to securing them in their customary rights. After a period of fratricidal war among the sons of Dost Muhammad, the Afghán territories were concentrated in the hands of Sher Alí, who was acknowledged as Amír by Lord Lawrence. A commercial crisis took place in 1866, which seriously threatened the young tea industry in Bengal, and caused widespread ruin at Bombay. Sir John Lawrence retired in January 1869, after having passed through every grade of Indian service, from an assistant magistracy to the viceroyalty. On his return to England, he was raised to the peerage. He died in 1879, and lies in Westminster Abbey.

Lord Mayo, 1869–1872.—Lord Mayo succeeded Lord Lawrence in 1869, and urged on the material progress of India. The Ambála *darbár*, at which Sher Alí was formally recognized as Amír of Afghánistán, although in one sense the completion of what Lord Lawrence had begun, owed its brilliant success to Lord Mayo (1869). The visit of His Royal Highness the Duke of Edinburgh in 1869–1870 gave deep pleasure to the natives of India, and introduced a tone of personal loyalty into our relations with the feudatory princes. Lord Mayo reformed several of the great branches of the administration, created an Agricultural Department, and introduced the system of Provincial Finance. The impulse to local self-government given by the last measure has done much, and will do more, to develope and husband the revenues of India, to quicken the sense of responsibility among the English administrators, and to awaken political life among the people. Lord Mayo also laid the foundation for the reform of the salt duties. He thus enabled his successors to abolish the old pernicious customs-lines which had for long walled off Province from Province, and strangled the trade between British India and the Feudatory States. He developed the material resources of the country by an immense extension of roads, railways, and canals. He carried out the beneficent system of public works which Lord Dalhousie had inaugurated. Lord Mayo's splendid vigour defied alike the climate and the vast tasks which he imposed on himself. He anxiously and laboriously studied with his own eyes the wants of the farthest Provinces of the empire. But his life of noble usefulness was cut short by the hand of an assassin, in the convict settlement of the Andaman Islands, in 1872.

Lord Northbrook, 1872–1876.—His successor was Lord Northbrook, whose ability found pre-eminent scope in the department of finance. During his viceroyalty, a famine which threatened Lower Bengal in 1874 was successfully averted by a vast organization of State relief. The Maráthá Gáekwár of Baroda was dethroned in 1875 for misgovernment, and for his attempt to poison the British Resident at his Court. But his dominions were continued to a child of his race. The Prince of Wales made a tour through the country in the cold weather of 1875–1876. The presence of His Royal Highness evoked a passionate burst of loyalty never before known in the annals of British India. The feudatory Chiefs and ruling houses of

India felt for the first time that they were incorporated into the Empire of an ancient and a splendid dynasty.

Lord Lytton, 1876–1880.—Lord Lytton followed Lord Northbrook in 1876. On January 1, 1877, Queen Victoria was proclaimed Empress of India at a *darbár* of unparalleled magnificence, held on the historic 'ridge' overlooking the ancient Mughal capital of Delhi. But while the princes and high officials of the country were flocking to this gorgeous scene, the shadow of famine was darkening over Southern India. The monsoons of 1876 had failed to bring their due supply of rain, and the season of 1877 was little better. This long-continued drought stretched from the Deccan to Cape Comorin, and subsequently invaded Northern India, causing a famine more widely spread than any similar calamity known in Indian history. Despite vast importations of grain by sea and rail, despite the most strenuous exertions of the Government, which incurred a total expenditure on this account of 11 millions sterling, the loss of life from actual starvation and its attendant train of diseases was lamentable. The deaths from want of food, and from the diseases incident to a famine-stricken population, were estimated at 5¼ millions.

Afghán Affairs, 1878–1880.—In the autumn of 1878, the affairs of Afghánistán again forced themselves into notice. Sher Alí, the Amír, who had been hospitably entertained by Lord Mayo, was found to be favouring Russian intrigues. A British envoy was refused admittance to the country, while a Russian mission was received with honour. This led to a declaration of war. British armies advanced by three routes,—the Kháibar (Khyber), the Kuram, and the Bolán,—and without much opposition occupied the inner entrances of the passes (1878). Sher Alí fled to Afghán Túrkistán, and there died. A treaty was entered into with his son, Yákub Khán, at Gandamak (May 1879), by which the British frontier was advanced to the crests or Afghán edge of the passes, and a British officer was admitted to reside at Kábul. Within a few months, the British Resident, Sir Louis Cavagnari, was treacherously attacked and massacred, together with his escort (September 1879), and a second war became necessary.

Yákub Khán abdicated, and was deported to India; Kábul and Kandahár were occupied in force, and a national rising of the Afghán tribes, which imperilled the British garrison at Kábul, was decisively repulsed by Sir Frederick Roberts (1879-80).

Marquess of Ripon, 1880-84.—At this crisis a general election in England resulted in the defeat of the Conservative Ministry. Lord Lytton resigned along with the Home Government, and the Marquess of Ripon was appointed his successor in April 1880. In that summer a British brigade suffered defeat at Maiwand, between Kandahár and the Helmand river, from the Herát troops of Ayúb Khán,—a defeat promptly retrieved by the brilliant march of General Sir Frederick Roberts from Kábul to Kandahár, and by the total rout of Ayúb Khán's army on 1st September 1880. Abdur Rahmán Khán, the eldest male representative of the stock of Dost Muhammad, was recognized by us as Amír. The British forces retired from Kábul, leaving Abdur Rahmán in possession of the capital (1881). Ayúb Khán again took the field. His success, however, was short-lived, and Abdur Rahmán is still sovereign in Afghánistán (July 1895). Lord Ripon availed himself of the unbroken peace which has prevailed in India since 1881 to enter on a series of internal reforms. The years 1882 and 1883 will be memorable for these great measures. By repealing the Vernacular Press Act, he set free the native journals from the last restraints on the free discussion of public questions. His scheme of Local Self-Government has opened a new era of political life to the natives of India. At the same time, by the appointment of an Education Commission, with a view to the spread of popular instruction on a broader basis, he has sought to fit the people for the safe exercise of the rights which he has conferred. He also laid the foundations for the great measure of land-legislation for Bengal which was passed into law under his successor, Lord Dufferin. In 1882, Lord Ripon's Finance Minister, Sir Evelyn Baring, took off the import duties on cotton goods, and the whole Indian import duties were, with a few exceptions, abolished. This distinguished financier left India in the following year (1883), to assume the high office of British Representative at Cairo, amid the universal regret of the Indian people.

In 1882, a contingent of Indian Native troops was sent to take part with the British forces in the successful occupation of Egypt. They displayed conspicuous powers of endurance in the campaign, and of gallantry in the field. A chosen band of the Indian officers and men were afterwards sent to England, and received an enthusiastic welcome from all classes of the people. Early in his rule Lord Ripon had re-established the Department of Agriculture; and he took measures to guard the country against famine. In 1884 he deputed officers to England, to give evidence before the Parliamentary Committee, with a view to the extension of Indian railways. Lord Ripon retired at the end of 1884. Some of his measures for the promotion of local self-government, and especially his proposal to give to the higher class of Native judges a larger amount of jurisdiction in the case of offences committed by British-born subjects, were considered by the European community to be unsuited to the actual condition of India. But whether or not in advance of the time, it is now realized that they point out the directions in which progress must sooner or later take place. Lord Ripon loved the people, and was greatly beloved by them.

Marquess of Dufferin, 1884–88.—The Earl of Dufferin succeeded as Viceroy, 1884. In the spring of 1885, Lord Dufferin held a magnificent Darbár at Ráwal Pindi for the reception of the Amír of Afghánistán, and strengthened our friendly relations with that ruler. In the summer, a war with Russia seemed imminent, and the Native States came forward with loyal offers of their armies and resources to the British government. Towards the end of 1885 the persistent misconduct of King Thebau in Upper Burma, his ill-treatment of British subjects, and his rejection of all conciliatory offers, led to an army being sent against him, under General Prendergast. The King was dethroned and removed to India. On the 1st January, 1886, his territories were annexed, and soon afterwards were constituted a British province together with Lower Burma under a Chief Commissioner. Early in 1886, also, a great camp of exercise was held on the memorable battle-plain of Pánípat in the Punjab: and the fortress of Gwalior was given back by Lord Dufferin to the Mahárájá Sindhia. During 1887 Upper Burma was being gradually reduced to order, and the *dakait* bands were dispersed. In the same year the Jubilee (or fiftieth year of the reign) of the Queen-Empress Victoria was celebrated with universal enthusiasm. A Commission inquired into the question of more largely employing Native officers in the higher branches of the Administration. The Earl of Dufferin retired in 1888, and was created Marquess of Dufferin and Ava for his services.

The Marquess of Lansdowne, 1888–1894, succeeded Lord Dufferin. Under Lord Lansdowne's rule (with Sir Frederick, afterwards Lord, Roberts as his Commander-in-Chief) the defences of the North-western frontier of India were strengthened, and the Passes from Afghánistán secured against any possible invaders. At the same time, the Native chiefs were allowed to take a more important position than before in the armies of India. A number of them had come forward with offers of money and troops to aid in the defence of the country. Under Lord Lansdowne these offers were accepted. Many of the Feudatories now maintain regiments, carefully drilled and armed, which in time of war would serve with the troops of the British Government. These regiments, kept up free of cost to the British Government, are a free-will offering to it from the loyalty of the Native princes, who have greatly prospered under British rule. They served with distinction in China in 1900. The institution by Lord Curzon of the Imperial Cadet Corps for young Indian chiefs and nobles, without necessarily leading to a military career, may give additional force and interest to the association of British and Native troops.

Progress of Self-government.—While the Native princes are thus zealous to aid the Sovereign Power, the peoples and races in the British provinces have been learning the first lessons of local self-government. Municipal Councils and District Boards have, during the past forty years, been gradually created throughout India. Their members consist chiefly of Native gentlemen, many of whom are elected by their fellow citizens. These Municipal Councils and District Boards now manage many branches of the Local Administration. Their legal powers and their practical ability to do good work are increasing. At the same time, a 'National Congress' of delegates from all parts of India has since 1886 been held each December in one of the provincial capitals, such as Calcutta, Madras, Bombay, and Allahábád. This Congress discusses plans for opening a larger share in the work of legislation and in the higher branches of the executive administration, to natives of India. In 1892 the British Parliament passed an Act which increased the number of the members of the Legislative Councils, and introduced a stronger non-official element. Under that Act the Local Governments in India worked out a system of electing members to the Legislative Councils in accordance with the needs and conditions of each province. The year 1893 will be memorable for the first general election of representative members to the Indian Legislative Councils. Side by side with this political movement, efforts (which to a partial extent were embodied into legislation by Lord Lansdowne) are being made to reform certain evils in the social and domestic life of the Hindus, arising out of the customs of child-marriage and of the enforced celibacy of Hindu widows. The whole tendency of these efforts, under the guidance of the social reformer Mr. Malabari, is to protect young Indian girls and to improve the status of Indian women.

Fall in the Rupee, 1893–95, leading to Financial Settlement, 1899.—The continued fall in the rupee, from its nominal value of two shillings to an actual value of about 1*s.* 2*d.*, seriously embarrassed the Indian finances. India had yearly to remit about 18 million pounds sterling in gold to England, chiefly in payment of interest on loans, railway material, army charges, &c., and this sum, which would have amounted to 180 million rupees with the rupee equal to two shillings, would amount to 360 millions of rupees with the rupee at one shilling. The remedy proposed by the Government of India was bimetallism; that is, to establish a fixed ratio between silver and gold for purposes of coinage by international agreement. But as England and the Western nations could not combine to carry out that scheme, the Indian mints were closed for free coinage in 1893, in order to render rupees scarce and so to raise and to keep up their sterling value to 1*s.* 4*d.* This expectation was not realized, and the rupee continued to fall. In 1895 it sank to about 1*s.* 1*d.* A Royal Commission was then appointed to inquire into Indian finances, with a view, if possible, to reducing expenditure. After the presentation of its report a gold standard was established (1899), and fixity of exchange was secured. The rupee has since remained at 1*s.* 4*d.*

Army Reforms, 1890–95.—The old system, by which the Indian armies were commanded by three separate Commanders-in-Chief in Bengal, Madras, and Bombay, had become antiquated, owing to the quicker communication between the three Presidencies by means of railways, steamers, and the telegraph. For a long time the Commander-in-Chief in Bengal had been also Commander-in-Chief for all India. It was therefore determined to have only one central Commander-in-Chief, with four Lieutenant-Generals under him at the head of the four great military divisions of Northern and Southern India. The separate Commands-in-Chief for Madras and Bombay were abolished. The change was gradually carried out 1890–95.

Religious Riots, 1893.—In 1893 the old religious strife between the Hindus and Musalmáns broke out afresh. A series of fanatical riots took place at the festivals of the two faiths in many of the British provinces and Native states of India, from Burma to the North-west and Bombay. In some of these tumults, especially in the city of Bombay, much blood was shed, men were killed, and houses were burned. By the end of 1893 the excitement had calmed down again.

The Earl of Elgin, 1894–98.—In January, 1894, Lord Elgin succeeded Lord Lansdowne. Owing to financial straits, caused by the continued fall in the rupee, a five per cent. customs duty was imposed in 1894 on goods imported into India. After much discussion, this duty was extended to Manchester cotton-cloths of the finer qualities, with which the Indian mills do not compete. A curious panic was caused during the summer of 1894 by the secret smearing of multitudes of trees in Northern India, and hidden and ominous meanings were ascribed to it. But the practice was found to be a harmless act of certain devotees to call popular attention to the shrine of their god.

The Opium Commission, 1893-95.—In 1893 a Royal Commission was issued to inquire into the results of using opium in India, and the possibility of prohibiting it. After examining many witnesses in England and India, eight of the nine Commissioners reported in 1895 that the results of using opium in India were much less harmful than had been supposed in England. It was found that opium sent scarcely any criminals to the Indian jails, scarcely any patients to the Indian hospitals, and scarcely any lunatics to the Indian asylums. It was proved that opium does not act, as alcohol does in Great Britain, as a cause of crime, disease, and death, while it is largely used as a remedy for fever and malaria. Parliament agreed with the Royal Commission's Report, and declined to prohibit the use of opium in India.

The Indian Frontier Lines, 1890-95.—During the Governor-Generalships of Lord Lansdowne and Lord Elgin a series of measures were taken to settle the boundaries of the Indian Empire at its south-eastern and north-western extremities. In the south-east the territories of Upper Burma, annexed in 1886, were moulded into a peaceful and prosperous British Province. The frontier line between Burma and China and Siam was marked out, and the spheres of British influence on the Burmese side and of French influence from the Tonquin side were defined. In the extreme north-west of India, the frontier between the British dominions and Afghanistan was fixed. The State of Kashmir entered on a new development by the settlement of its land-revenue and of the cultivators' rights, on equitable principles, by a highly skilled British officer whom the Mahárájá employed for that purpose. British influence was firmly established in the outlying provinces of Kashmir to the north, along the line of Hunza, Nagar, and Gilgit. On the Afghan frontier a successful expedition against the Waziris in 1895 ended in the settlement of the Afghan boundary line, and in the recognition of the British authority by the intervening hill tribes. A friendly treaty was made with Afghanistan by our envoy, Sir Henry Mortimer Durand, in 1894; and in 1895 a son of the Afghan Amir for the first time visited England. He received a magnificent reception, and visited the chief centres of British industry and commerce. The Central Asian boundary between the spheres of influence of Russia and Great Britain on the Pamirs was also defined by treaty in 1895.

The Chitral Expedition, 1895.—In the beginning of 1895 a dispute occurred beyond the extreme north-western angle of India for the succession to the rulership of Chitral. The British political officer then at Chitral found himself involved in the struggle, was besieged in the Chitral fort, and defended himself with great gallantry against overwhelming odds. A powerful force was advanced from the Punjab to relieve him, while a smaller body of Indian and Kashmir troops marched to his aid across the snows from Gilgit. After the two expeditions had overcome great physical obstacles, from the height of the passes and the then almost inaccessible situation of Chitral, the enemy abandoned the siege of the fort. Our political officer at Chitral and his little garrison were saved, and the British influence was confirmed in that remote mountainous corner which, by the recent agreement with Russia, had come within fifty miles of the Russian sphere of influence in Central Asia.

Lord Curzon of Kedleston, 1898.—In 1898 the Earl of Elgin was succeeded by Lord Curzon of Kedleston, who had already considerable experience of Indian needs. He formally assumed the office of Governor-General at Calcutta on January 6, 1899. Special commissions of inquiry were at once appointed with view to a series of schemes of administrative reforms, embracing Education in every branch, Police, Irrigation, and Railways. He undertook also a series of visits to Native States and parts of India never previously visited by a Viceroy, and was received everywhere with a cordiality which witnessed to the sense of security and strength which proceed from incorporation in the great unity of the Indian Empire. To him is also due the sustained policy of archaeological conservation and restoration, which will preserve to the peoples of India the great monuments, political, military, and religious, of the past as abiding memorials of the different ages of the long history of the land.

Military Reforms.—These were continued and amplified. The Madras Army was reorganized, a large addition of British officers was made to the Native force, a transport service was created, and the entire Indian Army was re-armed. British troops were dispatched from India to South Africa, where they did valuable service in Natal at the beginning of the Boer War; and Native troops were sent to China, where they joined in the relief of the besieged Legations at Peking.

Agrarian Policy.—Considerable reforms were undertaken under Lord Curzon in the system of Land Revenue Assessments, as well as special measures to arrest agricultural indebtedness. Especially notable is the Land Alienation Bill in the Punjab, by which an endeavour has been made to check the evils of growing debt and the consequent expropriation of the agricultural population. Much industrial legislation, 1901–1903, had the same object, of ameliorating the condition of the poorer classes; and as administrators of a reasoned policy, agricultural and financial, Sir Denzil Ibbetson and Sir Edward Law have done highly beneficial work. A Board of Scientific Advice has also been founded, and experiments in agricultural research and education have been planned and inaugurated.

The Bubonic Plague.—The last decade of the nineteenth century was generally one of misfortune and distress. Early in October, 1896, the bubonic plague was certified to exist in the Bombay Presidency. It rapidly spread, in spite of hygienic precautions, and before the end of the year nearly half the population had fled. In 1897 and 1898 it increased in Poona and other parts of Western India, and the measures used to disinfect dwellings and treat plague-cases caused riots in several districts. In 1899, 1900, and 1901 the increase was very great in Bengal as well as in other parts of India, and it was not till 1902 that it showed any signs of diminution, and that only temporarily. The self-sacrificing work of doctors, nurses, ministers of religion and officials was warmly eulogized by the Government. Unhappily at the time of writing the plague is in Western and Central India as severe as ever.

The Famine, 1899–1900.—At the same time India has been visited by a series of most severe famines, which affected five provinces of British India as well as many Native States: an area of over 400,000 square miles, and a population of about sixty millions. Relief was everywhere organized, and as many as 26 per cent. of the population were in receipt of assistance during the worst period in some parts of the country. In the five provinces the number of persons rose at one time to over four and a half millions, in all India to over six millions. During the whole period, owing to the strenuous exertions of the Government, the general mortality was less than in previous famines, and the distress more amply and swiftly relieved. A commission, under Sir A. MacDonnell, was appointed to consider the whole circumstances, and reported in May, 1901, making valuable suggestions for dealing with future outbreaks.

Creation of North-west Frontier Province.—After long consideration it was decided at the end of 1901 to create a separate administration from the Punjab in a new North-west Frontier Province, under a Chief Commissioner directly subordinate to the Government of India. The creation was the occasion for the declaration of a policy of neither neglecting nor crushing the frontier tribes, but of military concentration and tribal conciliation. Military garrisons were withdrawn from transfrontier posts, and tribal militia and levies were welcomed and utilized in their place. The military bases were at the same time connected with the frontier posts by a system of light railways.

Afghánistán and the Frontier.—In September, 1901, the Amir Abdur Rahman of Afghánistán died. He was succeeded by his son Habibulla, who began his rule well by an amnesty, and showed a disposition to maintain cordial relations with the British Government. The Viceroy's visit to Nepál in 1901 was evidence of the friendly disposition of another neighbouring State with which in earlier days there had been war. Troubles in Waziristán, among the Mahsud Waziris, where outrages on British subjects had been constant, were met by several small punitive expeditions; but the Viceroy, by measures of blockade followed by retaliatory sallies, secured a satisfactory settlement.

The rectification of the Tibetan border was completed in 1902, when an addition of 350 square miles was made to British territory.

Death of Victoria, Empress of India.—An epoch in the history of British India may well be thought to have ended with the life of the great Queen of England under whom the Indian Empire had, through the energy and devotion of her servants, both European and Native, and through many years of stress and suffering, advanced so greatly in wealth and unity and power. On January 22, 1901, closed the long life of devoted service to India as well as to England and of deep personal sympathy with all the highest aims of the Indian peoples. Nowhere in all the countries which she had ruled was there a more genuine sorrow, a more profound sense of loss, than in India—the corner-stone, as the Viceroy said in his commemoration of her, of the world-wide Empire which had been created in her day. She was felt to have been a true mother of her people. She had learnt in old age the Indian language: she had continually advised her representatives in the country with words of wise counsel and of tender sympathy for the people whom she had charged them to rule. At a meeting in which all classes and creeds were represented it was decided to commemorate her great services to India by a Victoria Hall in Calcutta, to contain and concentrate in memorial the historic interests of the different ages of the past of the great Indian Empire. The memories of heroic effort, the results of self-sacrificing service, associated with a long history, and consummated in the reign of one who gave so conspicuous an example of the highest public and private virtues, are fitly to be summed up in a permanent memorial in the capital city of the Indian Empire.

The Coronation Darbár, 1903.—After a year of mourning, and after a postponement due to his own sudden and dangerous illness, Edward VII, who had himself visited India in 1875, was crowned at Westminster on August 9, 1902, in the presence of many Indian princes among the representatives of the peoples united under his sway. A contingent of Indian troops, representing almost every part of the great Empire, was conspicuous in the military pageants which accompanied the period of rejoicing. The Indian commemoration of the Coronation took place at Delhi on January 1, 1903, when King Edward VII was proclaimed by the Viceroy as Emperor, on the same site as that on which Lord Lytton had announced the Imperial title of Victoria. Over a hundred rulers of separate States, whose united population amounts to sixty millions of people, from the Arab sheiks of Aden on the west to the Shan chiefs of the Mekong on the borders of China, were assembled to testify their allegiance to their common Sovereign, in the presence of his brother the Duke of Connaught.

There solemnly, through the mouth of his Viceroy, the Emperor renewed to all his feudatories and subjects throughout India the assurance of his regard for their liberties, of his respect for their dignities and rights, and of his devotion to their welfare. In impressive words the Viceroy declared the duties of the officials, the aims of the Government, the needs of the people, and anticipated, under the unchallenged Supremacy of the Paramount Power, an India 'of expanding industry, of awakened faculties, of increasing prosperity, and of more widely distributed comfort and wealth.' It was felt that a ceremony of unique grandeur had symbolized the unity of the mightiest Empire of the East.

With this great ceremony, which was happily followed by a considerable reduction of taxation—the first that had been made in India for twenty years—the new reign was inaugurated.

INDEX.